March 2020

The
Sociological
Review
Monographs

Contents

On Other Terms

Edited by Annemarie Mol and John Law

Words to think with: An introduction

The Sociological Review Monographs
2020, Vol. 68(2) 3–22
© The Author(s) 2020
Article reuse guidelines:
sagepub.com/journals-permissions
DOI: 10.1177/0038026120905452
journals.sagepub.com/home/sor

John Law
Open University, UK, and Sámi Allaskuvla [Sámi University of Applied Sciences], Norway

Annemarie Mol
Universiteit van Amsterdam [University of Amsterdam], The Netherlands

> . . . my answer to the question, 'Can an African ever learn English well enough to be able to use it effectively in creative writing?' is certainly, 'Yes.' If on the other hand you ask, 'Can he ever learn to use it like a native speaker?' I should say, 'I hope not.' It is neither necessary nor desirable for him to be able to do so. The price a world language must be prepared to pay is submission to many different kinds of use. (Achebe, 1965, p. 347)

In 1991 one of us, Annemarie, was riding in a lift in Chicago – where this particular *thing* is called an elevator. 'He is going slowly', she said. Other people looked puzzled. This wasn't because she had breached the silence usually observed in lifts: this was a university campus and it was okay to talk to strangers.[1] The moot point was the *he*: in English a lift or an elevator does not have a gender: it is an *it*. This is not the case in various related languages. For instance, in French *it* is '*un* ascenseur' and not '*une* ascenseur' – a *he*, not a *she*, and certainly not an *it*. The confusion was settled with a friendly: '*Ohhhh* . . . you mean the elevator!!' But the mismatch offers an interesting lesson. It suggests that the theoretical proposition, so strange at the time, that *things* might be *actors* was easier to invent in French than in English. In French things are more person-like than in English because they have a crucial attribute that marks persons (or does it?) – that they are *a man* or *a woman*.

There is further way in which French makes it easier to imagine that *things act* than English. This is that *faire* (to do/make something) and *act* (to do/accomplish something) are also different. In English *acting* is usually done from a particular place, a centre. The French *faire*, by contrast, tends to point at events that occur without a prime mover: goings-on that happen thanks, or due to, efforts distributed between the participants. For example, in English *I cook*, while in French *je fais cuire*, 'I make cook': my *faire* is relevant, but it is the *food* that cooks. In English cooking is *done to* passive food, while in

Corresponding author:
Annemarie Mol, Amsterdam Institute of Social Science Research, Department of Anthropology, University of Amsterdam, Postbus 15509, Amsterdam, 1001 NA, The Netherlands.
Email: a.mol@uva.nl

French food itself is actively *doing* the cooking. It doesn't do so all by itself. I facilitate it along with the pan, the heat beneath it, and other bits and pieces. In other words, in French cooking is a process involving different elements that *invite* or *make* each other act; that *afford* each other to do what they do; or in some cases simply *allow* it. The lesson is that in French 'acting' is not a solitary affair but involves a range of f/actors which/ who make each other *faire faire: faire cuire* (make cook); *faire bouger* (incite moving); *faire penser* (encourage thinking). *Faire faire*, indeed, translates into English in a range of different ways.[2] It is possible to *explain* all this in English as we have just done. But at the same time, this short account suggests another reason why *actor-network-theory* was invented in French rather than in English, and why it was easier to imagine 'actors' as 'networks', as *acteur-réseaux*, in Paris than in London or New York.[3] The linguistic repertoires available in French simply make it more likely that actors of all kinds, human and otherwise, might act together, forming a network in which each contributes to the *doings* of all the others. Analogous arguments can be made for other agency-decentring terms such as 'discourse', 'assemblage' or 'rhizome'.

But if French allows for ways of thinking that are a lot less obvious in English, this raises a larger question. Might there not be further interesting words and ways of wording lying dormant in other languages? Dormant, that is, from the perspective of academic writing done in English. And such is the question that animates the present monograph edition of *The Sociological Review: what kinds of intellectual inspiration might we find in 'non-English' linguistic repertoires?* This is an urgent question. For here is the problem: when 'international' academic conversations restrict themselves to using the intellectual tools available in English, they become limited and parochial. To say this is not to say that the horizons of monolingual academic work are necessarily *national*: English is first language in many countries. Neither is it to suggest that they are *univocal*: the coexistence of *lift* and *elevator* reminds us that 'English' is itself diverse. But even so, academic conversations become limited and parochial because to work in English alone is to forgo the verbal richness afforded by moving between languages and working *inter-linguistically*.

For instance, in English a person is, by tradition, either a 'man' or a 'woman', but until recently 'man' was also a generic term that encompassed 'woman' and hid her from view. Feminist critique has interfered with this, which shows that with enough effort linguistic repertoires may be transformed. But Dutch would have made the task easier. For while it is no less sexist overall, it offers a helpful third term. Alongside *man* (man) and *vrouw* (woman), the Dutch harbours the term *mens* – human being. There is no *mankind* in Dutch, instead there is *mensheid*. Things are not *man-made*, but *door mensenhanden gemaakt*, made by the hands of *mensen*. The word *mensen* is a linguistic gem in that it helps to avoid subsuming *women* to *men*. This term also offers speakers of Dutch an easy way of avoiding the obligation of specifying whether a particular person is a *man* or a *woman*: a *mens* is not marked first and foremost by his/her – their – gender.[4] Other languages take this a step further. Rather than offering ways of escaping from binary gender categorisation, they avoid it altogether. They typecast people in other ways, for instance by age, occupation, or wealth. Indeed, one ends up asking what is so interesting about gender. Oyěwùmí tells us that before Yoruba was infiltrated by English terminology (she calls this 'Western') it did not even have words for *man* and *woman*.[5]

Different languages, then, are concerned with *gender* to differing degrees. At the same time, *gender* itself is a term that deserves attention. In the 1960s and 1970s, English-language academic work painstakingly distinguished *gender* from *sex*. This made it possible to disentangle the social and the biological differences between *men* and *women*. The former could not be explained by the latter, but had historical, social and cultural roots.[6] By now this claim is a commonplace. But the dominance of English in the social sciences means that along with this the term 'gender' has travelled into other languages and squeezed alternative linguistic possibilities. Take, for instance, the French expression, *rapport de sexe*: this foregrounds neither the supposed characteristics of individuals nor their supposed identities, but instead stresses the way in which people who have been slotted into one or other of two sexes are made to *relate*.[7] Or take the German *Geschlecht* and the Dutch *geslacht*: neither separates the biological from the social. This means that while the terms *Geschlecht* and *geslacht* allowed scholars to engage in historical, social and cultural investigations of masculinity and femininity, they also, early on, encouraged them to investigate how biological disciplines such as anatomy, endocrinology, genetics and physiology enact 'sex' in different ways.[8]

So this is the tension. As they attune to *international* discussions scholars working in other languages import English terms that do useful work in the context of particular debates. However, this means that the potential intellectual value of the words of their own languages is at risk of disappearing, and it is this disappearance that concerns us here.[9] In this monograph we do not address this by analysing the effects *of* English on whatever it risks eroding. Instead, we foreground the possible value *for* English of importing some of the intellectual resources embedded in other tongues. Our question is how, when, and where *other terms* might enrich academic texts written in English. This in turn raises a series of further questions. For instance, is it possible to simply import *words* and *ways of wording* into the 'imperialist tongue', or do vested academic interests and conventions prevent this? Do particular ways of understanding 'language', 'theory', 'analysis' and 'discussion' set limits to what can be said and done in (English-language) academic writing? And if so, how might these understandings be adapted and tweaked? And if importing additional linguistic resources into English is indeed possible, then what is actually worthwhile importing? What kinds of lessons might 'English' usefully learn?

We do not address these questions in general. Instead, each of the contributions to this monograph explores what it takes and what it adds to think in *other terms* by presenting a detailed analysis of a case: a specific 'foreign' word and some of the practices in which it figures. In the last section of this introduction, we briefly present those cases. But first we make two short detours. We start by offering a rough sketch of the institutional arrangements within which English functions as an academic superpower. Then we reflect on how best to frame our concerns about the erosion of multi-linguistic intellectual life and the promise of enriching English with *other terms*.

Submitting

A classic way of contributing to the 'international' academic literature is to *submit* an article to an English-language journal. The term is telling: for as they *submit*, would-be authors are bowing to the authority of a journal. Its editors and referees judge whether the subject-matter of the submission is relevant, its argument properly made, its empirical grounding solid, its references well chosen, its originality sufficient – or whatever other criteria they take to be important. Alongside the judgement of the text as a whole, individual sentences are also judged. These should be *well-phrased*. Neither too long nor too short, nor should they be too abstract or informal. There should not be so much jargon that reading becomes an ordeal, but still enough to mark a text out as academic rather than a piece of journalism. And, of course, the text should be written in *proper* English. *Received* English. Depending on where the journal is based, this may be British or American English. Inflections which reflect how people speak in New Zealand, South Africa, India or any of the many other *Englishes* are unlikely to be welcome. And it is not just editors and referees who keep authors in check. So, too, do software spellchecks. On the screen as we draft this text, Microsoft Word (set to 'English [United Kingdom]') underlines the word 'Englishes' with a red wavy line: the plural is being marked as *wrong*.[10] And the price for those who would want to avoid linguistic submission tends to be high, as there are structural feedback loops in place. 'International' (that is English-language) journals and their ISI or ISCI scores are central to many systems of research assessment. This leads to a straightforward conclusion: publish in English or perish.[11]

The homogenisation that goes into academic submission echoes the consolidation of national languages that took place in many nation-states from the late eighteenth century onwards. Out of all the linguistic variants that were – and to some extent still are – in use within national borders, just one was elevated above the rest and crowned as the official national language. In the process, the others were downgraded to the lowly status of *subsidiary languages*, or to the even lower one of *dialects*. The specificities differed between countries, but the linguistic standardisation of France became the exemplary case of *normalisation*.[12] Committees of experts in Paris were given the task of consolidating *the French language*. They set the norm. People brought up to speak Breton were not forced to submit to this norm, but because French became the working language for such 'national' endeavours as parliaments, schools, universities and newspapers, holding on to Breton meant being silenced, excluded, left without a voice. The norm was not imposed as a formal rule, but following it allowed a person to achieve much more in public life. In different variants, national languages established themselves in most other countries of Europe and pressed other languages or dialects to the periphery.[13] Sometimes this was not a matter of normalisation alone, but took more forceful, regulatory shapes. For instance, in Scandinavia Sámi languages were ruled out and state languages harshly imposed: children were sanctioned if they spoke in the school playground as they did at home. Elsewhere, more subtle pressures led to similar effects: John's grandfather spoke a version of Lowland Scots until shamed into giving this up as a young man. Europeans also imposed their national languages on the people in their colonies, and after independence many former colonies went on to adopt a single national language.[14] In others it remained common practice to shift between four or five languages in daily life – a customary skill in large parts of the world. Nevertheless, most *states* are monolingual, or work with two languages at most.

Similar mechanisms are now at work on a global scale: a single language, English, has come to dominate in many 'international' settings including air traffic control, software development, multinational corporations and international organisations, from the World Health Organization to the European Central Bank. And the same is true for science. The natural sciences were there first: *Nature* and *Science* – and many more journals – appear in English. In the social sciences there is somewhat more linguistic variation with lively discussions and excellent journals and book series in fields such as sociology, social anthropology and ethnology in French and German. Even so, texts written in French or German do not move as easily as their English equivalents. Yes, French travels to Senegal and other former francophone colonies; or to universities in Brazil or Mexico; or to departments of Romance Language Studies in the US.[15] German, in its turn, is read in Germany, Austria and Switzerland, and by a diminishing number of people further afield for whom it is a second or third language. But the dominant language travels a good deal more easily and in many places English has become the *sine qua non* for an academic career. In most of the academic world a reading knowledge of English is essential and writing in English is often obligatory as well. Translations are few and far between – waiting to be translated is likely to take forever.[16] Meanwhile, one's ideas may have been attributed to an author who has written about them in English.[17] Hence, publishing directly in English comes to be an asset. For a university post in the Netherlands it is by now obligatory and in the Scandinavian countries this tends to be the case as well. In Taiwan or Japan, 'international' publications also help. There are (still?) exceptions to this English rule. In South America most university students and their teachers work and write in Spanish or Portuguese. And, although the industry of 'Chinese English'-into-'English English' editing is huge, large numbers of Chinese scholars get by very well without English, too. That said, the level of normalisation is impressive. In 2005, three quarters of the social science papers that were published globally appeared in English, distantly followed by German and French (around 7% each), while no other language scored more than 2%. Japanese, with more than 8% in 1945, had fallen off the chart.[18]

English, then, has come to stand for *international*. But as Ammon (2012, p. 342) observes: 'English is just not a real lingua franca in the sense of being a non-native language for all its users as was Medieval Latin, but an asymmetric global language, whose advantages are unequally distributed.' For (this is obvious but often gets forgotten by monolingual speakers) those who learned English when they were young need a lot less *effort* to read and write in that language – *their* language – than those who did not. This effort is not equally distributed. For those who have been growing up with Norwegian or Dutch, English is less alien than for those whose first tongue is Hungarian or Vietnamese. But, in one way or another, the task of crafting texts in a language that one does not live in day-by-day forms a substantial overhead for all those who have to do this. It takes added effort, it means making mistakes, and it means being put right. It also means never being sure: only a few people get to really *master* what to them is at first a foreign tongue. To compensate for lack of mastery, you may ask for editorial assistance. But for this you need financial resources or friends who are willing to help. And such support only goes so far: editors cannot sharpen a point that you were unable to articulate in the first place. Nor can they compensate for your failure to be in-the-know if you have not read up on what is currently *hot* in the places from where the journals issue forth. Academic fashions change pretty fast![19] And then, last but not least, there are obdurate linguistic mismatches. What you hope to say may be alien to English. If it is then you face the question as to what to squeeze, what to transform, what to betray, and what to hold on to.[20] That is, you face matters to do with *content*, and it is these that lie at the heart of the present volume. But in which terms to address them? For – this much is obvious by now – terms always carry intellectual baggage; they do *work* of one kind or another. And this is why we do not rush to outline our concerns but instead approach them in a roundabout way. So in what follows, we briefly present four English-language expressions that are simultaneously helpful and frustrating. Difficult to avoid, they also carry intellectual baggage that we would like to leave behind. These notions that both express and distort our concerns are: *language, translation, equivocation* and *(non-) native speaker*.

Framing the issues

It makes sense to say that to write academic texts in English is to make use of the possibilities but also to hit up against the limits of a particular *language*. It is also useful to say that alternative intellectual tropes are embedded in other *languages* such as French or Mandarin. However, the term 'language' also suggests that *words* and *ways of wording* can be categorised and organised into distinct and separate slots, but there are good reasons for resisting this idea. One is that it arose along with the nation-state agendas of normalisation that we have described above. To use the term *language* is, at least implicitly, to reproduce the divide between a dominant national language and subordinate regional languages and dialects. A further problem is that *languages*, like the nation-states that they serve, all too easily seem to have distinct boundaries that clearly demarcate them from other languages. The implication is that fluidities within and overlaps between different ways of speaking are marginalised (as, for instance, with the gradients between the 'dialects' of 'German' spoken along the Rhine, all the way from Switzerland, via various *Länder* in Germany, to the mouth of the river in the Netherlands).[21] In addition, and this is what is most important in the present context, to talk of *language* is to imply that it is possible to disentangle how people talk (or sign or write) from the *practices* in which they do so. It is to suggest that vocabularies and grammars (or signs and syntax) lead lives of their own on a plane removed from their mundane incarnations.[22]

So the word *language* is useful because it underscores the fact that the ingredients that allow a person to speak (or sign or write) are not invented then and there but precede any particular utterance. It reminds us that relating to others in verbal ways depends on shared linguistic repertoires. However, there is a lurking risk that 'language' is taken to coincide with the words in dictionaries and the syntax found in grammar textbooks, while the irregular specificities of words-being-used-in-practice are treated as mere idiosyncrasies. Indeed, the discipline of linguistics was crafted on the distinction between what De Saussure (1960) called *langue* (language, linguistic system), a relatively stable object amenable to scientific research, and *parole* (word, linguistic utterance), day-to-day parlance too elusive to be caught in schematic overviews. If we were obliged to accept this divide, we would say that this monograph is about 'parole'. However, in conformity with recent movements in linguistics, we prefer to avoid the distinction altogether.[23] Why should scientific enquiries restrict themselves to the study of stable objects? They might just as well attend to phenomena that are situated, specific or idiosyncratic.[24] And as social scientists we have a further reason for leaving the *langue/parole* division behind. Our primary concern is not with words 'themselves' but with what linguistic repertoires *do* and *facilitate* in the worlds around them. This is why the authors gathered together in this monograph work ethnographically. Our focus is on situated practices populated by diverse f/actors, including words and ways of wording, which are all shaped by and help to shape events as they unfold.[25]

Once again, it is possible to say all this in English. However, other linguistic traditions may offer alternative sources of inspiration. For interestingly, not all such traditions have a word for 'language'. Ariel Heryanto (2007) explores this for the case of Indonesia. Here many 'languages' were spoken but the word *language* – or rather the word *taal*, which has similar abstracting propensities – was introduced to the archipelago by the Dutch. The colonial administration worked in Dutch, and for interaction with the colonised mostly used another *taal* – a trade language called *Maleis* ('Malay' in English). When Indonesia liberated itself from colonial rule in the late 1940s, it elevated *Maleis*, with necessary adaptations, to the status of its national language, calling it *bahasa Indonesia* (the 'Indonesian language'). As *Maleis* had no word for *taal*, the term *bahasa* was imported from Javanese to fulfil this nation-building task. In Javanese, however, *bahasa* had never been used for anything like an abstracted 'language'. Instead this word alluded to a wide range of polite and cultivated ways of *doing* which included *speaking properly*. And this earlier incarnation of the term intrigues us. For yes, it was part of the celebration of Javanese high culture, but interestingly it also took *talk* to be an integral part of *practice*.

Our argument, then, is that if we frame the dominance of English by talking of the power of the 'English language' we are casting our concerns in a particular *English* intellectual mould. While this mould is not confined to English (think *langue* and *taal* and the present-day meaning of *bahasa*), it still awkwardly suggests that signs and syntax can be disentangled from practices in a meaningful way. This separation fits the project of nation-building. It makes sense in settings where a dead 'language' such as Latin, shorn of present-day extra-textual practices, is taught and translated. It also facilitates the comparative study of 'languages'. But for our purposes, the term is a mixed blessing. Yes, the term 'language' is a useful and sometimes unavoidable shortcut for those who want to explore the added richness of *inter-linguistic* social sciences. But the point of such an exploration is not to learn about 'languages'. It is instead to better attune to wider realities of which 'languages' are just a part. To the worlds, the practices in which the social, the material and the semiotic intertwine.

A second term that is both useful and problematic is *translation*, a contested focus across a whole range of disciplines.[26] The texts in this monograph often use this term when they allude to inter-linguistic travel. This makes it possible to say that the Dutch word 'lekker' *translates* into English as 'tasty' – or, depending on circumstances, as 'nice' or 'good' or 'delicious'.[27] It also helps with the detection of the *mistranslations* and *untranslatables* that form the focal point of the contributions to this monograph. For translators, words that are difficult to *translate* tend to take the form of obstacles in need of taming.[28] By contrast, in this monograph we use such frictions as sources of inspiration.[29] Terms such as *translation, mistranslation* and *untranslatable* help to underscore this, but at the same time carry awkward agendas. For instance, they imply that what is at stake is the interplay between 'languages', and that the challenge (impossible to meet) is to replace the elements of one linguistic system with those of another. As a part of this, as we just rehearsed, they disentangle what is being said in the realities studied from what is being done. But there is more. Translating 'words' also detaches texts from their contexts. And this is a problem because texts are never simply about the concern they address or the object to which they may be referring. They are also located in a particular place and time: they are linguistically, geographically and historically situated. And in academia they are located within disciplinary debates and, whether explicitly or not, are in conversation with a corpus of work written by others. This means that however adroitly words and sentences are translated, their original contexts are lost, left behind. After translation texts arrive in another set of debates, and in a different historical moment.

In the social sciences, for instance, the French texts that became influential in the social sciences beyond France in the 1970s and 1980s may have been *about* the subject, discourse, habitus, or actor-networks, but they were at the same time a response *to* other authors who were mostly active in Paris. When Foucault wrote he was revolting against Sartre. When Bourdieu wrote he was in the business of disproving Foucault. When Latour wrote he was fighting Bourdieu. But when these authors were translated from French into German, their texts entered another arena. They were made to support, attack or otherwise relate to the work of scholars such as Habermas, Luhmann, or Beck and they were made to respond to academic concerns quite unlike those that had originally inspired them in France.[30] And the same was true when the French was translated into English. The Foucault of the US was never quite the same as the Foucault of the UK, and in neither case were these the Foucault that circulated in French. But, and this is crucial: *none of this was Foucault's own problem.* Give or take a few lectures in Berkeley, Foucault worked in France. He wrote in French. To a large extent he was able to focus on the audience that attended his weekly lectures in the *Collège de France.* And while his translators may have struggled with the connotations crucial terms might have for their new audiences, they also had an original French text to work with. It was their primary task to minimise its betrayals.[31]

The situation is quite different for authors who write in English whilst otherwise living in another tongue. Here, there is no 'original' to which one might try to be faithful. Rather than starting off in (say) Danish, they are writing directly in English from the beginning. Hence, the term *translation* does not really catch what is at stake. Instead, in order to get published such authors need to engage with debates conducted in English rather than in their own tongue. Indeed, in the Scandinavian countries or the Netherlands where much academic work is done in English, 'local' debates have been seriously eroded. The socio-material conditions on which they used to depend – journals, publishers, classes in which texts in the local language are read – have dwindled or, in some cases, disappeared. Writing in English, then, is not so much a matter of *translating* terms but of *attuning* from the outset to English terms. And this is not just a linguistic issue because to be publishable texts also need to align with current, English-language debates. This means that if a 'foreign' author seeks to convey something difficult to express in English terms, the question is not simply how to *translate* her own terms. It is also how to convince others – readers, editors, reviewers, publishers – of the *pertinence* of those concerns. If concerns are not already being addressed in English-language social science, it tends to be difficult to get them across.

This is an issue with many layers, because articulating and demonstrating the pertinence of what is written does not begin with the writing itself, but much earlier. This means that it does not just hinge on linguistic skills but also on whether it is possible to secure the financial and institutional support necessary to do research in the first place. This task, however, is again linguistically biased, for often grant applications have to be written in English so that they are amenable to 'international' peer review, while, as we noted above, the quality of one's earlier work is bound to be judged with the use of (English-language oriented) ISI or ISCI metrics. Overall, then, being 'international' rests on being able to craft and sustain arguments that, somehow or other, speak to English-language academic colleagues. This means that the concern that we seek to address in this monograph is not just, or not even necessarily, about gaps between *languages* and the limits of *translation*. It is also that all kinds of *issues* or *concerns* that present themselves to academics for whom English is a second or third language simply fall outside of the scope of 'international' academic life. In this monograph we do not offer institutional solutions to this problem. However, the authors assembled here do provide contributions that are pertinent in a range of different ways. They demonstrate that intellectually speaking there is much to be gained from opening up conferences, journals, book series, grant-giving bodies and university curricula to issues that have salience in *other terms* even if they do not immediately fit with *English* agendas.

The third term that is both problematic and relevant to our concerns is *equivocation*. This term is central to a particular way of doing anthropology that does not hunt for what human beings have in common, but instead explores differences between the realities they live with. Differences, one might say, that are simultaneously social, cultural, material and linguistic and that, as they are all-encompassing, may be called ontological.[32] *Equivocation*, then, is a term for talking about gaps and clashes between *words* that belong to different *worlds*. Usually the focus is on the equivocation between the words/worlds of Western-language anthropologists on the one hand, and the indigenous subjects described in their anthropological studies on the other. The argument is that *we* anthropologists should not squeeze *their* realities into *our* grids but hold back in our attempts at translation. Instead, it is more respectful, informative and worthwhile to attend to the gaps and the clashes. Bracketing off and suspending *our* common sense makes it possible, at least to some extent, to get a sense of *their* reality, their ontology. If we can manage this, it will lead to surprises that give *us* cause for thought; and at the same time it will make us modest when it comes to claiming authority over or about *them*. In short, the argument is that rather than being downplayed, equivocations should be foregrounded. Rather than being ignored, they should be controlled and cared for.[33]

Unsurprisingly, this insistence on the otherness of *other terms* is a source of inspiration for many of the contributors to this monograph edition. They do not rush to translate their terms, but attentively explore the relevant *equivocations*. However, once again this is a term that has its limits. This is because, as we have seen, it was designed for a context in which academics, *we*, write about the practices of other people, *them*, and seek to respect the differences between *their* realities and *ours*. This is the situation in which many anthropologists find themselves, but it is not where we start out here. Yes, the contributors to this monograph have done fieldwork in languages other than English – in Hungarian, Chinese, Dutch, Russian, Japanese, Spanish, Arabic, Brazilian Portuguese, Sámi – and yes, they write about that fieldwork in English. But while in a few cases one co-author has English as a first tongue, for most it is their second or third. This means that our authors are not a comfortable part of *us*, but since they write in English, neither are they simply *them*. Here *we* are also *them* working hard to *pass* as *we*. This double position is crucial for it shifts the locus of equivocation. Instead of grappling with the gaps between *them* and *us*, *they/we* are being torn from within. The implication is that authors may need to erase a part of their own *otherness* – even in the present volume.[34] This predicament may hurt, indeed it often does, but it also has its rewards. If these tensions are accepted, explored and celebrated, if they are controlled and cared for, they become occasions for learning.[35] For when *their* terms may be used by *us*, this means that 'other terms' shift in status. From figurations being analysed, they become tools that allow for analysis. From topics of investigation, they become instruments that help investigation. No longer confined to 'the field' they also become part of 'method'.[36]

So *language, translation* and *equivocation* all help to outline the concern that this monograph seeks to address, but none of them quite fits. Here is another try. Our argument might be that while *native speakers* have the advantage of child-learned English, *non-native speakers* are able to draw interesting lessons from their first language. Is this a good way of putting it? Interestingly, in the expression *native speaker of English* the term *native* has shifted. It no longer designates people living in places invaded by European explorers, and neither does it carry pejorative undertones. But *native* still evokes natality and therefore suggests that people are *born* with and have 'innate access' to their language.[37] Hence, people for whom English is their *native language* seem to have – and often claim – special authority over this language as if this came to them by birthright. This authority is linked to the projects of nationalism we touched on above.[38] It also assumes that English is internally consistent and coherent rather than a shifting babble of creative acts of speaking, signing and writing.[39] But if English is the language in which 'international' academic life is to be conducted, then these assumptions all need to be undone. Authority over this language – or rather this set of 'languages' – cannot remain in the hands of those who happened to learn to talk in one of its versions when they were children. Others may also speak *in* it. Just as important, they may also speak *about* it. *They may add to it and interfere with it.* Such is Chinua Achebe's point in the epigraph with which we started this Introduction for the related issue of English in novels.[40]

Yes, the absorption of *other terms* into the imperialist language carries dangers. It may lead to imperialist appropriation. In the history of English this has often happened – think, for instance of how academics writing in English ran away with the Maori term *hau*.[41] But the best remedy against this, or it seems to us, is not purification. We do not suggest that languages should close themselves off in their own nativist corners. Instead, those concerned should have the confidence to speak up and call out when their/our words are being abused. Which depends on them/us being granted a say – in English. And on offering a warm welcome to *other terms*. To words and ways of wording that allow the articulation of events not so easily said and done in English. For the *voicing* of concerns that might otherwise elude *our* attention.

On other terms

Like its articles, the title of this monograph is in English. But if we try to translate 'On Other Terms' into the other languages of our authors the phrase rapidly becomes multivalent. So as a first brief exemplification of what can be learned by attending to what transforms in translation, we start the volume with a collectively written note. It presents the stories behind the multi-lingual title variants printed on the cover.

What the other texts in this publication have in common is that they introduce one or more non-English words that help them to address pertinent issues, related to current events or concerns.[42] Hence, you may read these texts in two ways. Each explores some aspect or other of what it takes to make space for multi-linguistic academic writing. But each also talks about a particular extra-textual concern that their non-English words of choice readily articulate. Hence, they are concerned with the *saudade* of migrants or wayfarers; the possibility of *búskomor* politics beyond optimism; the *raza* of prize bulls and modest cows – and so on. You may not yet know what these words stand for or evoke – but that is the whole point. Reading on will satisfy your curiosity. Below, for a first sense and overview, are some introductions. They follow the order in which the chapters appear. There is no grand theoretical rationale for this order. Instead, we have carefully crafted a juxtaposition of texts in which each colours those that follow and feeds back into those that preceded it. We start with a text which will warm you to our topic. And we end with one which warns against a romantic trust in *other terms*. And in between these, you find explorations of terms to do with landscapes, common property, balancing, politics, cattle, cleaning, knowing and burning. Burning indeed.

Bruno Magalhães is concerned with those who cross borders – and in particular the border between Venezuela and Brazil – and with the Brazilian-Portuguese term *saudade*. This term evokes sadness and missing. Border crossers may miss their home, their family and friends, their schooling. But sometimes, and crucially, *saudade* is not about missing anything in particular, but just about missing, overall. This vagueness is used by those on the move to shield themselves from power and its abuses and to make space for their wandering hopes. Against this background, Magalhães muses on the bias towards conceptual precision that runs through both policymaking and academic social science. Each wants to pin things down. Are people who cross the border 'migrants' or 'refugees'? And where do they want to settle themselves? In this place or that? Siding with people who wander, Magalhães offers an impassioned defence of imprecision and of vagueness. (English-language) social science, he says, would do well to foster multiple and messy arts of living, rather than trying to collapse the world into fixed categories.

Solveig Joks, Liv Østmo and John Law are also invested in fluid ways of knowing, this time in the context of colonial struggles about landscape terms and practices in northern Scandinavia. The indigenous Sámi term *meahcit* points to practical and productive taskscapes (Ingold's term) for hunting, fishing, or gathering berries. *Meahcit* take the form of uncertain and unfolding relations between lively and morally sensible human and non-human beings; they do not divide between nature and culture. But *meahcci* (the singular of *meahcit*) is mistranslated by the dominant colonial states as (terms close to) 'wilderness', reflecting an agricultural logic that puts wildernesses in contrast to land that is 'cultivated'. The relationality lost along the way also emerges in the relatively verb-oriented character of the (North) Sámi language. And it speaks from the material character of Sámi knowing, which is less about centring knowledge in documents and rooms, and more about talk unfolding in practical settings. The authors argue that Sámi ways of talking and living lands and relations offer a resource for an English-language social science that is itself struggling to articulate situated and relational ways of knowing.

Liubov Chernysheva and Olga Sezneva are concerned about 'the commons'. Or rather, they are concerned with things held in common that in English-language social science are called 'commons'. But is this term, with its specific English history, always adequate? Among its alternatives is the Russian word общее, *obshcheye*, that grows out of quite different realities. To exemplify these, Chernysheva and Sezneva take us to several forms of 'communal' housing in post-Soviet St. Petersburg. There, they describe different ways of sharing spaces such as corridors and kitchens. Sometimes positively appreciated, sometimes leading to fierce disputes, *obshcheye* takes different material forms in different circumstances. The term is also related in varied ways to other terms for things communal which may be either negative or positive depending on the circumstances. In short, *obshcheye* is a term in tension. In a conclusion not unlike that of Magalhães, the authors ask: how important is it to seek coherence in academic linguistic repertoires? Non-coherence may well be more true, subtle and versatile.

Wen yuan Lin seeks to move beyond the limits of English language social science critique. He starts out with the paradox that if we critique critique, we remain within the existing war-like structure of academic criticism. So how to escape this logic of antagonism? Lin takes us to a Taiwanese practitioner of Chinese medicine, Dr Hsu, who successfully intervened in the SARS epidemic. Dr Hsu did not fight the virus, but sought to restore imbalances in the flows of energy in and through the body reflected in SARS. As a part of this he sought to determine *shi* (shì, 勢), a term evoking propensity to change. Working with each particular body's *shi* allowed Dr Hsu to nudge the flows of energy in that body back into balance. Similarly, rather than attacking Western forms of biomedical reasoning he sought to rebalance the relations between these and Chinese medicine by publishing statistically valid papers in English-language biomedical journals. Taking these lessons on board, Lin suggests that *shi*-inflected reasoning might also help to rework disturbing imbalances in the social sciences. It could move these away from their English domination and preoccupation with antagonistic versions of critique.

Endre Dányi's article is a meditation on how to respond intellectually and politically to the erosion of liberal democratic politics, and like Lin, is a reflection on the limits of critique. When the institutions of liberal democracy were working, they harboured internal differences which suggested the possibility of positive transformations. This allowed scholars to infuse their analysis with pragmatist optimism. But when populism takes over and parliamentary institutions are eroded, as has happened in Hungary, this no longer works. Seeking a way out, Dányi explores a novel, a film and an exhibition that exemplify *búskomorság*. Like 'melancholy' this word alludes to a mood that is sad and sombre. But while melancholy is a personal affliction, *búskomorság* is collective and political. It is about recognising the hopelessness of the situation and yet not despairing. It is about acknowledging that things are in ruins and yet carrying on. Allowing for a fragmented form of critique, *búskomor* politics is a politics of working in the cracks.

Marisol de la Cadena and Santiago Martínez Medina write about cow-making practices and words on farms and in cattle markets in Colombia. *Res* is (something like) an unremarkable 'common bovine' (the English plural might be 'cattle') fit for milking or the slaughterhouse. Its parents' pedigree – and that is stretching the word – is most likely known only by its owner. An *ejemplar*, by contrast, exemplifies a breed with a long, written pedigree detailing its genealogy. Both have *raza*, but for an *ejemplar, raza* can be translated as 'breed', while the *raza* of *res* is a shifting label to describe cows that are 'mixed' in ways that differ from one context to the next. A 'breed' is a cow or bull backed up by sufficient documentation. Hence, while all *animales tienen raza*, not all have breed. What makes the translation of *raza* really tricky is that this word applies not just to animals but also to people. The dislocation is stark: English does not talk of 'breeds' of people, and biologists have officially given up on human 'races'. One of the issues that this mismatch throws into relief is that in much of Latin America 'race' has less to do with fixed attributes like skin colour (elites may be white locally, and their skin may look 'brown' to Euro-American eyes) than with documented lineage or the paperwork of university degrees.

Annemarie Mol underscores the way that words have resonances that elude translation. Since she studies *schoon* in the Netherlands she writes about *clean* in English. But what to do, she wonders, with the way *schoon* is marked by ironic commentary in Dutch popular culture? And how to bring one's field sites to life in English without first learning what particular words mean for English-language audiences by doing similar fieldwork in English – but then again in how many versions of English should that be? It is far from obvious how to make ethnography work if author and readers do not find similar things remarkable and take similar things for granted. Mol goes on to claim that theories to do with clean – notably the anthropological mantra that 'dirt is matter out of place' – are informed by the English language. In Dutch this idea would never have arisen, as *vies*, the most prominent antonym of *schoon*, is never spatial but always visceral. And while *schoon* may have to do with hygiene, or have moral overtones, quite like the French *propre*, it has also an aesthetic ring to it, that sounds even stronger in the German *schön*. This leads Mol to wonder if rather than striving after the purification of their conceptual apparatus, academics might not care more about making this *schoon* in the sense of beautiful.

Lili Lai and Judith Farquhar challenge Western epistemology by presenting three ethnographic moments in the practice of Chinese minority medicines. The herbalists they follow work with knowledge of local herbs and their preparation; but also of diet; and of both living family and ancestors. But they insist that there is much they do not know. In this context, the authors meditate on the Chinese term *zhi*, 知, and discard its usual translation as 'knowledge' in favour of 'knowing'. They do this because Western 'knowledge' is infused with dreams of domination, while in the *zhi* of the herbalists 'knowing' and 'not knowing' are woven into ethical but uncertain processes in which practitioners cultivate the self in order to come near to things. These 'things' are not external objects waiting to be known, but contexted and emergent manifestations or expressions of patterning, *li* 理, running simultaneously through the practitioner and the world. The term *li* is often but unhelpfully translated as 'principle', but 'texture' makes more sense – *li* also translates as 'grain' as in the grain of wood. This does not exist in and of itself, but expresses itself, momentarily, in situated practices, where not-knowing is as important as knowing. The authors' final message is that if social science were to work in this way then other worlds would await it.

Amade M'charek takes us to what many Europeans might think of as 'irregular' or 'undocumented' migrants. She does this by travelling to southern Tunisia, and to the Arabic term *harraga* (الحراقة). A literal translation into English would be 'those who burn'. The metaphorical translation 'undocumented migrants' misses the point because *harraga* is not a group of people but the *activity* of moving out of the Maghreb in defiance of rules and regulations. It is about *burning borders*, traversing them, while keeping links to the people and places from where one came. Those who engage in *harraga* are crafting connections to *expand* the spaces in which they live. As M'charek explores these connections, she draws out the colonial and postcolonial links between southern Tunisia and France. So, for instance, it is trivially easy for salt, extracted under exploitative conditions, to move across the Mediterranean. Doctors and IT experts are also welcome in Europe. But not so those who lack the appropriate diplomas: the EU expects the Tunisian authorities to police the boundaries and stop travellers short. All of which reverberates in an artwork by Mohsen Lihidheb, an artist who resists *harraga* because it is an expression of neo-colonial relations that drain Tunisia and erode it.

Like the rest of us, Shiaki Kondo and Heather Swanson are concerned with the narrowing of English-language social science, but they also warn that non-English words may carry unwelcome political baggage. The Japanese 鮭鱒論 (*sake masu ron*, or 'salmon trout theory') is a case in point. It arose in Japanese anthropology to understand how people in the North of Japan (including the indigenous Ainu of Hokkaido) but also people on the North American Pacific coast interacted materially and spiritually with salmon. This was contrasted with the growing of rice in Southern Japan that was more precarious, and therefore praised as more artful, more generative of creativity – and altogether more 'Japanese'. Kondo and Swanson therefore warn against the colonial and racist stains that were built into *sake masu ron*. At the same time they do not want to simply discard the term. Instead, they wonder how to salvage it as a potentially good phrase for thinking of regions that are not so much given by spatial proximity, but rather emerge from environmentally facilitated multispecies ways of living. This, then, is their question: how to import promising terms into English without losing sight of their complex and often problematic origins?

The spectrum of terms and topics assembled here is wide, but at the same time these are just a few examples. Once the doors to *other terms* are opened, many more will follow. Sceptics may complain that this will turn social science into a *cacophony*. But such are the fears of those who stand to lose their privileges; privileges, in this case, to do with the reality that *their* terms rule. In a wider sense, there is no need to worry that all meaning will be drowned in an excess of words: authors will continue to attune their text to their readers. They don't, after all, want their message to be lost in the noise. What will change, however, is the timbre or the tone of how we coordinate and relate to one another; the rules of the academic game will start to shift. As a number of our authors indicate, moving between linguistic repertoires means giving up on the idea that *words to think with* should be stabilised into univocal *concepts* – whether or not the language is English. For solid concepts may seem to promise reassurance, but their apparent clarity is as misleading as it is stifling. How to best engage in a wider, less provincial conversation? Instead of avoiding multivocality, we might want to seek out terms that offer intellectual inspiration or suggest evocative forms of resistance. Instead of seeking to define our words, we might do better to exemplify them. But if we do this then we will need to explore words in practice; in their material-semiotic networks, discourses, assemblages or rhizomes. And instead of translating everything that is foreign into English, we might give some space to *other terms*, so that they are able to say, name, and evoke what they *hope* to say, name, or evoke. This is the quest of the contributions to this volume. Taken together, they seek to encourage and contribute to a new kind of 'international'.

Funding

The authors received no financial support for the research, authorship, and/or publication of this article.

Notes

1. For an analysis that uses lifts as a case for how people manage to shun others, see Hirschauer (2005).
2. For discussion of *faire faire* we thank Antoine Hennion; and for a further linguistic analysis see Kokutani (2005, p. 209).
3. Even though it was very quickly translated into English. See Callon (1986). And for early discussion of the misunderstandings that arose from this translation see the contributions to *Actor Network Theory and After* (Law & Hassard, 1999).
4. This also means that while transsexuality is possible in English – a man may become a woman or vice versa – intersexuality runs up hard against the assumptions embedded in the English language. See Hirschauer (2017).
5. Oyěwùmí (1997). For a range of rich and detailed analyses of how languages 'do' gender, see the contributions to Hellinger and Motschenbacher (2015).
6. See, for instance, Haraway (1989).
7. Descarries (2014).
8. Hirschauer and Mol (1995) and Mol (2015).
9. This loss is a specific example of a more general phenomenon in which 'small languages' are shaped and arguably impoverished in interaction with their larger neighbours. See, for instance, Asad (1986, p. 158), who argues that Arabic became more like European languages in the nineteenth century, and Joks, Østmo and Law in the present volume for examples of how Sámi has been shaped by the languages of its dominant Scandinavian national languages.
10. For discussion of the plurality of Englishes, see, for instance, Pennycook (2017).
11. See Arnold (2017) and de Lima Costa and Alvarez (2014).
12. For this analysis and the use of the term *normalisation*, see Canguilhem (1966).
13. Traditionally, linguistics prioritised the analysis of spoken language; but in state formations the particular formations and impostions of ways of writing are crucially relevant as well. See the contributions to Weth and Juffermans (2018).
14. See Makoni and Pennycook (2007).
15. See François Cusset (2008). Hamel (2013) suggests that in the natural sciences French holds its own in publications and teaching, but not in its distribution or reception.
16. Translations from English into other languages are far more numerous than translations from other languages into English. For discussion and statistics, see Heilbron (1999) and Ronen et al. (2014).

17. For further discussion, see Ammon (2012).

18. These numbers come from Ammon (2012, p. 339). For further discussion see Lillis and Curry (2010) and de Lima Costa and Alvarez (2014) and for the natural sciences, Gordin (2017). The larger context of linguistic 'globalisation' is that on some estimates only 10% or less of languages are 'safe'. See Ostler (1999).

19. On the difficulties of publishing in the multiply-disadvantaged circumstances of the University of Jaffna during the Sri Lankan civil war, see Canagarajah (1996).

20. This is a long-standing debate in a wide range of literatures. For a classic reference see Benjamin (1997), Asad's forcible intervention in the context of colonialism (1986), and for recent discussion in anthropology, see Viveiros de Castro (1998).

21. See also Tsu (2010).

22. This comes with a risk of linguistic determinism – even among those who recognise the historic malleability of languages. This risk threatens the otherwise truly stimulating studies of Anna Wierzbicka, who provides in-depth analyses of the obsession of 'English' with accuracy, proof and empiricism, concerns that started to seep into it at the time of the scientific revolution. See e.g Wierzbicka (2006, 2010).

23. For prominent examples, see Becker (1995) and Pennycook (2010).

24. Pennycook (2017).

25. This mistrust of the idea that scientific research means studying another explanatory plane arose in various intellectual fields at more or less the same time. For actor-network arguments against 'depth' see Callon and Latour (1981) and Latour (1986). For a similar argument in language studies, see Pennycook (2010). There are obvious intellectual ancestors, notably Wittgenstein's *Philosophical Investigations* (1953).

26. These include linguistics; literary studies; translation studies; biblical studies; parts of cultural studies; parts of postcolonialism; parts of cultural anthropology; parts of indigenous studies; the extensive literatures on teaching English as a foreign language; and the many language- and region-specific historical and cultural studies.

27. For the case of 'lekker' pursued along 'language trails' (in the Netherlands and beyond), see Mol (2014).

28. There are many versions of and positions with respect to this argument, but the straightforward observation is that translators typically find that the richness of one language rubs up against inadequate vocabularies in another. Linguists talk of 'exuberance' and 'deficiency' (Becker, 1984), while anthropologists may discover epistemological (Hanks & Severi, 2014) or ontological difference (Viveiros de Castro, 2004).

29. For an inspiring set of examples of thinking with untranslatables for philosophy texts see the many contributions to Cassin (2014).

30. For an analysis of Bourdieu in which translation is explored as a shift between different local debates, see Bourdieu (2002).

31. Most theories of translation assume there is indeed an original that can (even if maybe it should not) be betrayed in the 'target language' of the translation, and there is a long history which takes it for granted that perfect translation is impossible, and proceeds to debate the merits of different forms of betrayal. For a recent anthropological summary see Hanks and Severi (2014). As a part of this, notions of 'original' and in particular of original 'authorship' have been questioned in a movement that argues that translation is also a creative process. See Venuti (1998).

32. Viveiros de Castro (2004, 2015).

33. That equivocations may be hard to control but still deserve to be cared for is argued in Yates-Doerr (2019).

34. See, for instance, Law and Lin (2017).

35. As it happens, Viveiros de Castro moves between Portuguese, French and English, and *passes* time and again, so it would be interesting to hear him comment on what the three intellectual traditions he straddles afford him.
36. For earlier explorations of what it is to import field terms into analysis, see Van de Port and Mol (2015) and Mann and Mol (2019). The argument that field terms may be used as analytics owes much to the work of Marilyn Strathern, see e.g. Strathern (1991).
37. For this argument see Tsu (2010) who also pithily suggests that '[n]ative speaker is to language what color has been to race' (p. 197).
38. These extend beyond English. See, for instance, the discussions by Chow (2014) and especially Tsu (2010) in the context of nation-building, power and the multiple forms of Chinese.
39. See Becker (1995) on the creativity of what he calls languaging; Chow (2014, fn 19), who writes of languaging that it is a process that 'combines attunement to context, storing and retrieving memories, and communication'; Hanks and Severi (2014), who argue that language works through self-interpretation which means that translation is ubiquitous; and Spivak (1993/2000), who warns that subjugated others are not homogeneous.
40. Achebe (1965).
41. For an analysis of the appropriation of the Maori idea of 'hau' into gift theory, see Stewart (2017). And for debate on the use of the term HAU for the journal of that name, Mahi Tahi (2018).
42. Our focus is on what non-English words may do in academic settings. For a great collection of transpositions and transformations of words from one setting to another *outside* academia, see the contributions to Gluck and Tsing (2009).

References

Achebe, C. (1965). English and the African writer. *Transition, 75/76*, 342–349.

Ammon, U. (2012). Linguistic inequality and its effects on participation in scientific discourse and on global knowledge accumulation – With a closer look at the problems of the second-rank language communities. *Applied Linguistics Review, 3*(2), 333–355.

Arnold, D. (2017). South Asian studies: Britain and the burden of alterity. *South Asian Review, 38*(3), 69–78.

Asad, T. (1986). The concept of cultural translation in British social anthropology. In J. Clifford & G. Marcus (Eds.), *Writing culture: The poetics and politics of ethnography* (pp. 141–164). University of California Press.

Becker, A. L. (1984). Biography of a sentence: A Burmese proverb. In D. Brenneis & R. K. S. Macaulay (Eds.), *The matrix of language: Contemporary linguistic anthropology* (pp. 142–159). American Ethnological Society.

Becker, A. L. (1995). *Beyond translation: Essays toward a modern philology.* University of Michigan Press.

Benjamin, W. (1997). The translator's task. (S. Rendall, Trans.). *TTR – Traduction, Terminologie, Rédaction, 2*, 151–165.

Bourdieu, P. (2002). Les conditions sociales de la circulation internationale des idées [Social conditions for the international circulation of ideas]. *Actes de la Recherche en Sciences Sociales, 5*, 3–8.

Callon, M. (1986). The sociology of an actor-network: The case of the electric vehicle. In M. Callon, J. Law, & A. Rip (Eds.), *Mapping the dynamics of science and technology: Sociology of science in the real world* (pp. 19–34). Macmillan.

Callon, M., & Latour, B. (1981). Unscrewing the Big Leviathan: How actors macrostructure reality and how sociologists help them to do so. In K. D. Knorr-Cetina & A. V. Cicourel (Eds.),

Advances in social theory and methodology: Toward an integration of micro- and macro-sociologies (pp. 277–303). Routledge and Kegan Paul.

Canagarajah, A. S. (1996). 'Nondiscursive' requirements in academic publishing, material resources of periphery scholars, and the politics of knowledge production. *Written Communication, 13*(4), 435–472.

Canguilhem, G. (1966). *Le normal et le pathologique* [The normal and the pathological]. PUF.

Cassin, B. (Ed.). (2014). *Dictionary of untranslatables: A philosophical lexicon.* Princeton University Press.

Chow, R. (2014). *Not like a native speaker: On languaging as a postcolonial experience.* Columbia University Press.

Cusset, F. (2008). *French theory: How Foucault, Derrida, Deleuze & co transformed the intellectual life of the United States* (J. Fort, Trans.). University of Minnesota Press.

de Lima Costa, C., & Alvarez, S. E. (2014). Dislocating the sign: Toward a translocal feminist politics of translation. *Signs, 39*(3), 557–563.

De Saussure, F. (1960). *Course in general linguistics.* Peter Owen.

Descarries, F. (2014). Language is not neutral: The construction of knowledge in the social sciences and humanities. *Signs: Journal of Women in Culture and Society, 39*(3), 564–569.

Gluck, C., & Tsing, A. L. (Eds.). (2009). *Words in motion: Toward a global lexicon.* Duke University Press.

Gordin, M. D. (2017). Introduction: Hegemonic languages and science. *Isis, 108*, 606–611.

Hamel, R. E. (2013). L'anglais, langue unique pour les sciences? Le rôle des modèles plurilingues dans la recherche, la communication scientifique et l'enseignement supérieur [English, the only language for science? The role of multi-linguistic models in research, scientific communication and higher education]. *Synergies Europe, 8*, 53–66.

Hanks, W. F., & Severi, C. (2014). Translating worlds: The epistemological space of translation. *Hau: Journal of Ethnographic Theory, 4*(2), 1–16.

Haraway, D. J. (1989). *Primate visions: Gender, race and nature in the world of modern science.* Routledge and Chapman Hall.

Heilbron, J. (1999). Towards a sociology of translation: Book translations as a cultural world-system. *European Journal of Social Theory, 2*(4), 429–444.

Hellinger, M., & Motschenbacher, H. (Eds.). (2015). *Gender across languages* (Vol. 4). John Benjamins.

Heryanto, A. (2007). Then there were languages: Bahasa Indonesia was one among many. In S. Makoni & A. Pennycook (Eds.), *Disinventing and reconstituting languages* (pp. 42–61). Multilingual Matters.

Hirschauer, S. (2005). On doing being a stranger: The practical constitution of civil inattention. *Journal for the Theory of Social Behaviour, 35*, 41–67.

Hirschauer, S. (2017). Gender (in) difference in gender (un) equal couples: Intimate dyads between gender nostalgia and post genderism. *Human Studies, 40*(3), 309–330.

Hirschauer, S., & Mol, A. (1995). Shifting sexes, moving stories: Feminist/constructivist dialogues. *Science, Technology and Human Values, 20*(3), 368–385.

Kokutani, S. (2005). Sur l'analyse unie de la construction 'se faire + infinitif' en Français [The unified analysis of the French construction 'se faire' + infinitive]. In H. B.-Z. Shyldkrot & N. Le Querler (Eds.), *Les périphrases verbales* [Verbal periphrases] (pp. 209–227). John Benjamins.

Latour, B. (1986). The powers of association. In J. Law (Ed.), *Power, action and belief: A new sociology of knowledge?* (Vol. 32, pp. 264–280). Routledge and Kegan Paul.

Law, J., & Hassard, J. (Eds.). (1999). *Actor network theory and after.* Blackwell and the Sociological Review.

Law, J., & Lin, W.-y. (2017). Provincialising STS: Postcoloniality, symmetry and method. *East Asian Science, Technology and Society*, *11*(2), 211–227.

Lillis, T., & Curry, M. J. (2010). *Academic writing in a global context: The politics and practices of publishing in English*. Routledge.

Mahi Tahi. (2018). *An open letter to the HAU journal's board of trustees*. www.asaanz.org/blog/2018/6/18/an-open-letter-to-the-hau-journals-board-of-trustees (last accessed 20 January 2020).

Makoni, S., & Pennycook, A. (2007). Disinventing and reconstituting languages. In S. Makoni & A. Pennycook (Eds.), *Disinventing and reconstituting languages* (pp. 1–41). Multilingual Matters.

Mann, A., & Mol, A. (2019). Talking pleasures, writing dialects: Outlining research on Schmecka. *Ethnos*, *84*(5), 772–788.

Mol, A. (2014). Language trails: 'Lekker' and its pleasures. *Theory, Culture & Society*, *31*(2/3), 93–119.

Mol, A. (2015). Who knows what a woman is. . . On the differences and the relations between the sciences. *Medicine Anthropology Theory*, *2*(1), 57–75.

Ostler, R. (1999). Disappearing languages. *The Futurist*, *33*, 16–22.

Oyěwùmí, O. (1997). *The invention of women: Making an African sense of Western gender discourses*. University of Minnesota Press.

Pennycook, A. (2010). *Language as a local practice*. Routledge.

Pennycook, A. (2017). *The cultural politics of English as an international language*. Routledge.

Ronen, S., Gonçalves, B., Hu, K. Z., Vespignani, A., Pinker, S., & Hidalgo, C. s. A. (2014). Links that speak: The global language network and its association with global fame. *Proceedings of the National Academy of Sciences*, *111*(52), E5616–E5562.

Spivak, G. C. (2000). The politics of translation. In L. Venuti (Ed.), *The translation studies reader* (pp. 398–416). Routledge (Original work published 1993).

Stewart, G. (2017). The 'hau' of research: Mauss meets Kaupapa Māori. *Journal of World Philosophies*, *2*(1), 1–11.

Strathern, M. (1991). *Partial connections*. Rowman and Littlefield.

Tsu, J. (2010). *Sound and script in Chinese diaspora*. Harvard University Press.

Van de Port, M., & Mol, A. (2015). Chupar frutas in Salvador da Bahia: A case of practice-specific alterities. *Journal of the Royal Anthropological Institute*, *21*(1), 165–180.

Venuti, L. (1998). *The scandals of translation: Towards an ethics of difference*. London.

Viveiros de Castro, E. (1998). Cosmological deixis and Amerindian perspectivism. *Journal of the Royal Anthropological Institute*, *4*(3), 469–488.

Viveiros de Castro, E. (2004). Perspectival anthropology and the method of controlled equivocation [translation of Introdução ao método do perspectivismo]. *Tipití*, *2*(1), 3–22. http://amazone.wikia.com/wiki/Introdu%C3%A7%C3%A3o_ao_m%C3%A9todo_do_perspectivismo (accessed 23 July 2010).

Viveiros de Castro, E. (2015). Who is afraid of the ontological wolf? Some comments on an ongoing anthropological debate. *The Cambridge Journal of Anthropology*, *33*(1), 2–17.

Weth, C., & Juffermans, K. (Eds.). (2018). *The tyranny of writing: Ideologies of the written word*. Bloomsbury Publishing.

Wierzbicka, A. (2006). *English: Meaning and culture*. Oxford University Press.

Wierzbicka, A. (2010). *Experience, evidence, and sense: The hidden cultural legacy of English*. Oxford University Press.

Wittgenstein, L. (1953). *Philosophical investigations*. Blackwell.

Yates-Doerr, E. (2019). Whose global, which health? Unsettling collaboration with careful equivocation. *American Anthropologist*, *121*(2), 297–310.

Author biographies

John Law is Emeritus Professor in Sociology at the Open University, and visiting Professor at the Sámi University of Applied Sciences at Guovdageaidnu in Norway. He has written widely on material semiotics, and his books include *After Method* and *Aircraft Stories*. He works on colonial environmental controversies, research methods, modes of knowing, and postcolonial knowing relations. His home page is at www.heterogeneities.net.

Annemarie Mol is a Professor of Anthropology of the Body in the University of Amsterdam. She wrote about the coordination of different enactments of an allegedly single disease in hospital practice; theorised *care* as intertwined with, rather than opposed to, technology; explored how our theoretical tropes change if, instead of continuing to celebrate human thinking, we foreground human eating; and is currently embarking on an enquiry into *clean* as a *good*. All the while she reflectively attends to words and styles of writing.

The Sociological Review Monographs
2020, Vol. 68(2) 23–26
© The Author(s) 2020
Article reuse guidelines:
sagepub.com/journals-permissions
DOI: 10.1177/0038026120905470
journals.sagepub.com/home/sor

The
Sociological
Review
Monographs

Translating a title: On other terms

**Liubov Chernysheva, Endre Dányi,
Marisol de la Cadena, Judith Farquhar,
Solveig Joks, Shiaki Kondo,
Lili Lai, John Law, Wen-yuan Lin,
Bruno Magelhães,
Santiago Martínez Medina,
Amade M'charek, Annemarie Mol,
Olga Sezneva, Heather Swanson,
Liv Østmo**

Present-day academic work is mostly done in English. What happens, or so the contributions to this monograph ask, when we open a few windows, let in some air, and invite elements drawn from other linguistic traditions into our texts? Doing so does not simply mean welcoming other *words*. Along with this it also changes the conditions, the *terms*, that stipulate what is, and what is not, good – proper, interesting, international, academic – writing.

To exemplify the way in which the traffic between languages is rarely smooth, here we briefly present some of the conundrums that have arisen as we, the authors, have picked up the phrase that figures as our title – *on other terms* – and tried to translate it – rewrite it – into the *other* languages that we introduce in the articles in this monograph.

In Hungarian, the first phrase that comes to mind is *más szóval*, which literally means 'with other word' (singular!). This is often used in everyday language, when someone wants to find a better way of saying something. Then there is *más feltétellel*, which means 'under other conditions'. This sounds more like a legal expression, specifying under what circumstances something can be used. On the cover, you will find *más szóval* because this captures an interesting tension between sameness and difference. It suggests that by using a *different* word it becomes possible to say the *same* thing, but better.

Corresponding author:
Annemarie Mol, Department of Anthropology, Amsterdam Institute of Social Science Research, Universiteit van Amsterdam, Postbus 15509, Amsterdam, 1001 NA, The Netherlands.
Email: a.mol@uva.nl

Interestingly, this in turn suggests a melancholy kind of perseverance. When we say 'in other words', we acknowledge that our first attempt to express something was not quite right, and our second attempt might not work all that well, either. At the same time, we think it is still worth trying.

'On other terms' may translate into Spanish as *en otros términos*, which can indicate a new agreement – or a new goal – to be settled after discussion. But while everybody would understand *en otros términos* (and would also 'get' that it originated in translation) the more comfortable translation of our title is *en otras palabras*. This often means 'different but the same' and it is used in conversations to clarify, and in a sense impose, the main message of the speaker. They each have their own valence, so which to go for? We are lucky, here, in that we have a Portuguese contribution as well – and this, give or take a few letters and a different pronunciation (invisible in written form), presents options that are 'different but the same'. So, in the end, for the Spanish we went for *en otros términos* – along with the linguistic discomfort this produces. The new agreement is yet to happen, the new goal to follow – and the hope is that the present volume gets us started as it discloses differences between *terms* and acknowledges the analytical inspiration of *other words*. Other words, indeed – or, as the Portuguese has it: *outras palavras*. This translation has the added advantage that *palavras* are first and foremost spoken words (like the French *paroles*). Having those in our title suggests that our texts might not contribute to theories so much as weave stories. That their point is not to reveal structures and systems and solid boundaries, but to move about and discover new versions and variants, different ways of wording and living.

Translating 'On other terms' word by word into the Sámi language would yield: *nuppiin sániiguin daddjon*. This is a phrase commonly used when a person has said something and wants to make it more explicit, and therefore uses other words, repeating the same thing differently. But the use of this phrase disguises the difficulties of translating between different languages. Since that is our concern, since we focus on differences in understanding things, we prefer as our Sámi title *eará áddejupmi*. Which means: different understanding. Not the same thing repeated to make it clearer or to insist on it. But something else instead.

Finding a good Russian analogue wasn't easy. In the end, we had two variants: Иным языком and При ином раскладе. The first lays emphasis on language – языком – and uses the instrumental case, one of the six cases available in Russian. (In Latin this would be the comitative.) It denotes a tool, an instrument, by which one agent affects another. It sounds nice and organic in Russian. But, it singles out the linguistic as a tool. This is why we prefer the other option, При ином раскладе. The word расклад dictionaries translate into English as either 'deal' or 'scenario'. It has a very clear sense of spatiality and complexity and it is also conditional: things could be different under different circumstances – different расклад. Circumstances that we hope to contribute to with this monograph.

Other circumstances are also implied in the Arabic version of our title. Read from right to left, the words that compose it are في قرائن اخر. Transposed into the Roman alphabet this makes: *fī qaraatin akhra*. This phrase has a fitting double meaning. It translates back into English as 'in another context' – the circumstances also mentioned in the Russian version of our title. But then, second, it also translates in a way that foregrounds one of the activities implied in, or required for, the otherness at stake here. More particularly, the activity of reading: 'in another reading'.

Then there is Chinese. To indicate that there are many ways of translating 'On other terms' into idiomatic Chinese, on our cover you find two Chinese titles. The first, in complex characters, traditional script, is 議約 (*yì yuē*). This translation underscores our concern that, as English is dominant in international exchanges, we are somehow squeezed into English ways of understanding each other. English terms have become the major conditions of possibility for expressing worlds that themselves have different linguistic legacies. They organise our cross-linguistic (mis)translations. But could things be done on other terms, negotiated differently? Hence 議約: the first word, 議 (*yì*), means negotiate or discuss, and the second word, 約 (*yuē*), means an agreement or 'terms and conditions'.

The second translation we propose is 易言之 (*yi yan zhi*). This works in both traditional and simplified characters. Translated back into English, 易言之 (*yi yan zhi*) would, literally glossed, present itself as 'changing the words to speak of the thing'. Here, then, 'the thing' at issue is transformed as language shifts. The insistence, this time, is not on the conditions that English sets for international exchanges. It is, instead, on the ontologies that are embedded in words that are spoken.

The Japanese version of the title is 別の言葉で. Transliterated into Latin script this becomes: *betsu-no-kotoba-de*. If, throughout, this book had dealt with academic discourse, we might have used 用語 (*yougo*) instead of 言葉 (*kotoba*) as *yougo* is the word for 'word' that tends to be used in grammars and other academic and professional contexts. But since quite a few articles deal with vernacular terms, we chose *kotoba*. This translation misses the connotation of 'terms' as 'contract' and also that of 'relation', of being 'on good terms with' another person. But it also adds something. For in ancient times *koto* 言 used to mean event or happening (事 which also reads as *koto*). Hence, 'saying' was an event, it was 'happening'. '*Koto-no-ha*' or '*kotoba*' (the edge of the words) was a weaker variant. Present-day *kotoba* is rendered in Japanese as 言葉, which literally means 'leaves of words'. This calls up multiplicity and richness in meaning.

A rich story that is. The next is a lot simpler. For in Dutch our title is: *Op andere termen*. This illustrates the fact that 'languages' are not tightly closed off from one another. For the English *other* and the Dutch *ander* may sound a bit different, but it is still apparent that they had a common ancestor. Like the English *terms*, the Dutch *termen* means both 'conditions' and 'words'. *Op andere termen* – like *on other terms* – means under other conditions and suggests the possibility of other rules to go by. While a second reading suggests that otherness might have to do with words.

In English, finally, our title makes trouble from the start. It is not everyday English in any of the sites we know of. But there are traces in it of legal English: contracts are framed by 'terms and conditions'. As a contract is drafted there may be negotiations about that framing, while if there is breakdown the question arises as to whether one or more of its 'terms and conditions' have been breached. In more daily settings, if one is concerned about the way one's life is taking shape, one may be encouraged 'not to live on someone else's terms' but rather 'on one's own terms'. However, when asked to translate back *outras palavras*, or *más szóval*, a speaker of English would more likely come up with 'in other words' or (more emphatically) 'to put it differently'. At the same time, this idea, that 'it' may be put differently resonates in 'other terms'. Our title, then, juxta-poses conditions, framings, 'your own terms' and words. This combination of concerns has been our fractal focus from the start. As a title, *On other terms* opens up questions to do with practices and their implicit rules; questions to do with words and the worlds they help to verbalise and form a part of.

Note

The affiliations for the authors are as follows: University of Amsterdam, The Netherlands (Liubov Chernysheva, Amade M'charek, Annemarie Mol and Olga Sezneva); Bundeswehr University Munich, Germany (Endre Dányi); University of California Davis, USA (Marisol de la Cadena); University of Chicago, USA (Judith Farquhar); Sami University of Applied Sciences, Norway (Solveig Joks, John Law, Liv Østmo); Hokkaido University, Japan (Shiaki Kondo); Peking University, China (Lili Lai), The Open University, UK (John Law); National Tsing-Hua University, Taiwan/R.O.C (Wen-yuan Lin); Pontifical Catholic University of Rio de Janeiro, Brazil (Bruno Magelhães); Alexander von Humboldt Biological Resources Research Institute, Colombia (Santiago Martínez Medina); Aarhus University, Denmark (Heather Swanson).

Funding

The authors received no financial support for the research, authorship, and/or publication of this article.

Moving on with *saudade*: On bordered countries and vague terms

The Sociological Review Monographs
2020, Vol. 68(2) 27–44
© The Author(s) 2020
Article reuse guidelines:
sagepub.com/journals-permissions
DOI: 10.1177/0038026120905472
journals.sagepub.com/home/sor

Bruno Magalhães

Pontifícia Universidade Católica do Rio de Janeiro [Pontifical Catholic University of Rio de Janeiro], Brazil

Abstract

This article is about how people moving along state borders – I call them wayfarers – refuse the assumption that they ought to live either a sedentary or a nomadic lifestyle inside or outside states, whether as citizens or as Others. In particular, it looks at how the term *saudade* helps mobile people to manage friction without falling back into such binaries. The Oxford English Dictionary defines *saudade* as a desire 'for something' and describes it as a characteristic of the 'Portuguese or Brazilian' people. Here, we shall attend however to the *saudade* evoked by Venezuelans and Warao (defined by the same dictionary as 'members of a South American Indian people inhabiting Guyana, Suriname, and Venezuela'). This article patterns a contrast between two ways of evoking the term in comments about movement made by my informants: the first, Precise *Saudade*, asks for precision about that of which people feel *saudade*. The second way of evoking the term, Vague *Saudade*, is, as its name suggests, more comfortable with being vague. The argument put forward by this article is that scholarly and policy texts on 'migrants', 'nomads' and 'refugees' need to make more room for Vague *Saudade* when translating the talk of wayfarers. It may be tempting to dismiss vagueness as showing ambiguity and imprecision. Yet, as the stories that follow are meant to highlight, Vague *Saudade* can be useful to wayfarers in several ways: to engage in care, to protect others, to protect themselves and to engage in conversations about alternative worlds. To grant monopoly to Precise *Saudade*, it is argued, risks hindering wayfarers' ability to do these things. I find this is relevant to how we translate wayfarers, and I suggest it is also germane to how we translate in research.

Keywords

border, migration, nomad, refugee, *Saudade*, translation, vagueness

Corresponding author:

Bruno Magalhães, Pontifical Catholic University of Rio de Janeiro (IRI, PUC-Rio), R. Marques de Sao Vicente, 225 – Gavea, Rio de Janeiro, RJ 22793-260, Brazil.
Email: brunoepbm@gmail.com

This text is about the term *saudade* – a word found in many Portuguese languages, including the Brazilian version I was raised to treat as my own. In particular, it is about how Venezuelans and Warao evoke *saudade* to talk about their journeys between Venezuela and Brazil. These people – I call them wayfarers – are my source of inspiration. Priests and nuns, UN and army envoys, clerks and police officers, as well as experts on 'refugees', 'migrants' and 'nomads', also show up in the narrative. Even a Portuguese king plays a role. And I am also present, in the middle, stitching ethnographic snippets to texts about vagueness in translation to build a plot.

That plot is simple. I contrast and rebalance two ways of evoking *saudade*. The first – I call this Precise *Saudade* – is *saudade about this or that*. It is *saudade of* Venezuela,[1] *of* a home,[2] *of* a lifestyle,[3] *of* a 'traditional habitat'[4] or *of* a family left behind.[5] The United Nations High Commissioner for Refugees (UNHCR, 2018) evokes it to translate a Venezuelan girl as saying, 'I miss *Venezuela* every day. I miss *my mom*, I miss *my friends* and I miss *my school*.' Along with this first *saudade about this or that*, a second way of evoking the term – I call it Vague *Saudade* – is much more difficult to translate into English because it allows the term to wander. Vague *Saudade* is both about a lot of things and about nothing in particular. Put into English literally, it would lead us to a phrase like but not quite the same as, 'people feeling missing' – full stop.

This article argues that writings about migrants, nomads and refugees need to make more room for Vague *Saudade*. To push people to be precise about *saudade* helps authorities to 'triage immigrants' (Silva et al., 2018, p. 20), 'profile those leaving Venezuela and overview key migration drivers' (Mixed Migration Centre [MMC], 2019, p. 7). It helps humanitarian agencies to classify wayfarers according to the global 'Glossary on Migration' (International Organization for Migration [IOM], 2019). To attend to Vague *Saudade* is not so useful for these practices. Still, it does seem to be used by wayfarers – as a form of politeness, to engage in care, as a shield to avoid religious conversion and as a way of doing mobility that I did not know how to translate. To write about wayfarers feeling *saudade* of home, being homesick or missing the Orinoco would foreclose these uses. In short, I argue that to grant hegemony to Precise *Saudade* would jeopardise the wellbeing of Warao and Venezuelans who rely on Vague *Saudade* to 'fare'.[6]

To support this claim, I first cut a way through debates that look for precision about *saudade*. I also explain why I use the word 'wayfarers' – a term I borrow from the anthropologist Tim Ingold (2007, 2011, 2018).[7] Next I explore a series of ethnographic vignettes in which Vague *Saudade* makes space for faring that would be blocked by Precise *Saudade*. Finally, I do not so much conclude as suggest how the conversation could go on along with studies about the role played by vagueness in texts about 'other terms'.

To cut a long story short, there are many reasons why aiming at precision is desirable in research, but there are reasons to be vague too. Some forms of scholarly writing seek to curtail vagueness at all costs, even though they cannot completely succeed, but research writing does not need to move towards perfect precision as its pole star. As researchers-qua-translators, we might want to be vague not because we are unable to be precise. We might want to be vague *to foster* multiple arts of living (Omura et al., 2018; van de Port & Mol, 2015). The next sections seek support for these arguments in the streets of the Venezuelan town of Santa Helena.

Two ways of evoking *saudade*

Santa Elena de Uairén is a busy frontier town linking Venezuela with Brazil. The diamonds that made it a mining centre in the 1930s have long since disappeared, but languages fared better. Spanish, Pemóng, Warao, Portuguese and Global English are all spoken there. The wayfarers speaking these languages are also multiple. A UN survey counted fewer than 4000 Venezuelans entering the state of Roraima in 2016 (International Organization for Migration [IOM], 2018b), but by June 2018, when I got to Santa Elena, a second survey had counted more than 100,000 (Brazilian Federal Police [BFP], 2019). According to the Brazilian authorities, some were Venezuelan asylum seekers, others were Venezuelans migrants and others still were not primarily Venezuelans. These were identified as Barí, Yukpa, E'ñepa and Warao – described as 'the largest indigenous group from Venezuela in Brazil' (UNHCR, 2018).

Choosing terms to write about these wayfarers is neither neutral nor simple, but for now I simply want to give a sense of their hardships. Within Brazil, federal, state-level and municipal authorities were locked in skirmishes (Magalhães & Silva, 2018). After Roraima's governor appealed to the Supreme Court to close the borders, a Brazilian court temporarily suspended entry in 2018. In 2019, Nicolas Maduro also found reasons for closing the border on the Venezuelan side (Magalhães & Silva, 2018). As both countries tightened controls, wayfarers continued to move to and fro on paths and waterways in the Parima mountains and the Orinoco river, as they had been doing for years (Magalhães & Silva, 2018).

That is not to say that those journeys were easy. Some wayfarers managed to share houses in Pacaraima, Boa Vista and other Brazilian cities, but many were sleeping under bridges and on cardboard at street corners. Human trafficking, prostitution, drug smuggling and the collapse of food and medical supplies were all issues before they arrived, but some newspapers and politicians nevertheless blamed the wayfarers. During 2018, xenophobic attacks were almost routine: improvised barracks were destroyed, shelters were attacked, and wayfarers were beaten on the streets. It was difficult to talk to them after reading the sad news (*El País*, 2018a).

For better or for worse, newspapers also told tales of solidarity. The armed forces started building shelters and the UN sent envoys to coordinate a humanitarian response among local charities. American and European money funded much of the work. It was used to buy medicine and food, and it was also used to classify people as migrants or refugees. I was an active cog in this machine. I followed wayfarers as they looked for shelter, and I worked as an impromptu interpreter in registry offices and police stations. I met UN and Army envoys in local headquarters and situation rooms. I listened while priests and nuns told me of their good intentions. And I tried to learn from wayfarers too. I shared meals and words with those I met on the streets and tried to help however little I could. Sometimes this help included following them back and forth along roads. I met Ms J on one of these trips, along the road between the Venezuelan Gran Sabana and Pacaraima.

> Ms J: I wasn't expecting it. I really just called my husband and ran. I couldn't say
>   goodbye to my mother, to my grandmother, to my family, to anyone. We had

to leave it all there, the few baby clothes we had . . . the crib. I will feel *sau-dade*, but what could I do? It was not long before I graduated. But it couldn't wait. If my son had been born there, he might not be alive today. They don't have incubators . . . no surgical gloves, no equipment. And he was born at 32 weeks! He had to go straight into the incubator. And I had to wait quite some time. He is finally feeling better now. He is finally with me.

Here it is, *saudade*. Reading this conversation in retrospect, I still find it hard to tell how many versions of this weird Portuguese word there are in this little extract alone. For Ms J does not specify what she is going 'to miss'. Instead, she navigates the need to translate her Spanish 'extrañar' ('to feel the absence of', perhaps) using the word *saudade* associated with Portuguese. She tells me, all in one go, about her university, her mother, her father and her grandmother, about the crib and clothes she had bought for her baby, and about the son she was eager to meet. Because we can both say *saudade*, Ms J and I engage in this translingual practice (Canagarajah, 2013). To evoke the term vaguely helps us to go on chatting without having to pin down any one thing of which she feels *saudade*.

Not all wayfarers I met talked about *saudade* and, those who did, did not always evoke it like Ms J. Instead, they spoke in ways I would feel ok translating as being *saudade of* this or that, such as family or home. For instance, take this remark by Mr E, a Venezuelan wayfarer I met in the main and only square in Santa Elena de Uairén. We were sitting side by side on a bench, trying to hide from the sun in the shade of an almond tree and waiting to board the dodgy lorry that was to take us to Brazil. 'Você não vai sentir saudade?' I ask him, making conversation in Portuguese. Or, in one translation, 'Aren't you going to miss it?' Mr E answers me, mixing words in Spanish and Portuguese as he plays along.

Mr E: Sí. Sure, I'll miss home (*por supuesto, voy extrañar a casa*) but I'll try not to think about it. Leaving is easy. What is hard is not to get sad. Venezuela has many problems . . . but I will feel *saudade* of it, for sure.

Mr E and I get to share a bench and talk. Mr E gets to tell in Spanish about feeling *saudade* ('of Venezuela') and about missing *home* ('voy extrañar a casa'). I could translate Mr E's reply as 'Yes, of course I'll feel *saudade of this and that*' without giving a second thought to the terms being used. In one way, this translation would be practical. It would allow me to tell the story of a homesick Mr E missing his home and his homeland to a bigger English-speaking audience.

Maybe this is why Precise *Saudade* is becoming widespread in writing about the plight of wayfarers. In a newsreel in Portuguese, Brazil's broadcasting company tells us the reception granted to Venezuelans 'is not enough to stall the *saudade* of home' (Empresa Brasil de Comunicação [EBC], 2019). Reporting on a festival in Roraima, the UN office for refugees says in Portuguese that Venezuelans got together 'to kill a little of their *saudade* of home' (UNHCR, 2019a). Also in Portuguese, the Associated French Press (2018) describes '"Venezuelan Indians in Roraima" rebuilding life in Brazil while "*Saudosos* do Orinoco"'. Curiously, even in interviews in Spanish, *saudade* comes up as *saudade of* things. Asked why he left Venezuela, one interviewee replies: 'I would not stay in Venezuela starving to death.' And he concludes: 'I feel *saudade* of my family, but I will not leave' (Costa, 2019). It is impossible to know whether the word was smuggled in by the translator, but it shows up as *saudade of* relatives.

Precise *Saudade* has also found its way into the work of some Brazilian scholars. In a chapter on *Forced Migration Present in the South of Bahia* (Santos & Santos, 2018) the authors interview Ramon, a young Venezuelan. Ramon's *saudade* is big, the authors tell us (p. 269), but not just big of nothing in particular. The authors make a point of saying that '*Saudade* is big, *mainly of his grandmother*' (p. 269, my emphasis). In another text, a Venezuelan named Sonora is interviewed. The author tells us that '*saudade* and suffering mark the life of Venezuelans who migrate to Brazil' (Costa, 2019). Vague *Saudade* appears briefly but is not allowed to stay for long. The author asks Sonora what she misses most and, sure enough, Sonora is able to pin things down. 'I miss my home', she says. 'I had a house I struggled to build with my husband. I feel *saudade* of my home and of my mother' (Costa, 2019).

In all these snippets, Precise *Saudade* tries to settle things down: *saudade* of a person, a place or some other thing isolated, distinguished from others, and said to be important. Yet, though Precise *Saudade can* be evoked, it does not *have* to be: commenting on her journey, Ms J talks about baby clothes, college, cribs, home and parents and then she tells me she is feeling *saudade*. She does not single out anything – and neither do I push her to do so. Vague *Saudade* helps to keep the conversation going by giving space to wander around the term. The next section continues the case in favour of Vague Saudade by interfering with the search for precision about mobility and about the word *saudade*.

On not being precise about *saudade* (and mobility!)

Precision has lurked over writers since the first attempts to turn *saudade* into a concept. It is said that a Portuguese monarch, the fourteenth century king Duarte, was the first philosopher to seek a precise meaning for *saudade*. Dom Duarte's take on the word involved building a border between '*suydade*' as a pleasant feeling,[8] and other feelings he framed as inferior, such as *nojo* ('disgust') and *pesar* ('sorrow'). But it was also about borders in a literal sense. Portugal was trying to assert its independence from Castille and create an identity as a European nation (Teletin & Manole, 2015), and Duarte almost single-handedly established the distinction between Portuguese and other languages (Cerqueira, 1991). The book in which he seeks to define *suydade* – celebrated by many as the first philosophy book in Portuguese – is full of remarks about 'our costumes' and 'our language' (Cerqueira, 1991). Ironically, Dom Duarte reserved *suydade* for the Portuguese quite literally by royal decree ('it seems to me this name of *suydade* so unique of the Portuguese language that neither Latin nor another language that I know of has a name for such similar feeling') (Cerqueira, 1991).

Duarte was long dead when the Portuguese carracks arrived on the Indian coast. He was alive, however, when his father led the Portuguese fleet in its attack on Ceuta, starting the Portuguese expansion along the African coast and across the Atlantic Ocean. I guess *saudade* helped to spread the Portuguese colonial empire. Thus philosopher Afonso Botelho (1990) argued that the sociotechnical array that made Lisbon's long distance control possible would have been of no use if 'souls' had not been equipped by *saudade* ('If any person by my service and a warrant from me breaks, from her I feel *suydade*, certain him that from such departure I bear no resentment and . . . that I would be sad if he did not go') (Cerqueira, 1991, p. 457).

I do not want to go into etymology, but I find it revealing that the desire to be precise about *saudade* has walked hand-in-hand with attempts to set borders. The continuing discussion of the origins of the concept, Latin or Arabic, is telling in this regard. Philologist Barbara Cassin and her colleagues argue that 'the origin of soidades is the Latin plural *solitates* (solitudes)'. Portuguese scholar Michaelis de Vasconcellos (1922) might concur. Vasconcellos does not write of *saudade* though. She writes (proudly, perhaps?) about '*The Portuguese* Saudade'. On the other hand, we have scholars that defend an Arabic origin of the word in *saudah*. Deonísio da Silva (2014) notes that, in Arabic, the expressions *suad, saudá and suaidá* mean blood trampled and black inside the heart. Apparently, Arabic medicine diagnoses a liver disease making patients melancholic as *as-saudá*, and the Arabic سُوَيْداء (*suwayda*) influenced *saudade*.

I have little Latin and no Arabic at all. Neither am I a philologist, so I am not defending any side. Instead, what I am protecting is doubt. We might say that the word comes from Latin, *tout court*! And this might well be so. But maybe we would be losing something with a clear-cut statement like this. We might be losing the vagueness in *saudade* that helps speakers to fare well without caring too much for these things we now describe as 'Arabic' and 'Latin' cultures.

Did 'the erudite' turn *saudade* into a concept, or did 'ordinary speakers' give the term its meaning by mistaking *solitate* (solitude) with *saudar* (to greet) (Cassin et al., 2014)? Is *saudade* in Brazil the same as in Portugal (DaMatta, 1993)? Is it felt in the heart or understood in the mind (Farrell, 2006)? Can it be translated into other languages or not (Matos & Truzzi, 2015)? All these debates about *saudade* seem to be driven by a concern to divide and clarify. Perhaps there are good reasons for looking for answers to these questions. But I am pretty sure that attempts to tame the vague in *saudade* have fed inside/outside distinctions, with violent consequences for those on the losing side.

Against this background, I take joy in learning that none of these attempts at clarification has been very successful. The multiplicity of *saudade* is illustrated by studies of how the word was evoked by Portuguese settlers in Brazil in correspondence with their families in Europe. In it, we find *saudade* of clothes, utensils, musical instruments, salt cod, sardines, cheeses, parents, wives, siblings and children and of the smell of rosemary infused in love letters (Matos & Truzzi, 2015). *Saudade*, I suggest, never seems to have been about any *one* thing. Neither, or so George Monteiro (2013) has argued, does it translate into a single word in any other European language. For Monteiro, the German 'sehnsucht' would be limited to people. French 'souvenir' would leave too much space for sad memories (2013). The Greek 'nostalgia' would reduce *saudade* to the absence of the homeland, as would the English 'homesickness' (2013).

Is Monteiro saying that other languages need several words to catch the meaning of *saudade*? Maybe, but I prefer to read him in other terms. My preferred reading is that there are all kinds of things persons may relate to in a *saudade* way, and that these do not need to be pinned down; that what is poetic in *saudade* is the room it gives for wandering and that – perhaps – this is how we should leave the term.

I would like to take this way of reading into texts about mobility as well. Precision also seems to lurk in policy and scholarly texts that use terms such as nomads, migrants and refugees. Consider, for instance, how Brazilian scholars and UN agencies working at the border feel the need to 'disentangle' the 'mixed nature of Venezuelan migration flows'. The International Organization for Migration (2011, p. 82), defines 'regularization' as 'any process by which the authority in a State allows non-nationals in an irregular or undocumented situation to stay lawfully in the country'. A UNHCR officer adds that 'the purpose of regularization has been primarily to clear processing queues, to resolve *fait accompli* cases of long-term migrant residence and to bring migrants back to the formal sector so that they can be protected and taxed' (Papadopoulou, 2005, p. 2). Both agencies suggest this is particularly challenging for Venezuelan and Warao wayfarers. 'Venezuelan migration to Brazil presents features of "mixed" migration, given the motivations and expectations of migrant groups, which include, at least, economic migrants, migrants for humanitarian reasons and asylum seekers' (IOM, 2018a, p. 82). Adding to the complexity, 'the issue of indigenous refugees has distinct components from non-indigenous ones, especially related to their cultural habits, which must be respected' (UNHCR, 2019b, p. 17). Allegedly, migration flows (of this kind), classified as 'mixed', 'hold a strong connection to irregular migration, and present a major challenge to States' (Silva et al., 2018, p. 20; see also M'charek, this volume).

No doubt categories are often important for humanitarian work and may help to protect wayfarers (IOM, 2018a, 2018b; UNHCR, 2019b). Nonetheless, the terminology is suspect. In Refugee Law, if you cross an international border because you chose to do so or find a better job then you are counted as a migrant. Against this, if you were forced to leave your country or are afraid to return for fear of persecution then you become a refugee (Scheel & Squire, 2014). To make things more complicated, in Brazilian law you are also a refugee if you have left a country in which there are grave and generalized human rights violations, and you are entitled to a humanitarian visa if fleeing an economic and environmental crisis.

States have been classifying people as migrants and refugees for so long that these distinctions sound almost common sense. But the binary division has also attracted criticism. Some criticize the migrant/refugee divide for neglecting 'internally displaced people' (Cohen, 2007), for helping less to protect people than to sustain bureaucracy (Scalletaris, 2007) and for making migration sound opportunistic or even criminal (De Goede, 2018; Huysmans, 2006). Yet others ask whether this binary divide makes sense: in short, they note 'there is no clear border between mobility that is forced or voluntary, driven by economic drives or by fear of persecution' (Scheel & Squire, 2014) and that this is better understood as a continuum (Casas-Cortes et al., 2015).

And there are many more binaries in texts about mobility. For example, Brazilian authorities and humanitarian agencies also distinguish between 'settled and nomadic peoples'. This is explicit in texts on Warao 'nomadic mobility', but also in comments about 'temporary', 'circular' or 'pendular Venezuelan flows'.[9] The problem here is that the division is taken to be a difference between natural lifestyles. One that is sedentary is said to involve production in one place: people become sedentary when they live in fixed territories. In turn, a nomadic lifestyle involves travel(ling) from place to place, with no permanent home (Gilbert, 2014). This has recently been nuanced: having a 'home', 'habitat' or 'abode' for part of the time does not mean you are not nomadic, if this does not become fixed or permanent (Gilbert, 2014).

As with the migrant/refugee binary, this nomadic/settled divide is central to humanitarian and border policies, but it is suspect. Critics note that some mobile peoples have actively resisted settlement and have been coerced into staying put, while many have used contact with settled people to move more rather than less. Despite the progress narrative which sees *homo sapiens* starting as hunter-gatherers, moving into nomadism and finally settling into civilization, critics also remind us that settled people have lived in towns with no agriculture and that nomads may stop to harvest before moving on (Scott, 2017).

The terms that policy writers use to sustain the migrant/refugee and the nomad/settled binaries are not the same. But both express a proclivity to think of people as if they were in need of native soil and fixed roots like trees. Treating the inside as the norm and being outside as exceptional (Walker, 1993), they take also settlement to be the norm against which nomadism is to be contrasted (Isin, 2018; Scott, 2017). Perhaps this is why some scholars caution that versions of migration theory fall prey to 'methodological nationalism', assuming nationalist belonging as an 'invisible background for research' (Wimmer & Schiller, 2002, p. 302); or that some versions of citizenship theory reduce belonging to formal citizenship and reduce agency to action mediated through representative politics (Isin & Nielsen, 2008).

I want to steer away from these divisions by formally introducing the notion of wayfaring that I have used above. I borrow this from anthropologist Tim Ingold's (2007, p. 75) remarks on how different persons – I have in mind his contrast between 'Inuit' and 'British', in particular – relate to the world in which movement occurs. Ingold claims that the Inuit engage in movement as 'an ensemble of itineraries' (Collignon, 1996, p. 98, as cited in Ingold, 2007, p. 172, fn. 1). By contrast, for the British sea lords, movement is 'a course determined by the latitude and longitude of successive points *en route* to the intended destination' (Ingold, 2007, pp. 75). Inuit move 'along paths' while British sea lords sail 'across' oceans. For the English-speaking sailor, 'every destination is a terminus, every port a point of reentry into a world from which he has been temporarily exiled whilst in transit' (p. 77). For the wayfarer, movement has no final destination, 'for wherever he is, and so long as life goes on, there is somewhere further he can go' (p. 77; see also Ingold, 2011, pp. 148, 154–155; Ingold, 2018, p. 71). This is why my protagonists are wayfarers. In my eyes their movements are not about arriving or re-entering 'normality', but rather about faring well along the way, feeding their bellies and their spirits through active engagement with their paths. To grant monopoly to Precise *Saudade* would hinder their ability to do just that.

Moving along with *saudade*

Vague *Saudade* may be useful to wayfarers in several ways. The next vignette hints at one of these uses I found while crossing countries. As we enter the next scene, I am sitting in the back of a small car being driven at high speed, squeezed between a Venezuelan woman on my left and a father carrying his child on his lap on my right. Piles of bolivars[10] used to pay for the ride were partially blocking the drivers' view. I am not sure if he noticed I was apprehensive or if he wanted to pass the time, but the man with the child,

Mr D, started talking to me. He told me he had just been back from Brazil to pick up his daughter, who was staying with her aunt in Ciudad Bolivar. He told me that he had finally got a job as a construction worker in Boa Vista, and was bringing the girl to stay with him and her mother. I said that it must have felt good to see her again.

Mr D: Oh my God! When I was getting close, my heart started to beat faster. Tum! Tum! Tum! [He gestures in what seems to me as a heart beating strongly in his chest]. Oh, my god [smiling]! It was nine months now: nine months without seeing her. We couldn't bring her before. It was hard! . . . When we finally got the money, the army people said they were closing the border and I couldn't go through. I had to call and tell her she couldn't come yet. I thought I would die of *saudade* [stressing the s, as he says the word]. But here you are, my daughter [hugging her]. And how big you are [he says while tickling her]. *¿Extrañaste mucho a su papá? 'Sentí saudade'*, she replies with an accent. He insists: 'Did you say you missed daddy?' She does not say a word. She looks at him, and she smiles.

How to read this? If I were asked if I missed a particular person, I might use the word *saudade* to give a generic reply, 'I felt *saudade*', full stop, without saying what I was feeling *saudade* about. I might do this not because I really missed the person concerned but because I wanted to be polite. I would be evoking Vague *Saudade* as a politeness device. Or I might evoke Vague *Saudade* as an affectionate way of teasing the person for whom I actually felt *saudade*: to show care for my interlocutor by pretending half mockingly that I did not miss him at all, even though I was thinking about him all the time.

I cannot be sure about what Mr D's daughter was doing. Translating her words in retrospect makes it hard to know what went on. It also raises questions about whether it is possible to do justice to emotions and gestures in research texts. Even so, I think there is a lesson to be learned from Mr D and his daughter, even if we take it as a hint: that evoking Vague *Saudade* – without isolating, distinguishing or ranking that of which I feel *saudade* – is valuable. Though Precise *Saudade* could be expressed, to translate Mr D's question as 'have you missed *your father*?' and the daughter's reply as 'I have missed *you*' would block the possibility of evoking the term to be polite or engage in care.

Vague *Saudade* seems to help Mr D and his daughter to engage in these practices. And there are other possibilities, like using it as a shield against religious conversion or avoiding being fitted too tightly into categories about 'cultures' and 'lifestyles'. For instance, for Ms V, a Warao wayfarer, Vague *Saudade* seemed to act as a shield in conversations about religion. When I met Ms V, she was living in a football stadium re-purposed as a public shelter by the municipal government in Boa Vista. Claiming shortage of funds, little had been done to adapt the stadium's infrastructure. Whole families were sleeping on thin mattresses while others slept in hammocks hung between columns and walls. In the overcrowded accommodation fights regularly broke out. A video recording shot inside the stadium shows a group of Warao sitting in a circle, praying in a mixture of Spanish and Portuguese under the guidance of nuns (Empresa Brasil de Comunicação, 2017, 31:17). Looking at this, one of the priests in charge remarked:

There are fights, skirmishes, naturally. That's why we ask the sisters to put these prayer circles together at least once a day. Praying together helps to create a sense of solidarity among them.

Maybe I am overstating the benefits of politeness between fathers and daughters. Sometimes, politeness comes from fear of being hurt or hurting someone (Cutting, 2007). Though I hesitate to be precise, I found hints of this in my conversation with Ms V. In my next vignette I was talking to Ms V as she held a little TV set against her stomach, watching a show and swinging gently in a hammock.

> The friends, they told me that here they gave clothes and food. Sometimes they ask us to pray to say thanks. And we pray. But sometimes, when they tell us it is time to pray, I know it is nice, but I don't want to do it because the *saudade* makes me sad. It makes me want to go back. But there is not much to do now. I have to wait here and see. But I don't want to talk about it. I'm going to be sad. I don't want to say anything.

I did not witness Ms V talking of *saudade* to nuns and would not want to turn her use of *saudade* into a grand theory about migrants' autonomy or indigenous resistance. Even so, to be polemical, I would say that being vague about *saudade* did seem to help Ms V to be polite while protecting herself from some not-too-polite attempts to convert her to Catholicism. Ms V did not tell me about confronting the nuns. Instead, she talked about refusing to pray in non-confrontational terms by evoking Vague *Saudade*. These first stories were meant to highlight the potential in Vague *Saudade*: if it can interfere with the way people show care and pray to Gods, maybe it can also interfere with the way people draw borders around ways of living.

Categorically stuck

I had read in anthropological accounts that some Warao sing to ward off evil spirits. It is not difficult to find verses on this, called 'Hoa' in Warao, translated into Spanish or English. When I met Mr T, a young Warao, not much older than I am, I could not resist asking if Warao songs really described the snakes turned into the demons of which I had read in books. This is how Mr T got to tell me about the risks of the road. We talked sitting on the pavement beside a highway in Roraima, eating a plate of rice, and nothing else, cooked over an improvised pot from which 12 other Warao were being served. Mr T was kind enough to offer me a bowl.

Me: I've talked to some [Warao] living on the streets. You don't like the shelters?

Mr T: It's not that the shelters are not nice. It's just that there are too many Venezuelans . . . Everywhere I looked, there was a Venezuelan. It is not that the shelters are bad. It is just that we have a different attitude. *Somos viajeros* ['we are voyagers'].

A 2017 report by Brazil's Federal Attorney's Office describes the Warao as 'a single ethnic group with seasonal practices' (Ministério Público Federal [MPF], 2017, p. 7). Quoting an ethnographic study in Spanish, the report says that they live a 'a transhumant life between the "morichales" and channel banks' (Garcia Castro & Heinen, 2000, as cited in MPF, 2017, p. 13).[11] It notes that archaeological and linguistic evidence suggests that the Warao have always moved as groups searching for food, visiting and bartering. It is only the distances and directions of movement that have changed since the 1920s as a result of state interference, disease, oil drilling, mining and environmental degradation. In the 1990s, the Warao started to move to Venezuelan cities to sell fish and handicrafts and to buy food and medicine, and more recently, with shortages in Venezuela, they have begun to seek more goods in Brazil (IOM, 2018a).

Although this art of living seems to work for some of the Warao, humanitarian agencies consider it a challenge. In 2018, the IOM published a report commenting on Warao's 'mobility patterns':

> . . . in general, there appears to be no clarity or concern of the Warao natives in relation to the choices or options available for the regularization or definition of their stay in Brazil. Many of the indigenous people only communicate issues related to the need to have food, receive health care and provide basic consumer goods for their families. For the authorities, there are doubts as to the attempt to fix and internalize the Warao in Brazil, especially if confronted with the manifest desire for continuous, pendular return to the Bolivarian Republic of Venezuela. (IOM, 2018a, p. 66)

I assume the warning is well-meant, but it reveals entrenched notions about how wellbeing is to be achieved. More 'precise official information' is required. Are Warao nomads, do they have a 'pendular' form of mobility that will lead them back to Venezuela, or do they want to stay in Brazil? Here is Mr T:

> Mr T: The Brazilians, like that, in general, they complain a lot. They speak like that: 'you can't stay here, you can't stay here'. But then, again, if we go and move somewhere else, they complain too. I tried to talk to go the forest there for a while, but you should see . . . the government came straight for my throat. There are lot of protocols you need, a lot of studies, they said. They arrived and already started asking a lot of questions . . . They came with all these rules and resolutions and conventions. They surround you from all sides . . . and then it is better to just keep moving.

For those used to thinking of life as happening in one place, Mr T's way of living adds fuel to fire. 'If they are refugees, why do they keep going back?' or 'they are using the shelters as holiday camps' – some Brazilians I met used phrases like these. At the beginning of this section, I mentioned how Mr T reacted when asked about shelters. Vague *Saudade* shows up when he tells more about the 'different attitude' of *viajeros* (voyagers, as I translate it).

> Me: I read that Boa Vista's mayor said you should not go to the forest because you might interfere with other tribes there. Was that it?
>
> Mr T: Yes. The mayor said we needed an anthropological study. We needed a report to know the differences between our cultures. And then I saw them showing to us, the anthropologist showing to us we were already living like that, floating, for many years, and always like that. Then, when I went back

to my people, I said: 'If we want to float through Brazil we need to stay in Roraima. Because that's how you will dialogue with the mayor here' . . . I said, 'listen . . . I know we will feel *saudade*, but how can we get help today if we are going on the road tomorrow? Power doesn't work like that. It doesn't float with us, no.'

Both reports note the Warao talk of themselves as '*viajeros*' (Spanish) or 'voyagers' and '*canoeiros*' (Portuguese) or canoe-people. Both stressed the risk of imposing sedentarism on the Warao. The IOM (2018a, p. 118) is careful about this:

> Nomadism denotes a mobile way of life, organized around cyclical or seasonal patterns, but carries a strong stigma of incivility. However, mobility can be established to enhance the well-being and survival of the indigenous peoples involved and therefore constitutes a life strategy related to differentiated cultural identities and dignity protected by numerous human rights instruments. It is always important to know the reason why indigenous peoples move and then apply these definitions.

Again, both reports say that the best way to protect wayfarers is to allow them to live according to their 'culture's life strategies': nomadic people should not be forced into settled living. They tell us to be careful not to classify the Warao wrongly, but they do not question the need to 'apply these definitions'. I am not out to pass judgement. Maybe these authors try to apply labels like nomadic and sedentary because they believe this will help the Warao. And maybe it would do this for some Warao, if not for all. But this is the problem right there: by writing like this, these texts foster a habit of thinking, a form of speech and way of acting that insists that people are either Warao in a precise way, or they are not culturally Warao at all. This way of writing freezes frame, so to speak. Comments of this kind make it sound almost as if they are saying that the Warao move today as they always have and as they always will.

Engin Isin (2018) has argued that the assumption that persons form 'peoples' and live as 'a people' is problematic. Mobile persons might refuse settling and still relate to states in such unique ways that it makes little sense to group them as wholes. Think of the differences between hunter-gatherers, slaves and pirates. And even these categories are too encompassing. Strangers, outsiders and aliens have been 'Other' to 'Citizens', but their ways of being political were very different and subject to change (Isin, 2002). As Isin (2018, p. 121) reminds us, 'barbarians included various peoples whose relationships to states were always in flux'. Such peoples, as he puts it, playing with binary thinking, 'came in and out of various barbarian positions' (p. 121).

This helps me explain why I do not want to translate Mr T as talking of *saudade about something*, even if that something is the road. I do not want to make it sound as if being on the road is some kind of lyrical condition, a symbol of the Warao's supposedly 'more natural lifestyle' – as if even when he is 'forced to abandon' his lifestyle, Mr T is actually treasuring the 'Warao tradition' of floating freely. Sometimes, I guess, being on the road can be emancipating. But this does not allow us to assume that that is always the case. As the Hoa songs hint, being on the road can be dangerous. There are snakes that turn into devils that I cannot even understand. A Warao who only feels *saudade* of the road, and does this all the time, does not strike me as a wayfarer moving along paths, but as an epic hero in a scary book, insisting on moving on against all odds.

More generally, this is also why I hesitate to translate my informants' stories, equivocating against Vague *Saudade* and in favour of Precise *Saudade* about this or that. To do so would be to turn the road – or Venezuela, or home, or a lifestyle, or a 'traditional habitat' or a 'culture' – into yet more criteria for setting people apart. It would foster the association between inside/normal and outside/abnormal that Mr T seems to avoid. Yes, crossing self-made and state-made borders can be tough. But the act of walking across, along or around these divides is not *essentially* anything, either good or bad. It depends on how much room we give people to live, not as problems to be fitted into categories, but as wayfarers moving along their paths.

Saudade: Instead of a recap or a stopping point, talking vaguely about new stuff

In this article I followed the word *saudade* in the talk and texts of Venezuelans, Warao, journalists, Brazilian authorities, Portuguese monarchs, scholars and humanitarian workers. I took issue with a way of evoking *saudade* that strives for precision and contrasted this with ways of evoking *saudade* that are comfortable with being vague. It is tempting to dismiss Vague *Saudade* as showing ambiguity and imprecision alien to seeking the truth. But Vague *Saudade* seems to help wayfarers in other ways: to care for others, to protect others, to protect themselves and to tell me about worlds I will never fully understand.

There is a hint in this: as researchers-qua-translators, if we care about a topic that we find difficult to talk and write about, we can give up. Or we can go on talking using placeholders, approximations and other words that make it possible to hedge meanings. The hint is as simple as it is easy to ignore. Vague language is often enough. Too much precision may be alienating. When talking about things that are new or sound strange, vague language may help to keep conversations flowing. Certainly, it is relevant to how we translate wayfarers, and I suggest it is also germane to how we translate in research.

Lest we forget, not too long ago it was perfectly fine to write about 'other cultures' without paying attention to how texts came to count as knowledge of those 'Others'. Things changed when scholars started to explore the authority of texts. Over time, the notion that authors are able to represent the way informants 'actually behave' has been unmasked as a stylistic accomplishment. Banishing the 'I' in writing and sanitizing reports of all things emotional are also among the literary techniques shown to sustain textual authority (Clifford, 1983; Clifford et al., 2010). Recently, critics of the literary norms of detached and impersonal writing have become more vocal in defence of emotionally invested forms of storytelling about international relations (Doty, 2004; Inayatullah, 2011; Leander, 2015; Vrasti, 2008). Yet there is much writing about how people move across borders that gives the impression that authors are not present. Stylistic assumptions of 'ethnographic realism' are still very much in vogue.

Taking precision as a default goal for research is one assumption that is proving hard to shake off. Yes, some authors have come to appreciate that not all textures of matter have sharp shapes. Some things are messy, and striving for precision risks distorting them into clarity (Law, 2004). Yes, there are now fascinating ways of thinking about methods and terms and texts and meanings. But, for all the lip service paid to change and fluidity, it is not hard to read about the death of the author, subject positions, discursive devices and reader-response theories and then, ignoring it all, to insist on learning what authors 'actually mean'.

This might sound like a matter of concern for half a dozen academics, but, at their worst, realist readings close down the space for multiplicity, for deliberate imprecision, for controlled equivocation, and for writing that does not try to determine the truth but seeks rather to move on with what is multiple. All these ways of relating to research, not to mention alternative arts of living, risk being subordinated to a search for 'the point'.

Guy Cook (2007, p. 24), the British applied linguist and defender of poiésis in writing, has described readers who obsess with quickly getting to the point as being like old-school theologians, devoted to finding God's true voice in endlessly many and endlessly cryptic scriptures. Cook quips caustically that '... like some religious exegetists, [readers of this persuasion] can be dogmatic, narrow-minded and fundamentalist'. This is a strong phrase. It is harsh. I would not put it so bluntly myself. I would find a vaguer way of saying it. But I would not disagree.

Acknowledgements

I would like to thank the Warao, Venezuelans and all the informants who agreed to talk to me and encouraged me to translate their stories into text. I could not have had more luck with the editors, reviewers and copy desk professionals who so graciously and patiently took part in shaping this narrative. If these words can even hope to save space for vagueness in writings about *saudade* and mobility, it is only because they allowed the text to move quite literally along with the terms.

Funding

The author declared receipt of the following financial support for the research, authorship, and/or publication of this article: This project has received funding from the European Research Council (ERC) under the European Union's Horizon 2020 research and innovation programme (grant agreement No. 682317).

Notes

1. *El País*, 2018a.
2. *O Estado de São Paulo*, 2019.
3. UNHCR, 2019b.
4. Associated French Press, 2018.
5. Costa, 2019.
6. The Wareo are an indigenous people who live in an area that includes Venezuela, Guyana, and Surinam.
7. Anthropologist Tim Ingold has argued that some persons – in his stories, these usually are not English speakers – seem to relate to the act of moving as 'moving along paths'. He uses the word wayfarer as a shortcut to write about people that relate to movement in this way. This helps him to contrast wayfaring – moving along paths – to other ways of relating to their movement that put more weight on the idea of getting 'from point A to point B'. Later I will have more to say about why I prefer to write about 'wayfarers' instead of writing about

'migrants', 'refugees' or 'nomads' and other terms used by scholars to talk about those on the go.

8. 'Suydade he sentida mais com prazer do que com tristeza' – 'felt more with pleasure than with sadness' (in Cerqueira, 1991, pp. 455–457).

9. States and international organizations have put together a rather intricate typology of migration forms based on time. 'Incomplete migration', 'pendular migration', 'transnational migration', 'transit migration' and 'circular migration' are just some of the labels policy makers have come up with to express this fragmentation of human lives into bureaucratic figures. 'Circular migration' is actively promoted by the International Organization for Migration. 'If occurring voluntarily *and linked to the labor needs* of countries of origin and destination', IOM (2019) Glossary on Migration reads, 'the fluid movement of people between countries, including temporary or long-term movement, may be beneficial to all involved.' In contrast, 'Incomplete migration' is used to refer to movement of migrants who rely on travel visas to engage in commercial activities. People who rely on this form of migration are sometimes described as 'false tourists'. 'Pendular migration', in turn, is used to refers to migrants who organize their lives as a back and forth pattern between a country of origin, where they live, and a host state, where they work, thus evoking permanent provisionality. 'Transit migration' refers to 'migration in one country with the intention of seeking the possibility there to emigrate to another country as the country of final destination' as is linked to negatively charged expressions, as illegal migration, bogus asylum seekers and transnational criminality (IOM, 2014; see also Scheel & Squire, 2014).

10. Venezuela's currency at the time.

11. *Morichales* are particular complex ecosystems dominated by the moriche palm.

References

Associated French Press. (2018). Índios venezuelanos refazem a vida no Brasil saudosos do Orinoco. https://istoe.com.br/indios-venezuelanos-refazem-a-vida-no-brasil-saudosos-do-orinoco/ (accessed 5 November 2019).

Brazilian Federal Police. (2019). Polícia Federal atualiza números da migração de venezuelanos em RR. www.casacivil.gov.br/central-de-conteudos/noticias/2018/outubro/policia-federal-atualiza-numeros-da-migracao-de-venezuelanos-em-rr? (accessed 5 November 2019).

Botelho, A. (1990). *Da saudade ao saudosismo / Afonso Botelho* (1st ed.). Instituto de Cultura e Língua Portuguesa.

Canagarajah, A. S. (2013). *Translingual practice: Global Englishes and cosmopolitan relations.* Routledge.

Casas-Cortes, M., Cobarrubias, S., De Genova, N., Garelli, G., Grappi, G., Heller, C., & Tazzioli, M. (2015). New keywords: Migration and borders. *Cultural Studies, 29*(1), 55–87.

Cassin, B., et al. (2014). *Dictionary of untranslatables: A philosophical lexicon.* Princeton University Press.

Cerqueira, L. (1991). Dom Duarte e o Sentido Ontológico da saudade. *Revista Portuguesa de Filosofia, 47*(3), 455–467.

Clifford, J. (1983). On ethnographic authority. *Representations, 2*(2), 118–146.

Clifford, J., Marcus, G. E., & Fortun, K. (2010). *Writing culture: The poetics and politics of ethnography.* University of California Press.

Cohen, R. (2007). Response to Hathaway. *Journal of Refugee Studies, 20*(3), 370–376.

Cook, G. (2007). This we have done: The vagueness of poetry and public relations. In J. Cutting (Ed.), *Vague language explored* (pp. 21–39). Palgrave Macmillan.

Costa, K. (2019). Saudade e sofrimento marcam a vida de venezuelanos que migraram para o Brasil. http://radioagencianacional.ebc.com.br (accessed 6 November 2019).

Cutting, J. (Ed.). (2007). *Vague language explored*. Palgrave Macmillan.

DaMatta, R. (1993). Antropologia da saudade. *Folha de S. Paulo.* www.folha.uol.com.br/ (accessed 28 January 2019).

da Silva, D. (2014). *De onde vêm as palavras: Origens e curiosidades da língua portuguesa* (17th ed.). Lexikon.

De Goede, M. (2018). The chain of security. *Review of International Studies, 44*(1), 24–42.

Doty, R. L. (2004). Maladies of our souls: Identity and voice in the writing of academic international relations. *Cambridge Review of International Affairs, 17*(2), 377–392

Empresa Brasil de Comunicação. (2017). *Caminhos da Reportagem: Em terra estrangeira* [Reporting Paths: In a foreign land]. https://www.youtube.com/watch?v=rKidW3I4Kq4 (accessed 12 February 2020).

Empresa Brasil de Comunicação. (2019). *Refugiados fazem curso do Senac para inserção no mercado de trabalho.* http://agenciabrasil.ebc.com.br/ (accessed 5 November 2019).

El País. (2018a, August 27). O 'monstro da xenofobia' ronda a porta de entrada de venezuelanos no Brasil. https://brasil.elpais.com (accessed 5 November 2019).

El País. (2018b, February 23). O venezuelano que fugiu de Maduro e da fome e vive um 'milagre' no Brasil. https://brasil.elpais.com (accessed 5 November 2019).

Farrell, P. (2006). Portuguese saudade and other emotions of absence and longing. In B. Peeters (Ed.), *Semantic primes and universal grammar: Empirical evidence from the Romance languages* (pp. 235–258). John Benjamins.

Gilbert, J. (2014). *Nomadic peoples and human rights.* Routledge.

Huysmans, J. (2006). *The politics of insecurity: Fear, migration and asylum in the EU.* Routledge.

Inayatullah, N. (2011). *Autobiographical international relations.* Routledge.

Ingold, T. (2007). *Lines: A brief history.* Routledge.

Ingold, T. (2011). *Being alive: Essays on movement, knowledge and description.* Routledge.

Ingold, T. (2018). *Anthropology and/as education.* Routledge.

International Organization for Migration. (2018a). Aspectos jurídicos da atenção aos indígenas migrantes da Venezuela para o Brasil. https://refworld.org (accessed 5 November 2019).

International Organization for Migration. (2018b). Migration trends in the Americas. https://robuenosaires.iom.int/ (accessed 5 November 2019).

International Organization for Migration. (2019). *Glossary on migration* (2nd ed.). International Migration Law, n. 34. www.iom.int/glossary-migration-2019 (accessed 28 January 2020).

Isin, E. (2002). *Being political: Genealogies of citizenship.* University of Minnesota Press.

Isin, E. (2018). Mobile peoples: Transversal configurations. *Social Inclusion, 6*(1), 115–123.

Isin, E. & Nielsen, G. M. (Eds.). (2008). *Acts of citizenship.* Palgrave Macmillan.

Law, J. (2004). *After method: Mess in social science research.* Routledge.

Leander, A. (2015). Ethnographic contributions to method development: 'Strong objectivity' in security studies. *International Studies Perspectives, 17*(4), 1–14.

Magalhães, B., & Silva, J. C. J. (2018). Pela coerência: como não lidar com a imigração venezuelana. https://puc-rio.academia.edu/BrunoMagalhães (accessed 5 November 2019).

Matos, M. I. S., & Truzzi, O. M. S. (2015). Presença na ausência: cartas na imigração e cartas de chamada. *História Unisinos, 19*(3), 338–347.

Ministério Público Federal. (2017). *Sobre a situação dos Indígenas da etnia Warao, da Região do Delta do Orinoco, nas cidades de Boa Vista e Pacaraima.* www.scribd.com/document/352654297/Parecer-Tecnico-n208-2017-WARAO-BOA-VISTA (accessed 28 January 2020).

Mixed Migration Centre. (2019). Waning welcome: the growing challenges facing mixed migration flows from Venezuela: a field assessment study in Colombia and Peru. https://reliefweb.int/sites/reliefweb.int/files/resources/072_venezuela.pdf (accessed 11 November 2019).

Monteiro, G. (2013). *Essay: An anatomy of Saudade.* https://portuguese-american-journal.com/essay-an-anatomy-of-saudade-by-george-monteiro/ (accessed 1 July 2019).

O Estado de São Paulo. (2019). Sem Maduro, desejo de voltar à Venezuela é dúvida. https://internacional.estadao.com.br (accessed 5 November 2019).

Omura, K., Otsuki, G. J., Satsuka, S., & Morita, A. (2018). *The world multiple: the quotidian politics of knowing and generating entangled worlds.* Taylor & Francis.

Papadopoulou, A. (2005). Regularization programmes: an effective instrument of migration policy? *Global Migration Perspectives*, No. 33.

Santos, F. O., & Santos, M. L. S. (2018). Venezuela e Brasil: a migração forçada presente no sul da Bahia. In R. Baeninger & J. C. J. Silva (Eds.), *Migrações Venezuelanas* (pp. 250–258). Universidade Estadual de Campinas:, Núcleo de Estudos de População Elza Berquó (NEPO) – UNICAMP.

Scalettaris, G. (2007). Refugee studies and the international refugee regime: A reflection on a desirable separation. *Refugee Survey Quarterly*, *26*(3), 36–50.

Scheel, S., & Squire, V. (2014). Forced migrants as illegal migrants. In E. Fiddian-Qasmiyeh, G. Loescher, K. Long, & N. Sigona (Eds.), *The Oxford handbook of refugee and forced migration studies* (pp. 227–240). Oxford University Press.

Scott, J. C. (2017). *Against the grain: A deep history of the earliest states.* Yale University Press.

Silva, J. C. J., Bógus, L. M. M., & Silva, S. A. G. J. (2018). Os fluxos migratórios mistos e os entraves à proteção aos refugiados. *Revista Brasileira de Estudos de População*, *34*(1), 16–30.

Teletin, A., & Manole, V. (2015). Expressing cultural identity through *saudade* and *dor*: A Portuguese–Romanian comparative study. In *Identity – concepts, theories, history and present Realities (a European overview).* Université de Aveiro.

United Nations. (2019). ONU Migração atua em diversas frentes para apoiar a gestão do fluxo venezuelano no Brasil. https://nacoesunidas.org (accessed 11 November 2019).

United Nations High Commissioner for Refugees. (2018). Venezuela situation: Responding to the needs of people displaced from Venezuela. https://reliefweb.int/report/colombia/venezuela-situation-responding-needs-people-displaced-venezuela-supplementary-appeal (accessed 11 November 2019).

United Nations High Commissioner for Refugees. (2019a). Desfile de beleza com crianças venezuelanas movimenta abrigo para refugiados e migrantes em Boa Vista. www.acnur.org/portugues/2019 (accessed 5 November 2019).

United Nations High Commissioner for Refugees. (2019b). Nota informativa para municípios sobre chegadas espontâneas de população venezuelana, incluindo indígenas. www.acnur.org/portugues/wp-content/uploads/2019/08/Nota-Informativa-para-Munic%C3%ADpios.pdf (accessed 11 November 2019).

van de Port, M., & Mol, A. (2015). Chupar frutas in Salvador da Bahia. *Journal of the Royal Anthropological Institute*, *21*, 165–180.

Vasconcellos, C. Michaëlis de (1922). *A saudade portuguesa: divagações filológicas e literar–históricas em volta de Inês de Castro e do cantar velho 'Saudade minha-Ôuando te veria?'* (2nd ed., revista e acrescentada). Renascença portuguesa.

Vrasti, W. (2008). The strange case of ethnography and international relations. *Millennium: Journal of International Studies*, *37*(2), 279–301.

Walker, R. B. J. (1993). *Inside/outside: International relations as political theory.* Cambridge University Press.

Wimmer, A., & Schiller, N. G. (2002). Methodological nationalism and beyond: nation–state building, migration and the social sciences. *Global Networks*, 2(4), 301–334.

Author biography

Bruno Magalhães is a postdoctoral fellow at the International Relations Institute of the Pontifical Catholic University of Rio de Janeiro (IRI, PUC-Rio) and an executive director of PUC-Rio's Digital Humanities Laboratory (#dhLab, PUC-Rio). He was also a postdoctoral visiting fellow at the University of Amsterdam, as a member of ERC-funded 'Project Follow', led by professor Marieke de Goede. He holds a PhD in Political Science and International Studies from the Open University, UK. His research focuses on how borders – inside and outside, normal and abnormal, good or bad, valuable or worthless, welcome or unwelcome, dangerous or safe – are practically accomplished, sustained, questioned, played with, circumvented and otherwise made irrelevant. For his doctoral research, he carried out an ethnographic study amid eligibility officers formally responsible for the work of Refugee Status Determination in Brazil. RSD is the work of the legal inquiry on which the Brazilian government, and most government these days, rely to set apart men, women and children classified as 'genuine refugees' and 'others' deemed deportable. The resulting monograph (*Inverting Skepticism: An Ethnography of Asylum Decision-making*, Palgrave, 2020, forthcoming) is a study of the practices on which the migrant/refugee binary lies, as in attempts to assess the legal fit, empirical support and narrative coherence of asylum applications, Bruno's current obsession is with following people, things and terms, like *saudade*, as they acquire different values in chains of translation.

Verbing *meahcci*: Living Sámi lands

The Sociological Review Monographs
2020, Vol. 68(2) 45–61
© The Author(s) 2020
Article reuse guidelines:
sagepub.com/journals-permissions
DOI: 10.1177/0038026120905473
journals.sagepub.com/home/sor

Solveig Joks
Liv Østmo
Sámi Allaskuvla [Sámi University of Applied Sciences], Norway

John Law
Department of Sociology, The Open University, UK, and Sámi Allaskuvla [Sámi University of Applied Sciences], Norway

Abstract
This article is about translating and mistranslating a Sámi landscape word. That word is *meahcci*. In what follows we start by exploring the logic of *meahcci*, contrast this with Norwegian land practices, with *utmark* – the term which is usually used to (mis)translate it into Norwegian – or such English-language terms as wilderness. We show that *meahcci* has nothing to do with agricultural logics, ideas of the wild, or cartographic spaces. Rather *meahcit* (in the plural) are practical places, uncertain but productive social relations with lively and morally sensible human and non-human beings in which there is no division between nature (Norwegian *natur*) and culture (*kultur*). *Meahcit* are taskscapes (Ingold) or places–times–tasks. Then we consider the relatively verb- or action-oriented character of the (North) Sámi language, and show that Sámi land practices and the patterns of words weaving through these enact contextual, processual and radically relational versions of space, time, interaction, subjectivities, objectivities, and the beings that live in the world. We also touch on the material character of this difference – the location of words and forms of knowing. We conclude by reflecting on what Sámi *meahcci* practices suggest for a hegemonic English-language social science that is also struggling to articulate situated and radically relational ways of knowing.

Keywords
human–non-human relations, landscape, *meahcci*, Sámi, spatiality

Starting

I am a Sámi who has done all sorts of Sámi work and I know all about Sámi conditions. I have come to understand that the Swedish government wants to help us as much as it can, but they

Corresponding author:
Solveig Joks, Sámi Allaskuvla, Sámi University of Applied Sciences, Hánnoluohkká 45, Guovdageaidnu, NO-9520, Norway.
Email: solveig.joks@samiskhs.no

don't get things right regarding our lives and conditions, because no Sámi can explain to them exactly how things are. And this is the reason: when a Sámi becomes closed up in a room, then he does not understand much of anything, because he cannot put his nose to the wind. His thoughts don't flow because there are walls and his mind is closed in. And it is also not good at all for him to live in dense forest when the air is warm. But when a Sámi is on the high mountains, then he has quite a clear mind. And if there were a meeting place on some high mountain, then a Sámi could make his own affairs quite plain. (Johan Turi, *Muitalus sámiid birra* [*An account of the Sami*], 1910/2012, p. 11)

Today, negotiations with *meahcci* are largely superseded by negotiations about *meahcci* . . . (Schanche, 2002, p. 169, our translation)

This article is about translating and mistranslating a Sámi landscape word. That word is *meahcci*.

Sámi people live in the subarctic north of Fennoscandia, in Sápmi. In the past they have hunted, gathered, fished and herded reindeer, and the landscape, *meahcci*, has been central to their lives. This is still the case for many. At the same time, for at least 300 years, Sámi people have been marginalised by sometimes brutal and racist forms of colonialism, whilst Sámi languages, practices and relations to the land have been squeezed.[1] As a part of this the word *meahcci* has been readily mistranslated and its practices have been ignored because they fit poorly with those of the colonising nation states and their languages.[2] (They fit equally poorly with the English language.) In what follows we start by exploring the logic of *meahcci*, and contrast this with Norwegian land practices and terms. Then we consider the relatively verb- or action-oriented character of the (North) Sámi language, and show that Sámi land practices and the patterns of words weaving through these enact contextual, processual and radically relational versions of space, time, interaction, subjectivities, objectivities, and the beings that live in the world. We also touch on the material character of this difference – the location of words and forms of knowing. We conclude by briefly reflecting on what Sámi *meahcci* practices suggest for environmental struggles with the powerfully colonising practices and language of the dominant Norwegian, and the (differently colonising) English of the social sciences.

Some cautions before we start. First, *meahcci* practices are highly variable, and there is no single, unchanging or essential 'Sámi culture'. The latter is diverse, has changed throughout its long history, and very substantially with the arrival of motorised transport and integration into market economies.[3] Second, since the relation between Sámi and their colonisers is one of long-term reciprocal (albeit asymmetrical) entanglement, any attempt to divide these is an analytical and political convenience rather than a binary essentialism.[4] Third, as a consequence of this colonial history, many Sámi people do not speak the Sámi language, and virtually all of those who do are bilingual. How this subordination is shaping the Sámi language is a matter for debate, but it is probably eroding at least some of the ways in which it is distinctive (Helander & Kailo, 1998, p. 66). Fourth, as an aspect of these changes, many Sámi have not grown up with *meahcci* practices, and would not, for instance, recognise the vocabularies of those who go fishing in *meahcci*.[5] And fifth, though related dynamics might be detailed for Sweden, Finland and Russia, here we focus primarily on Norway, and on the largest and the strongest of the remaining Sámi languages, North Sámi.[6]

Meahcit as taskscapes

Away from the coast and on the plateau much of Norwegian Sápmi is subarctic tundra, with lower areas in which there are small trees including birch and willow, marshes with rushes, cotton-grass and cloudberries, and low hills with heather, lingonberries and bilberries. There are rivers and lakes with fish including salmon, arctic char, trout and powan. And there are rocky outcrops, together with wildlife including summertime mosquitoes and midges, crows, magpies and ptarmigan, ducks and geese, hares, reindeer, moose and wolverines, while for at least six months of the year it is far below freezing (temperatures of −30°C are not uncommon). Potentially dangerous for those who do not understand and respect it, this is a landscape that indeed deserves and receives respect. At the same time, since prehistory it has also been a potentially richly rewarding set of relations, a place of sustenance and of safety for Sámi people. To understand this, we need to start by saying that *meahcci* has been and remains a *creative collection of practical places and relations* – a set of *activity spaces* (a term used by Valkonen & Valkonen [2018] drawn from Doreen Massey) or (Tim Ingold's felicitous term) *taskscapes*.[7] Though this plural would be somewhat unusual in Sámi, in the present English-language context it might be better to talk of '*meahcit*' (the plural of *meahcci*), locations where people undertake different tasks at different times that often continue to form an important part of their livelihoods such as fishing, berry picking, hunting and cutting firewood or sedge.

A number of points arise. The first is that though they might look so to outsiders, *meahcit* are *not* wilderness (Norwegian *villmark*) (Østmo & Law, 2018; Tervaniemi & Magga, 2018). They may rather be a part of home and a place of safety (Schanche, 2002, p. 156).[8] They are also a set of potentially *productive relations*. And crucially, those relations weave together what English-language common sense distinguishes as nature and culture and Norwegian as *natur* and *kultur* (Valkonen & Valkonen, 2018). Our first point, then, is that the term *meahcci* effortlessly avoids this much-questioned binary without the need for complex or counterintuitive conceptual footwork.

A second point: there are multiple *meahcit* because Sámi people practise different *productive activities* in different places and at different times. This also means that *meahcit* are concrete and specific, a reality that is also reflected in the language. *Muorrameahcci* is where you collect firewood, *luomemeahcci* is where you go cloudberry picking, and *guollemeahcci* is where there is a fishing lake, or you may go to *meahcci* to collect materials for *duodji* (Sámi handicrafts). However, none of these *meahcit* is a fixed place, for where you go and what you do always depends on circumstances. Unsurprisingly, there are also many specialist task-related terms. So *rohtu* is an area with woodland and plants close to a river where reindeer may graze early in the winter before there is too much snow.[9] And *jassa* describes an appropriately sized and sited patch of snow that lasts through the summer and is large enough to cool the air and partially protect reindeer against insect attack (Meløe, 1988). This time–space specificity multiplies itself further because different families or *siida* (small collectives of, for instance, reindeer herding families; Sara, 2009, 2011) undertake these tasks in different locations. This means (for instance) that it is wrong for people in one family to pick cloudberries in the place where another family traditionally goes to do this (Schanche, 2002, p. 166). Writing about this in English is awkward because if we use terms such as 'locations' (as we just have) topography tends to displace activity. But this is not what happens in Sámi because *meahcit* are task-related, shifting according to season and weather, and have little to do with cartographic space (maps are empty of experience), or indeed with calendar time. Instead, the relevant conceptual units are better imagined as *places–times–tasks* – combinations of actions, encounters and located potential resources. In short, the practices of *meahcci* bypass not only the nature/culture binaries of Norwegian and English, but also the abstractions that go both with clock time and two- or three-dimensional cartographic conceptions of the spatial.[10]

Third, *meahcit* are also about *unfolding encounters* with other more or less powerful actors (Helander-Renvall, 2010; Ingold, 1993; Mazzullo & Ingold, 2008; Tervaniemi & Magga, 2018) including people, animals, birds and fish, and what outsiders might think of as natural phenomena such as snowstorms or mountains, lakes or rivers, as well as invisible entities such as 'sacred places' or visible but 'occult' phenomena including messenger birds, or visions. Crucially, those encounters are *unpredictable*. 'The term "stability" is a foreign word in our language', writes reindeer herder Johan Mathis Turi (A. Oskal, 2008, p. 24). As Sámi people put it, '*jahki ii leat jagi viellja*', 'one year is not the next year's brother', which means that *meahcci* practices cannot be rigidly planned or controlled (Sara, 2009, p. 172; Schanche, 2002, p. 168). How circumstances will unfold can be anticipated, in part on the basis of long-term observation and experience growing out of practice, and such educated and contexted observation is crucial to survival. But the taskscapes of *meahcci* demand flexibility. If the water level in the river is right and this combines with other appropriate circumstances, then it is possible to fish salmon. If it is not, then there is no point (Joks & Law, 2017). The implication, once again, is that *meahcit* generate realities in which the order and the character and location of contingent encounters come before any fixed plan.[11]

Fourth, as we have seen, *meahcit* are constituted in encounters with *lively and powerful beings*. Though all of these may be powerful, Sámi people distinguish between *luondu*, beings that breathe such as animals, and those that do not, such as lakes (*jávri*).[12] If the snow is too icy, if the lake does not want to give fish, if a *sieidi* (a 'sacred place') is offended, then you cannot successfully hunt, graze your reindeer or catch fish. And whether or not these beings breathe, they are often *morally sensible*. The Sámi word *bivdit* catches this: it both means to ask or request, *and* to hunt, snare, or fish. You ask lakes or animals before you fish or hunt, and some animals – for instance wolves or bears – also have the power to divine your thoughts and intentions, which means that you may also need to disguise these.[13] Similarly, the beings in *meahcci* demand and deserve *respect*. Mikkel Nils Sara (2009, p. 173), citing Nils Oskal, notes that to think of a reindeer 'as a means for our own intentions and not as a means with its own dignity' is a dangerous insult, and Oskal himself observes (2000, p. 176) that fishing luck relates in part to how a lake and its fish are treated. So, after fishing you should bless a lake even if you have caught nothing, and you return the bones of any fish you have eaten to a nearby birch tree (Østmo & Law, 2018). In short, your actions, intentions and thoughts all have moral dimensions which in turn means that they have practical consequences too. As Schanche puts it, you negotiate *with*, not *about*, *meahcci* (see the second citation at the head of this article). This means that *meahcci* practices have nothing to do with interactions with insensate objects in a morally neutral empirical world. Rather, they participate in a world in which what unfolds is intended – or not.[14] To put it differently, they enact what we might think of as *extended sociality* – so long as we understand that 'sociality' is a way of talking about association, about what it is that goes with what, rather than implying a reduction to 'the social' narrowly conceived as a set of arrangements confined to human beings alone.[15] Alternatively, if we were to borrow Max Weber's (1978) terminology, we might say that these are practices of enchantment (*Entzauberung*) – though we would also need to strip this term of its negative and historically colonial imputation of 'magic' or 'witchcraft', connotations that remain painful in Sápmi to the present day.[16]

Mistranslating *meahcci*

As we noted above, Sápmi is colonial. Over at least three centuries there has been settlement, and the imposition of state frontiers, laws, citizenship, national languages, forms of economic extraction, agriculture and religion (Minde, 2003). There has been recent pushback, starting in the 1980s, with recognition of Sámi indigeneity and language, the creation of Sámi parliaments, and the return of state-owned land in part of north Norway to a body, the Finnmark Estate, with substantial Sámi representation (Broderstad, 2014; Johnsen et al., 2015). But still the pressures unfold: roads, mining, offshore oil and gas extraction, outside commercial and recreational fishing, fish farming, hydroelectric power, wind turbines, national parks, outdoor recreation, tourism and environmentalism, all are at work and all are squeezing *meahcci* practices.

In this context words become important. So, for instance, *meahcci* is habitually mistranslated as *utmark*. Like *meahcci*, this Norwegian term does not readily translate into English. Briefly, however, it is one half of a binary *innmark/utmark* division in which it is the uncultivated other of the farming that defines *innmark*. It is the unfenced area without permanent habitation beyond the fields of a farm where, for instance, cows may graze in summer.[17] This agricultural logic is complemented by a second logic which Norwegians call *friluftsliv* – roughly 'open-air life'. This indexes a set of originally nineteenth-century imaginaries and practices central to Norwegian national and personal identity, and *utmark* is where urban Norwegians practise *friluftsliv* by skiing, walking, climbing, camping, and seeking physical and spiritual renewal. Indeed, so important is *friluftsliv* that Norway has been criss-crossed for more than a century by much-used marked trails for walking and skiing (Ween & Abram, 2012), and new trails are being marked in and through Sápmi. All of this was codified in a 2009 'right to roam' *friluftsliv* law. Within certain limits, so long as you do not harm the environment and you clear up after yourself, this law allows you to walk or ski, gather wild berries and mushrooms, camp and make fires anywhere in *utmark*.[18] The word *villmark* (wilderness) is not in the text of the law but the logic of (a specifically Norwegian version of) wilderness is clear: there is that which is *cultivated*, and then there is that which is *wild* (the law mentions 'wild berries', 'wild mushrooms'). You may roam in the latter, but this is potentially fragile and needs to be protected and conserved (Schanche, 2002). Except that what counts as 'harm' is also contested in a way that protects and reproduces an *utmark* logic. So, for instance, the law permits the hunting of ptarmigan with dogs early in the autumn, but, back to *meahcci*, Sámi critics complain that it allows this before the young birds have fledged. And, more *meahcci* harm, this sometimes affects reindeer too.

So how does *utmark* relate to *meahcci*? It depends on who you ask. On the one hand, it doesn't. 'The Sámi term *meahcci* and the general meaning of this term are not identical to the definition of *utmark* in the *friluftsliv* law' (Sámediggi, 2007, section 2, our translation from Norwegian). These words come from the Norwegian Sámi parliament. On the other hand, if you ask the Norwegian national parliament, the *Storting*, they are (taken to be) the same: '*meahcci* shall be understood as identical to *utmark*'.[19] These are the words of the Norwegian national *friluftsliv* law. And since the Sámi parliament has only advisory powers, this means that in Norwegian law *meahcci* and *utmark* are indeed the same.[20] As many have noted (Schanche, 2002; Ween & Lien, 2012), this is colonialism at work, an *imposed but performative mistranslation*. And we have said enough about the logic of *meahcit* above to see why this is a problem. One, Sámi land practices *work* the land and have no notion of wilderness or a nature–culture distinction. Two, they don't imagine it as a bounded area, a cartographically delineated territory on a map, but rather as a series of circumstantial and practical task-related *meahcit* in the plural. And three, those *meahcit* involve encounters with lively, powerful and morally sensible beings. In all of these respects, *utmark* is alien to *meahcci*. It enacts landscape, space, time, human, non-human and extra-human relations very differently. It implies quite different understandings of rights and wrongs or normativities. And it also enacts different versions of *what it is to know*.[21] So how are the latter reflected in language?

The answer comes in several parts. First, in Sámi as in other Finno-Ugric languages, nouns are easily made out of verbs and vice versa.[22] For instance, the verb *njeaðgat* means 'snow blowing lightly on tracks' (Grenersen et al., 2016, p. 1185) from which *njeaðga* (a substantive derived from the verb) can be derived as a description of a particular form of snow. How to translate this? Modifying Nielsen (1962) (as cited in Grenersen) we suggest 'the wind blew a little, so that snow settled unevenly on tracks leaving them barely visible especially on the side from which the wind was blowing'. Second, Sámi nouns are often *relationally descriptive*. *Njeaðga* is a case in point, as is *muorrameahcci* which, as we saw above, is *meahcci* where firewood is collected. But proper names may also be descriptive. For instance, there have been avalanche skiing deaths on a mountain north of Tromsø called *Sorbmegáisá*, whose name aggregates *sorbmi* (accidental death) with *gáisá* (high mountain) (Grenersen et al., 2016, pp. 1191–1192). Third, often in Sámi the emphasis is less on nouns and more on verbs and actions. The Sámi authors of this article tease their British co-author by asking 'What is the wind doing in English if it is not blowing? Is it sitting in a tree?' (Østmo & Law, 2018, p. 359). Though this is self-evident and sounds strange, in Sámi it is grammatically possible to say '*biegga bieggá*', which might be rendered as 'wind [noun] is winding [the gerund of a verb]'.[23] But often in talking of wind the noun *biegga* is absent and instead people say something like '*eske iððes biekkai*' ('this morning was blowing'). Fourth, this relational subtlety is also assisted by a series of noun cases. These include: the illative, direction towards, into (as in '*mun manan meahccái*', which means 'I am going to *meahcci*'); the locative, which expresses physical relations or movement (as in '*mun lean meahcis*', which means 'I am in *meahcci* somewhere' and '*mun lean muorrameahcis*' which means 'I am in *meahcci* working with firewood'); the comitative, which is accompanying (as in '*mun lean mánáiguin meahcis*', which means 'I am together with the children in *meah-cci*' – though this sounds rather odd); and the essive which is a temporary or changing duration (as in '*dál lea diet guovlu meahccin fas šaddan*', which means 'now [*dál*] that [*diet*] the area [*guovlu*] has become [*lea šaddan*] meahcci [*meahccin*, essive] again [*fas*]', a phrase which might be used for talking of formerly cultivated land that has become *meahcci* because no-one lives there any longer).

The Sámi language also reflects and reproduces processes and relations in other ways. Mikkel Nils Sara characterises reindeer herding as a *compromise* between the herder and his reindeer that benefits both (Sara, 2009, p. 160; 2011, p. 148). Control is impossible (Sara, 2009, p. 161), so those relations depend on careful observation and communication between animal and human being. Sámi herders speak of *bohcco luondu* (initially mistranslatable as 'the nature [*luondu*] of herded reindeer [*bohcco*]') which, however:

> . . . includes features such as reflexes, reactions to external stimuli, typical behaviour in relation to other reindeer, natural surroundings and seasons, behavioural characteristics of groups of animals, and, finally, imprinted or learned affiliation to specific landscapes. (Sara, 2009, p. 160)

The linguistic point is that *bohcco luondu* is *not* an attribute of an animal ('the nature of reindeer') or a group of animals, but points to an *unfolding and uncertain process* which includes the relations between herders, animals, and the interactions of the latter with changing aspects of the environment. Sara makes a similar point about the word *oaivil* (2009, pp. 148, 171). Reindeer have *oaivil* (most easily mistranslated as 'opinions') as they respond to changes in the environment and remembering where they have moved before. If we continue the mistranslation, we might say that herders read these changing 'opinions', and in turn respond to them with their own. But this is a misunderstanding. *Oaivil* comes from *oaivi* which means 'head', and herders are actually watching the heads of their reindeer:

> Herders can predict the next move of the reindeer by watching what they are focused on and what they seem to sense. So by asking someone's *oaivil* one would thus express it literally, not as *what do you mean*, but rather *where is your attention*? So *oaivil* in the context of reindeer herding means the beginning of a movement, intention, or proposed direction, and not, as in translation, to a permanent position or opinion one has formed. (Sara, 2011, p. 148, italics in the original)

The mistranslation displaces the reader from relation, focus, unfolding and possible movement in favour of a more stable reality. To put it differently, it shifts emphasis from an interactive and fluid subjectivity to one that is more bounded in which people or reindeer now have attributes called 'opinions'. Something important is being lost here. So, for instance, the word *soabalašvuohta* means peaceful coexistence (Sara's 'compromise'), but in Sápmi this is a good rather than a second best. This is partly because in a context of continuing mutual dependence it is important to sustain social relations of all kinds, and to avoid putting yourself in a position where you have to complain about the behaviour of others. If we were to put this into social science language, we might say that extended socialities go with what we might think of as 'soft subjectivities'.[24]

Knowing/knowledge materials

So our argument is that while translation is possible (we are, after all, writing in English), it is not that easy. The connotations and the practices that go into the words in Sámi have to be more or less laboriously spelled out if they are moved elsewhere, because it is simply easier to talk process and unfolding and relations and soft subjectivities in Sámi than it is in languages such as Norwegian or English. Gerunds-from-verbs to nouns, and processes to objects, this is the politically consequential shift that tends to get reproduced in the more obvious (mis)translations. Ingold's 'taskscape' and Massey's 'activity space' qualify as valiant attempts to avoid this slippage, a slippage that is at work in the shift from *meahcci* to *utmark* or *villmark*, or to such English-language terms as 'wilderness' or 'tundra'. But there is also a crucial shift in the *material character* of knowing going on. As we saw earlier, *meahcci* practices weave through the uncertain encounters of taskscapes or what we might also think of as places–times–tasks, while *utmark* practices belong to the law, to agriculture, to environmental protection, to recreation and to cartography. The latter, to be sure, are far from identical, and the extent to which they differ from the logic of *meahcci* is not complete.[25] But while what may count as accurate knowledge in these different legal and scientific contexts is often contested, uncertain, and indeed messy in practice, they all have something in common. This is that they all work on the assumption that 'knowledge' is something that can be abstracted from the circumstances in which it is produced. The idea and the hope is that it can be gathered in one place, manipulated and consolidated into an adequate description of the world (a body of law, a national cartographic survey, or a set of scientific findings and theories) and then transferred elsewhere. These are institutions and material arrangements in which *knowing* as something like practical or embodied wisdom has been displaced by the goal of *knowledge*.[26]

This distinction between knowing as process on the one hand, and knowledge as (aspiration to) material abstraction and consolidation on the other, has been rehearsed in many literatures. Literary theory and anthropology have described the move from orality to literacy with its shifts from story-telling and prosody to a visual space, particular kinds of reflexivity, virtual objects, and aspirations to completeness (Ong, 1988; Rotman, 2008). Analogous arguments, often with a stronger political cutting edge, have been rehearsed in indigenous studies (Helander-Renvall & Markkula, 2017). STS has explored the rise of virtual witnessing and technologies such as quantification which combine and manipulate scientific representations in locations far removed from the places where observations were made (Lynch & Woolgar, 1990; Shapin & Schaffer, 1985). And as we will briefly show below, documentary studies make related arguments. Interestingly Johan Turi, the founder of Sámi literature, reindeer herder and hunter turned author, knew this perfectly well over a century ago. His 1910 publication, *Muitalus sámiid birra* [*An Account of the Sami*] (Turi, 1910/2012), makes just this argument. He opens his book (see the citation at the beginning of this article) by telling his reader that Sámi minds do not work well in rooms. But since that is what government minds do, Sámi people have no choice: they need to write about how they live (Grenersen et al., 2016, p. 1193). He adds a pithy and possibly ironic one-sentence epistemological observation about the relation between truth and the material character of knowing:[27]

Herein [this book] are all sorts of stories, but it is not certain whether they are true, since they haven't been written down before. (Turi, 1910/2012)

'Written down'. As Grenersen et al. (2016, pp. 1184ff.) show, the material difference between contexted *knowing* and written *knowledge* is also visible in the Sámi language, and in what follows we gratefully follow their argument. Thus, Sámi has many loan-words, including the noun *dokumeanta*, document, perhaps from Norwegian *document* with its originally Latin roots.[28] But there are other ways of talking that lead neither to loanwords nor to paper and electronic texts. *Duođaštit* (verb, though this may also be a loanword from the Finnish *todistaa*) means 'to testify, bear witness, confirm' (Grenersen et al., 2016, pp. 1184ff.).[29] Alongside this there is a verb, *vuohttit*, which means both 'to find traces, to observe, to get to know' (p. 1185) (here traces also means the tracks left by people, animals or sledges) and, in particular, getting to know 'people's attitudes and intentions when they act' (p. 1185). So:

> ... if you have a quarrel about two different reindeer herds that intermingle you 'look for traces' – *vuohttit* – in the terrain that prove your point. If you find these traces they can serve as a documentation – *duođaštus* – of the intentions and attitudes of the owner of the neighbouring herd. To interpret and 'read' traces, especially in snow and ice, is common knowledge among the herders. (Grenersen et al., 2016, p. 1185)

Their argument is that in indigenous contexts documents may not take the form of texts, but comprise 'stories, songs, festivals, performances, dances and physical inscriptions in other materials than paper' (Grenersen et al., 2016, p. 1186), including, for instance, physical inscriptions in the landscape as these are read by herders, or as they witness the movement of reindeer in a landscape in the process of communication and compromise that we have described above. So these authors are drawing our attention to the *material* character of the squeeze on Sámi practices and Sámi ways of knowing. For if landscapes count as texts or documents then they cannot be extracted from their places–times–tasks, taken somewhere else, gathered together and manipulated to generate overviews. Instead, the processes that generate the possibility of knowing well depend on circumstances that cannot be transmuted into knowledge. Apprehension, communication, and the storying that goes with knowing do not seek to be hypostatised into separable representations. In short, the lesson is that it is better to avoid transforming verbs into nouns.

Decolonising words and practices

To summarise, the practical and political domination of Sámi *meahcci* practices is indexed by and reproduced in language, for *meahcci* is not an area on a map, *utmark* or empty wilderness but *meahcit* in the plural are lived and worked taskscapes, activity spaces, or places–times–tasks. This means that *meahcit* slip over and through one another rather than being mutually exclusive patches of land. It also means that *meahcit* have nothing to do with *natur* (nature) or the idea that this is a set of realities separate from 'culture'. Instead *meahcit* are composed of – and in – lively encounters and relations with beings of all kinds endowed with their own will and their own moral sensibilities.

Importantly, those encounters are contingent and uncertain. Little can be planned in or with *meahcit*. Interactions unfold iteratively and unpredictably, and they have to be negotiated and renegotiated. This means that if the *Storting*, the Norwegian national parliament, passes a law that starts by declaring that '*meahcci* shall be understood as identical to *utmark*',[30] then this is a form of colonial violence because it is a mistranslation that can be – and is – imposed.

The politics of this division between different words-and-practices have been widely debated and contested. And those debates extend across colonially imposed linguistic frontiers which also work to divide Sámi people. But if we confine ourselves to Norway, how best to resist the state's environmental domination is a matter of contingent tactics. Rebellion, politics, direct action, art, civil disobedience, ignoring the law, silence, euphemism, irony, procrastination, false compliance, academic debate, collaboration with dissident scientists, all of these are present in the history of Sámi resistance. But Turi, as we earlier indicated, adds to all this an insistence on the importance of the *practices* and the *materials* of knowing. If governments know in rooms and texts, then Sámi know and quite differently on mountains (Turi, 1910/2012, p. 9). Words and the material practices through which they weave make the very *possibility* of knowing. The implication is clear. To be heard in a colonial context it is important to attend to and work on the material forms of knowing and talking. But what might this mean in practice?

Meahcci and *utmark*. There are endless disputes. Here's one (we follow Benjaminsen et al., 2015). The Norwegian government consistently argues that there is overgrazing by reindeer in the north. The herders, they say, allow reindeer numbers to grow in the pursuit of profit, and it is official policy to cull what are taken to be excess reindeer. The herders strongly disagree. They say that there is no overgrazing, that they relate to reindeer respectfully (we talked earlier about 'compromise'), that economic return is only one of many concerns, and not only does the policy make no sense but it also undermines good stewardship. This dispute is full of words and their mistranslations. Consider the Sámi word *guohtun*. The law translates this as Norwegian *beite* (pasture).[31] But as with *meahcci* and *utmark*, this is misleading. In Sámi '*guohtun* has two meanings: the grazing activities of the reindeer; and the access to pasture under the snow' (Benjaminsen et al., 2015, p. 226), and it is the second – in various specific and circumstance-dependent forms – that is the more common:

> In most cases, herders' use of *guohtun* refers to the availability of plants for grazing, that is, the structure and quantity of the snow cover that determines access to the plants buried under it. (Benjaminsen et al., 2015, p. 226)

The world of herders-and-reindeer-and-forage-and-snow-conditions and the words that belong to that world grow out of the kinds of subtle and context-bound relations that we have discussed above. Unsurprisingly, this means that *guohtun*, like *meahcci*, is often a compound word.[32] Whatever it is, *guohtun* is not pasture understood in an agricultural logic as a patch of land endowed with particular attributes, and neither can it be seen and surveyed from a distance. But, here's the problem, the relevant practices of environmental management mostly work in precisely this way. *Beite* becomes an abstracted, indeed cartographic, reality, generated from satellite data, which seeks to measure changes in areas covered by lichen by comparing time-series images – images that are then used to justify the narrative about overgrazing.[33]

So there are two worlds, two sets of words, two sets of practices, and two ways of thinking of landscapes as text with proximate knowing on the one hand, and the abstraction of knowledge on the other, that's the diagnosis. But this also suggests a possible political and analytical intervention in the *meahcci*-related conflict about reindeer numbers. This is to interfere in the practices themselves and try to create alternatives that render *Sámi* ways of knowing *meahcci* real to biologists and policymakers. Perhaps the biologists and those who make and administer policy need to come with Sámi people into the taskscapes of *meahcit* to discover how Sámi practices make and know the world. Such is one thought, a possibility that suggests the need for different forms of training for environmental biologists.[34] Perhaps, here's another, those who practise the fluidities of Sámi knowing can work with dissident biologists (for let us not imagine that biology is a monolithic whole). And, indeed, this is what has happened with the Benjaminsen et al. paper that we have been drawing on above. This was co-authored by biologists, an anthropologist and a herder-academic. Either way, however, we are suggesting the importance of attending to mundane words and mundane practices in the context of colonial asymmetry, and of seeking ways of creatively re-working those practices.

Shifting English-language social science

If *meahcci* and its practices are other to Norwegian, neither do they easily translate into English: instead, they do land on other terms. This, to be sure, is why Ingold talks of taskscapes, Massey of activity spaces, and we have written of places–times–tasks. The conclusion is that translation into English takes effort. To state the anthropologically obvious, if we want to bring the relational fluidity of *meahcit* into English we have to bring a lot of their linguistic and practical context into English too. So what does this excursion into Sámi suggest? Given the linguistic, material and institutional constraints within which English-language social science works, how might *meahcci* and the practices in which it is embedded, help us to think and to write a little differently? How might they sensitise us to possibilities that may not be confined to Sápmi? We end with some brief thoughts about land on the one hand and knowing on the other.

First, then, we follow such authors as Massey and Ingold to suggest that in many contexts land is a process, not a space. Or better, perhaps, to propose that lands are *processes* rather than spaces. Two (and following the same authors), we also suggest that in many contexts, lands are better understood as *unfoldings* instead of (or as well as) regions. They may not necessarily be mutually exclusive, but instead work by slipping and sliding through one another. And then, in addition, we suggest that we should be looking for lands that are social, relational and normative, with unfoldings that are being composed in liveliness, filled with it. If we borrow from Schanche once again, there are contexts where it is important to negotiate *with* the liveliness that makes up lands rather than *about* those lands.

Alongside these land-related thoughts, there are issues about knowing. So, for instance, we suggest that it might be wise to come to a stop when we encounter the word 'knowledge' and ask what this is doing and whether it is appropriate. 'Local knowledge'? 'Tacit knowledge'? 'Indigenous knowledge'?' 'Traditional ecological knowledge'? 'Biological knowledge'? As we have seen, the tug in English is to abstraction, and to the idea that what is known can be removed from people, travel, be assembled in one place, and manipulated. But the Sámi experience suggests that 'knowing' needs to be set alongside 'knowledge'. It also suggests that the normativities – sometimes colonial – embedded in the idea of 'knowledge' deserve to be explored as well. Then, and to extend this point, the Sámi language also teaches us that verbs and their gerunds might well serve uncertain and contexted knowings better than nouns. Perhaps, then, we should be talking about *landings* instead of lands. Or *taskscapings* instead of taskscapes. Or *processings* instead of processes. Though once again we quickly find that the English language and its institutions are snapping at our heels. 'Processing' has been captured by the more or less routine and predictable industrial conversion of 'raw materials' (including paperwork and people) into products or outputs. 'Landings' are what aircraft do when they arrive at airports. We might think of this as *fixing the gerund*, pinning it down and robbing it of its liveliness. So what is happening here? This question leads us to our final thought. This is that the gerund is being pressed into means–end schemes. In this English-language world it is the *end* that counts. What goes on along the way, the 'processing', all the work that leads to 'knowledge', is being rendered uninteresting. So resisting this is all of a piece with avoiding the divide between nature and culture, with foregrounding unfolding, and with imagining a non-reductionist version of the social. With softening the subject. With telling uncertainties. With verbing *meahcci*. Sámi singer, artist and author Nils-Aslak Valkeapää wrote: 'I have no beginning, no end, and there is also no beginning, no end in the work I do' (in Helander & Kailo, 1998, p. 87). Quite so. In this way of thinking we are where we are, we do what we can do, we attend to it, and we try to care for it. No beginning, no end.

Acknowledgements

We are grateful to Áile Aikio, Harrieth Aira, Svanhild Andersen, M. J. Barrett, Judith Farquhar, Kaisa Rautio Helander, Jorunn Jernsletten, Tore Johnsen, Britt Kramvig, Stein Roar Mathisen, Lovisa Mienna Sjöberg, Annemarie Mol, Nils Oskal, Steinar Nilsen, Stine Rybråten, Mikkel Nils M. Sara, Jon Todal and Sanna Valkonen, for discussion, reactions, responses, referees' reports and comments.

Funding

We are grateful to Forskningsrådet (the Research Council of Norway) which partially funded the research reported in this article.

Notes

1. See, for instance, Todal (1998), Oskal (2001), Schanche (2002), Minde (2003), Lantto and Mörkenstam (2008), Kraft (2010), Lantto (2010), Law and Joks (2017) and Kent (2014, Chapter 1).
2. We focus here on Norwegian. Unlike the other Scandinavian languages, Finnish and Sámi belong to the same Finno-Ugric language group. Though there are important similarities between these two languages both structurally and in terms of vocabularies (for instance the Finnish word *metsä*, forest, is related to the Sámi word *meahcci*), we do not explore these here.

3. For at least a thousand years there has been a distinction between those who live inland, and coastal or 'sea Sámi' (Helander, 1999), and many Sámi now live in urban environments, often far from Sápmi.

4. For further discussion see Law and Joks (2019, pp. 429–430). We thank Stein Roar Mathisen (private communication) for reminding us that 'Sámi' understandings of enchanted nature are widely shared in Norwegian folklore.

5. For discussion of herding and herding vocabularies, see Sara (2009, p. 158). We touch briefly on some of these terms in the next section.

6. This is spoken by around 20,000 people (Valijävri & Kahn, 2017, p. 4), though estimates vary.

7. Valkonen and Valkonen (2018) are drawing on Doreen Massey (1992). For Ingold's notion of taskscape in the context of his dwelling perspective, see Ingold (1993). For accounts of Sámi movement, encounters and understandings of landscape, see Ingold and Kurttila (2000) and Mazzullo and Ingold (2008).

8. If strangers appear, Sámi children may be told to go and hide in *meahcci* – though this was more common in the past.

9. Mikkel Nils Sara, personal communication.

10. The disjunction between the unfolding realities of *meahcci* and the abstractions implied by cartographic space and/or clock time has been widely explored. See, inter alia, Mazzullo and Ingold (2008) and Ingold (2018).

11. For the implications of this for salmon fishing in the context of state conservation policy which works with calendar time and cartographic location and therefore squeezes traditional net fishing, see Joks and Law (2017).

12. *Luondu* is often used to (mis)translate the Norwegian word *natur* (nature) with serious practical and political consequences.

13. See Sara (2009, p. 173). The first Sámi author, Johan Turi, who was a reindeer herder and hunter, details the complex strategies needed to disguise intentions on the part of the hunter. See Turi (1910/2012, p. 99). Note that some animals are also able to disguise their own intentions.

14. See Joks and Law (2017, p. 155). Or you may say that no catch was *intended*, and '*jávri addá dan maid addá*', 'the lake gives what it gives'. See Østmo and Law (2018, pp. 353, 354).

15. This argument is explored in the debates between Émile Durkheim and Gabriel Tarde dramatised in Vargas et al. (2008).

16. See Dana (2011) for this, explored in relation to *noaidi* (shaman) drums.

17. 'This law counts as *innmark* farmyards, housing plots, cultivated land, meadows, and enclosed pastures. Smaller pieces of uncultivated land that lie within cultivated land or meadows or are fenced together with such areas, are also considered to be *innmark*. . . . This law treats as *utmark* uncultivated land which, in line with the preceding paragraph, does not count as *innmark*' (Klima- og miljødepartementet [Norwegian Ministry of the Environment], 2009, paragraph 1a, our translation). For discussion of agricultural logic in another context, see Nadasdy (2003).

18. Klima- og miljødepartementet [Norwegian Ministry of the Environment], 2009, paragraphs 2 (walking and skiing), 5 (gathering), 9 (making fires) and 11 (leaving no traces behind). The limits apply, for instance, to making fires which is only permitted in winter.

19. Klima- og miljødepartementet [Norwegian Ministry of the Environment] (2009, section 1a, our translation). The (advisory) Norwegian Sámi parliament writes, to the contrary, that 'The Sámi term *meahcci* and the general meaning of this term are not identical to the definition of *utmark* in the *friluftsliv* law' (Sámediggi, 2007, section 2, our translation).

20. The *Storting* is Norway's sovereign national legislature. It has devolved some (usually advisory) powers to the *Sámediggi*, the Sámi parliament.

21. The politics of this (mis)translation are colonial, deeply significant, and run through other major controversies in Sápmi including: how *meahcci* is codified into Norwegian law as usufruct rights; how national parks are established and maintained; how the Norwegian state seeks to protect the environment beyond those national parks; and how its policies for conserving salmon stocks are created. See Ween and Lien (2012), Ween and Colombi (2013), Benjaminsen et al. (2015), Østmo and Law (2018) and Joks and Law (2017).

22. On Finno-Ugric languages see, for instance, Laakso (1997).

23. This phrase also sounds exceedingly odd in English.

24. One consequence of this is that Sámi may avoid speaking for others, and/or speak indirectly and implicitly. This is also a further source of colonial tension, for Norwegians sometimes misread silence as acquiescence whereas it is better read as a form of resistance. For discussion, see Lehtola (2018).

25. In part this is because, under the impact of colonial relations, agriculture has also been (more or less marginally) practised in Sápmi. For discussion of the relations between Sámi agriculture and *meahcci*, see Schanche (2002).

26. The realities of 'knowledge' are often more or less fluid in practice. For this explored in the idiom of Science and Technology Studies (STS), see Law (2004). For a related argument posed in an anthropologically phenomenological idiom see Ingold (2018), who argues that the fluid becomings of the North are ubiquitous.

27. See also Gaski (2011, p. 595).

28. There is also a verb *dokumenteret* (to document) and an abstract noun *dokumentašuvdna* (documentation).

29. See also Grenersen et al., p. 1185, though here they are quoting Nielsen (1962). Again, there are related words. So *duohta* is a noun which means sincerity, seriousness, or truth (p. 1185) and *duođaštus* (a further noun) means '"evidence, testimony, confirmation, character, testimonial, receipt"', which may take spoken form, or may simply count as evidence because of its character.

30. Klima- og miljødepartementet [Norwegian Ministry of the Environment] (2009, section 1a, our translation).

31. See Landbruks-og matdepartementet [Norwegian Ministry of Agriculture and Food] (2007) and Benjaminsen et al. (2015, p. 226).

32. *Rudneguohtun* is access through holes in the snow, *báikkuid guohtun* is access in certain locations, and *bieđggus guohtun* is dispersed access. (This is a paraphrase from Benjaminsen et al., 2015, p. 226.)

33. The biological argument drawing on this satellite derived material is that the area covered by lichen is declining and the lichen coverage is thinner (Benjaminsen et al., 2015, pp. 223–224). Then these measurements are put together with reindeer head counts to make the claim that there is overgrazing. There is much more that might be said about this case. For instance, even if the overgrazing argument is accepted, what has disappeared from this argument is the pressures on land use from expanding activities such as mining, tourism, wind turbine farms, and other forms of economic activity. Crucial in the present scientific context, however, is that the policy of limiting reindeer numbers derives from ecological equilibrium modelling, while as Benjaminsen and his colleagues show, an alternative approach, that of non-equilibrium modelling, developed to explore environments where the major constrains lie outside the system (for instance deriving from climate extremes) may well be appropriate to Sápmi and reindeer numbers. (On non-equilibrium modelling see also Krätli et al., 2015.) Perhaps it is no coincidence that this non-equilibrium modelling fits the intuitions of herders much more closely.

34. For related work and experiments in other contexts, see Tsouvalis and Waterton (2012) and Verran (2002).

References

Benjaminsen, T. A., Reinert, H., Sjaastad, E., & Sara, M. N. (2015). Misreading the Arctic landscape: A political ecology of reindeer, carrying capacities, and overstocking in Finnmark, Norway. *Norsk Geografisk Tidsskrift - Norwegian Journal of Geography, 69*(4), 219–229.

Broderstad, E. G. (2014). Implementing indigenous self-determination: The case of Sámi in Norway. In M. Woons & K. Leuven (Eds.), *Restoring indigenous self-determination: Theoretical and practical approaches* (pp. 80–87). E-International Relations.

Dana, K. O. (2011). Áillohaš and his image drum: The native poet as shaman. *Nordlit, 8*, 7–33.

Gaski, H. (2011). More than meets the eye: The indigeneity of Johan Turi's writing and artwork. *Scandinavian Studies, 83*(4), 591–608.

Grenersen, G., Kemi, K., & Nilsen, S. (2016). Landscapes as documents: The relationship between traditional Sámi terminology and the concepts of document and documentation. *Journal of Documentation, 72*(6), 1181–1196.

Helander, E. (1999). Sami subsistence activities – spatial aspects and structuration. *Acta Borealia, 16*(2), 7–25.

Helander, E., & Kailo, K. (1998). *No beginning, no end: The Sami speak up*. Canadian Circumpolar Institute.

Helander-Renvall, E. (2010). Animism, personhood and the nature of reality: Sami perspectives. *Polar Record, 46*(1), 44–56.

Helander-Renvall, E., & Markkula, I. (2017). On transfer of Sámi traditional knowledge: Scientification, traditionalization, secrecy, and equality. In A. Xanthaki, S. Valkonen, L. Heinämäki, & P. Nuorgam (Eds.), *Indigenous peoples' cultural heritage: Rights, debates, challenges*. Brill.

Ingold, T. (1993). The temporality of the landscape. *World Archaeology, 25*(2), 152–174.

Ingold, T. (2018). The North is everywhere. In T. H. Eriksen, S. Valkonen, & J. Valkonen (Eds.), *Knowing from the Indigenous North: Sámi approaches to history, politics and belonging* (pp. 108–119). Routledge.

Ingold, T., & Kurttila, T. (2000). Perceiving the environment in Finnish Lapland. *Body & Society, 6*(3–4), 183–196.

Johnsen, K. I., Benjaminsen, T. A., & Eira, I. M. G. (2015). Seeing like the state or like pastoralists? Conflicting narratives on the governance of Sámi reindeer husbandry in Finnmark, Norway. *Norsk Geografisk Tidsskrift – Norwegian Journal of Geography, 69*(4), 230–241.

Joks, S., & Law, J. (2017). Sámi salmon, state salmon: LEK, technoscience and care. In V. Singleton, C. Waterton, & N. Gill (Eds.), *Care and policy practices: Translations, assemblages, interventions* (pp. 150–171). Wiley-Blackwell.

Kent, N. (2014). *The Sámi peoples of the North: A social and cultural history*. Hurst and Company.

Klima- og miljødepartementet [Norwegian Ministry of the Environment]. (2009). Lov om friluftslivet (friluftsloven) [The friluftsliv law]. Lovdata.

Kraft, S. E. (2010). The making of a sacred mountain: Meanings of nature and sacredness in Sápmi and northern Norway. *Religion, 40*(1), 53–61.

Krätli, S., Kaufmann, B., Roba, H., Hiernaux, P., Li, W., Easdale, M., & Hülsebusch, C. (2015). *A house full of trap doors: Identifying barriers to resilient drylands in the toolbox of pastoral development*. International Institute for Environment and Development (IIED). https://pubs.iied.org/pdfs/10128IIED.pdf (accessed 18 December 2019).

Laakso, J. (1997). On verbalizing nouns in Uralic. *Finnisch-ugrische Forschungen : Zeitschrift für finnisch-ugrische Sprach- und Volkskunde, 54*(2), 267–304.

Landbruks-og matdepartementet [Norwegian Ministry of Agriculture and Food]. (2007). Lov om reindrift (reindriftsloven) [Reindeer Husbandry Act]. Lovdata.

Lantto, P. (2010). Borders, citizenship and change: The case of the Sami people, 1751–2008. *Citizenship Studies, 14*(5), 543–556.

Lantto, P., & Mörkenstam, U. (2008). Sami rights and Sami challenges. *Scandinavian Journal of History, 33*(1), 26–51.

Law, J. (2004). *After method: Mess in social science research*. Routledge.

Law, J., & Joks, S. (2017). Luossa and laks: Salmon, science and LEK. *Revue d'Anthropologie des Connaissances, 12*(2), aw-bi. www.heterogeneities.net/publications/LawJoks2016LuossaAndLaks.pdf (accessed 23 May 2017).

Law, J., & Joks, S. (2019). Indigeneity, science and difference: Notes on the politics of how. *Science, Technology and Human Values, 44*(3), 424–447.

Lehtola, V.-P. (2018). Evasive strategies of defiance – everyday resistance histories among the Sámi. In T. H. Eriksen, S. Valkonen, & J. Valkonen (Eds.), *Knowing from the Indigenous North: Sámi approaches to history, politics and belonging* (pp. 29–46). Routledge.

Lynch, M., & Woolgar, S. (Eds.). (1990). *Representation in scientific practice*. MIT Press.

Massey, D. (1992). Politics and space/time. *New Left Review, 196*, 65–84.

Mazzullo, N., & Ingold, T. (2008). Being along: Place, time and movement among Sámi people. In J. O. Bærenholdt & B. Granås (Eds.), *Mobility and place: Enacting Northern European peripheries* (pp. 27–38). Ashgate.

Meløe, J. (1988). The two landscapes of northern Norway. *Inquiry, 31*(3), 387–401.

Minde, H. (2003). Assimilation of the Sami: Implementation and consequences. *Acta Borealia, 20*(2), 121–146.

Nadasdy, P. (2003). *Hunters and bureaucrats: Power, knowledge and Aboriginal–state relations in the Southwest Yukon*. UBC Press.

Nielsen, K. (1962). *Lapp dictionary*. Universitetsforlaget.

Ong, W. J. (1988). *Orality and literacy: The technologizing of the word*. Routledge.

Oskal, A. (2008). Old livelihoods in new weather: Arctic indigenous reindeer herders face the challenges of climate change. *Development Outreach, 10*(1), 22–25.

Oskal, N. (2000). On nature and reindeer luck. *Rangifer, 20*(2–3), 175–180.

Oskal, N. (2001). Political inclusion of the Saami as indigenous people in Norway. *International Journal on Minority and Group Rights, 8*(2–3), 235–262.

Østmo, L., & Law, J. (2018). Mis/translation, colonialism and environmental conflict. *Environmental Humanities, 10*(2), 349–369.

Rotman, B. (2008). *Becoming beside ourselves: The alphabet, ghosts, and distributed human being*. Duke University Press.

Sámediggi. (2007). Sametingets retningslinjer for vurderingen av samiske hensyn ved endret bruk av meahcci/utmark i Finnmark [Guidelines for assessment of Sami interests in cases of changes in land use in Finnmark]. Lovdata.

Sara, M. N. (2009). Siida and traditional Sámi reindeer herding knowledge. *The Northern Review, 30*, 153–178. http://journals.sfu.ca/nr/index.php/nr/issue/view/2 (accessed 10 March 2019).

Sara, M. N. (2011). Land usage and Siida autonomy. *Arctic Review on Law and Politics, 3*(2), 138–158.

Schanche, A. (2002). Meahcci – den samiske utmark. *Dieđut, 1*, 156–171.

Shapin, S., & Schaffer, S. (1985). *Leviathan and the air pump: Hobbes, Boyle and the experimental life*. Princeton University Press.

Tervaniemi, S., & Magga, P. (2018). Belonging to Sápmi – Sámi conceptions of home and home region. In T. H. Eriksen, S. Valkonen, & J. Valkonen (Eds.), *Knowing from the Indigenous North: Sámi approaches to history, politics and belonging* (pp. 75–90). Routledge.

Todal, J. (1998). Minorities with a minority: Language and the school in the Sámi areas of Norway. *Language, Culture and Curriculum, 11*(3), 354–366.

Tsouvalis, J., & Waterton, C. (2012). Building 'participation' upon critique: The Loweswater Care Project, Cumbria, UK. *Environmental Modelling & Software, 36*, 111–121.

Turi, J. M. (2012). *Muitalus sámiid birra* [An account of the Sámi]. ČálliidLágádus (Original work published 1910).

Valijävri, R.-L., & Kahn, L. (2017). *North Sámi: An essential grammar*. Routledge.

Valkonen, J., & Valkonen, S. (2018). On local knowledge. In T. H. Eriksen, S. Valkonen, & J. Valkonen (Eds.), *Knowing from the Indigenous North: Sámi approaches to history, politics and belonging* (pp. 12–26). Routledge.

Vargas, E. V., Latour, B., Karsenti, B., Aït-Touati, F., & Salmon, L. (2008). The debate between Tarde and Durkheim. *Environment and Planning D: Society and Space, 26*(5), 761–777.

Verran, H. (2002). A postcolonial moment in science studies: Alternative firing regimes of environmental scientists and Aboriginal landowners. *Social Studies of Science, 32*(5–6), 729–762.

Weber, M. (1978). *Economy and society: An outline of interpretive sociology*. University of California Press.

Ween, G., & Abram, S. (2012). The Norwegian Trekking Association: Trekking as constituting the nation. *Landscape Research, 37*(2), 155–171.

Ween, G., & Lien, M. E. (2012). Decolonialization in the Arctic? Nature practices and land rights in the Norwegian High North. *Journal of Rural and Community Development, 7*(1), 93–109.

Ween, G. B., & Colombi, B. J. (2013). Two rivers: The politics of wild salmon, indigenous rights and natural resource management. *Sustainability, 5*(2), 478–495.

Author biographies

Solveig Joks is Associate Professor at the Sámi Allaskuvla/Sámi University of Applied Sciences, Norway. She is editor of the Sámi language interdisciplinary scientific journal, *Sámi dieđalaš áigečála*. Currently she is project manager of a three-year research project financed by the Research Council of Norway. The project deals with gathering practices in coastal Sámi areas in Norway, and investigates how traditional knowledges are expressed in Sámi languages, narratives and place names.

Liv Østmo was one of the founders of the Sámi Allaskuvla/Sámi University of Applied Sciences, Guovdageaidnu, Norway, and a former Dean. Recently retired, she has lectured and undertaken research on multicultural understandings. Over the last decade she has worked to document traditional Sámi environmentally-relevant knowledge in a range of contexts, both in written articles and reports, and in film-making.

John Law is Emeritus Professor in Sociology at the Open University, and visiting Professor at the Sámi Allaskuvla/Sámi University of Applied Sciences at Guovdageaidnu in Norway. He has written widely on material semiotics, and his books include *After Method* and *Aircraft Stories*. He works on colonial environmental controversies, research methods, modes of knowing, and postcolonial knowing relations. His home page is at www.heterogeneities.net.

Commoning beyond 'commons': The case of the Russian '*obshcheye*'

The Sociological Review Monographs
2020, Vol. 68(2) 62–80
© The Author(s) 2020
Article reuse guidelines:
sagepub.com/journals-permissions
DOI: 10.1177/0038026120905474
journals.sagepub.com/home/sor

Liubov Chernysheva and Olga Sezneva

Universiteit van Amsterdam [University of Amsterdam], The Netherlands

Abstract

How do the semantic logics that different words accommodate in different languages map onto studies of social realities internationally and interdisciplinarily? This article is an ethnographic study of *obshcheye* – a corpus of phenomena pertaining to communal life in Russia. Similar to the English term 'commons', it marks the zone of the public – that which is shared and collective. In contrast to the commons, it displays greater semantic polyphony, bringing together social, discursive and affective qualities. Our analysis demonstrates that various semantic subsets *of obshcheye* sensitize research differently from the commons by indexing different societal concerns. They tune us into a wide set of concerns – with time (not wanting to be 'Soviet'), ownership (worrying about what is 'no one's'), affective connectivity (one sits and waits for a conversation), and the act of caring for people and for spaces. Each word and each relationship in the semantic network reflects what is important to social actors as they go about ordering their lives together. The article concludes that *obshcheye* is so definitively a semantic network that expunging its conceptual heterogeneity and narrowing the multiple logics to encompass one in particular would amount to analytical reductionism and the impoverishment of social analysis.

Keywords

commons, concepts in social sciences, housing, Russia, semantic network

Commons as a model-system

There is a long-respected tradition in the western social sciences of relying on 'the model-system', 'an object of study that pools resources and is used by convention to stand in for a more general class of epistemic objects' (Krause, 2016, p. 198). 'Doctors', for example, stand in for the 'professions', the 'English working class' for 'class formation under capitalism', and 'Chicago' as representative of 'cities' in general. Consequently, studies about doctors are foundational for the sociology of professions, and studies about Chicago are foundational to urban sociology and urban ethnography (Krause, 2016, p. 198; see also

Corresponding author:
Olga Sezneva, Department of Sociology, University of Amsterdam, PO Box 15508, Amsterdam 1001 NA, The Netherlands.
Email: O.Sezneva@uva.nl

Abbott, 1988; Park et al., 1925; Thompson, 1963). One consequence of this is that analysis of western societies and institutions implicitly serves as a stand-in for the analysis of societies and institutions in general. The model-system thus serves as but one important way in which the hegemony of western social sciences is established.

Our ethnographic study of *obshcheye* – a corpus of phenomena pertaining to communal life in Russia – resonates with Krause's argument, but probes another aspect of system modelling: language. How do the semantic logics that different words accommodate in different languages map onto studies of social realities internationally and interdisciplinarily? Our key example is the English concept 'the commons', which has recently enjoyed a renewed interest in various social sciences. The concept is interesting in its own right while also possessing exemplary value. A strikingly large body of literature has emerged around realities and domains as different as academic work, biodiversity, culture, public art, ideas, information, native culture, scientific data, the airwaves, the environment, the sky, the village and water – all identified as 'the commons' (Hess, 2008, pp. 6–7; Hess also provides a helpful review of works on each topic). Commons-the-term has come to stand for the 'collective resources, qualities, and affects within a social and political order of being-in-common' (Swyngedouw, in Wagner et al., 2012, p. 635) and has 'a ubiquitous presence in the political, economic and even real estate language of our time' (Caffentzis & Federici, 2014, p. i91). By approaching the contemporary commons as a right through the question of 'who owns it?', researchers try to reimagine the conditions under which the commons can 'become the seeds of a society beyond state and market' and a viable response to ever-widening privatization (Caffentzis & Federici, 2014, p. i95). Precisely as an 'anti-capitalist' form of ownership and control, the commons are seen as engendering collective action, collaboration and self-governance – commons-like thinking (Benkler, 2004). This idea was even romanticized in the early 2000s, with new literature appealing to a need for a 'rediscovery of the commons' and 'our common wealth' (Sanders [2006] and Rowe [2002], respectively, cited in Hess, 2008, p. 11). In sum, there is a wide array of practices, ideologies and politics to which the term applies in academic literature.

Yet, it is rarely acknowledged that 'the commons' is also a term with a history. It broke from its moorings in early modern English property rights to serve as a model-system for the contemporary 'complex social and political ecologies' (Chatterton, 2010, p. 626) of the 'collective-pool resource' (Ostrom, 1990; for more recent reflections on the meaning of the concept, see Harvey, 2012), often in non-European contexts (Bakker, 2007; Kuttler & Jain, 2015). These 'travels' (Bal & Marx-Macdonald, 2002) affected the concept's 'epistemic flexibility' (Bal & Marx-Macdonald, 2002, p. 25). John Wagner, writing about water, notes that conventional definitions of the commons map poorly onto observable events (Wagner et al., 2012), and that there is a mismatch between academic and everyday uses of the word. Between the many academic contexts and the relative unfamiliarity of ordinary users of the commons with the term, it is not always clear what the commons actually articulates: ownership or common interest, common-pool-resources and their tragedy (Hardin, 1968), or whether commons really are about the affective states of 'togetherness' that collective resources recursively produce.

Rather than joining the critical chorus lamenting the blurring (Vaccaro & Beltran, 2019) of commons, we use our ethnography of *obshcheye* to think about the work that words do, and to demonstrate how a foreign language can be an intellectual resource for international social sciences. How might a word's own semantic logic in practice illuminate otherwise-hidden zones of the social realities we study? Concepts are not 'real' but rather more or less effective ways to organize reality in the service of interest-driven research; 'concepts are bound to carry around the concerns engrained in them when they were coined', activating different 'linguistic repertoires' and making 'different cuts' (Mann & Mol, 2019, p. 780). Concepts like 'commons' 'sensitise' research towards certain 'collective dynamics' and 'social imaginaries' (Wagner et al., 2012, p. 617). But, we argue, sensitizing is itself a complex issue in need of examination-in-context. Academic communities in different geographical locations may react differently to the ways a single word sensitizes: towards what end, by what means, and for whom? Diverse histories and institutions, the variability of tools, places and objects deployed in knowledge production (Knorr-Cetina, 1981), and ways of wording that have different relevance all matter.

These are the main concerns that our article addresses. It is set to ethnographically explore a specific case – the Russian word *obshcheye* (*общее*) – as a variation on the commons. Russian language displays extraordinary semantic wealth when it comes to collective life, its norms and the material resources that support it. This is no doubt attributable to the country's history, starting with the pre-revolutionary peasant *obshchina* (*община*) which subsumed 'the role of the elders, concepts of justice, problems of the family, ethical and aesthetic views, education of youth and children, attitudes towards women' (Lewin, 1990, p. 21; on the Russian peasant commune, see Mironov, 1985). A different shade of commonality found complex expression in the distinctly Soviet phenomenon of shared housing, the communal flat, where access, or ownership followed social belonging and trust, and was understood as shared – or not shared (Buchli, 1999; Gerasimova, 2002; Paxson, 2005; Utekhin, 2018). When communal flats went into decline in the post-socialist period, the sense of loss of 'the common good' abounded (Shevchenko, 2008), weakening memories of the mistrust and suspicion which also proliferated in them. The market reforms of the 1990s, while restoring private property, did not undermine public concern over collective life formulated either in terms of local communal affairs (*mestnaja obshchestvennost'*, *местная общественность*) or civic life (*grazhdanskaya zhizn'*, *гражданская жизнь*).[1]

We cannot do justice to the enormous literature pertaining to things that are common or collective in Russia. The social history of the *obshcheye* and what it stands for is extremely complex and cannot be fully explored here. We limit ourselves to an observation that *obshcheye* in Russian encompasses at least three vectors of tension: one between public and private domains, another between (private) property and common resources, and the third between collectivity and individualism. The result is an array of adjectives and nouns, which while relating to the same lexemes, nevertheless take on different meanings depending upon the practical needs of the user and situation. Thus, *obshcheye* offers, in our view, an interesting alternative exemplar to commons. Similar to the English word, it marks the zone of the public – that which is shared and collective. In contrast to the commons, it displays greater semantic polyphony, bringing together social, discursive and affective qualities. Importantly, it does this as a vital, socially embedded idea, not an object of intellectual revival.

Our analysis demonstrates that various semantic subsets *of obshcheye* generate different forms of sensitizing by indexing different societal concerns. This is consequential, as it pertains directly to a more general question of whether or not coherence should be a desirable quality in social scientific taxonomies. In the case of the commons, semantic heterogeneity is said to lead to an instability in conceptual boundaries, seen by many as a downside. *Obshcheye*, by contrast, is so definitively a semantic network – a set of different words whose meaning is defined relationally – that expunging its heterogeneity and narrowing the multiple semantic logics to encompass one in particular would amount to analytical reductionism and the impoverishment of social analysis. To focus on *obshcheye* is to enrich the sociology of the commons by infusing it with other semantics. It is also to understand better the different ways in which social life in common can be organized in a given place at a given time, in which materiality, discourse and practice may converge.[2]

The fieldwork

This article grew out of research that Liubov has been conducting in St. Petersburg, where she followed two urban communities representative of two types of urban living. One is a large-scale, newly constructed housing complex in a peripheral zone of St. Petersburg, the *novostroika* (Brednikova & Zaporozhets, 2016): typically, an agglomeration of towers and some basic amenities – roads, parking and courtyards, operating simultaneously as green and recreational zones. The community that Liubov studied is composed by approximately 70,000 people, the population of a small town, living in 33 high-rises each 29 stories high. The construction began in 2008 and continues to this day. The housing stock is designated as '*ekonom-klass*', and thus affordable for lower-middle class residents. All the units are privately owned by families or individuals, although a considerable number are rented out by the owners. We call it 'Placid Hollow', or 'The Hollow' (Figure 1).[3]

A second case is an example of a new but already well-known trend of forming small communes for collective living. The commune members call themselves *so-obshchestvo (сообщество)*, sometimes *ko-living (коливинг*, transliterated from English: co-living). As a rule, they share a single large flat in an old part of the city. Such flats may house 6 to 15 tenants at a time. Although nominally in the private ownership of a third party, the flats are rented and no tenant can make an exclusive claim to them. On the contrary, spaces are equally shared and decisions have to be made collectively with all residents participating. Liubov conducted research on one of these, which we call Agora (Figure 2).

Both communities practise active communication concerning rules, norms and expectations, have a strong appeal to the public good at some basic, mundane level, and provide numerous instances of coordination around cleaning, repairs and collective decision-making – all in a context that is commonly described as 'privatist', or privacy-oriented (Hirt, 2012). In Placid Hollow, these appear to be practices prompted by the living space itself, its lengthy hallways and malfunctioning rubbish chutes. Here, neighbours run a group page on VKontakte ('in touch'; vk.com, the Russian version of Facebook), exchange information, discuss technical and legal problems, lend and borrow pretty much everything they need with each other, and passionately debate the 'do's' and

Figure 1. 'Placid Hollow', May, 2016.

Figure 2. Kolomna district in St. Petersburg, where Agora is located.
Photo by Stanislav Zaburdaev.

'don'ts' of neighbourly behaviour. In the case of Agora, commoning is different. There, this is an explicitly proclaimed goal and the driving principle of the group, which wants to oppose 'traditional family values' and instead practise a more 'open' and collective life (according to *Obshchezhitiye XXI veka*, 2018, a TV programme).

Although the material collected by Liubov provided both authors with a clear sense that *obshcheye* was at the centre of the neighbourly life, the character of its exact material expression remained a puzzle. Where is *obshcheye* materially and spatial anchored and made empirically accessible? The answer came from national news, which reported incidents in different urban communities around the country. The reported incidents occurred when individual occupants renovated and beautified communal spaces in their buildings. These included lobbies, stairwells and stairs, landings, and the hallways that lead to private flats. For example, in the sunny climate of Rostov-on-Don, Mr Nikolaev, an artist and resident of a multi-unit house, painted walls and tiled the floors of the common stairs and the lobby, hung landscape paintings of his own production in gilded frames, and produced plasterwork in the style of the Italian Baroque (Gopalo, 2018). Nikolaev was sued by his neighbours, who dismissed his explanation that he was 'working *na obshcheye blago*' (*на общее благо*) – for the public good. They accused Nikolaev of using renovation to monopolize something that belonged to everyone. In a different case, when making plans to upgrade a dilapidated staircase in St. Petersburg, the initiator, a well-known blogger, immediately posted announcements of the so-called 'planned' renovation. Typed on his own typewriter, the announcements looked and read like typical announcements produced by a Russian bureaucratic office, in this case, the house management. Thus 'informed', the neighbours did not protest when privately hired contractors began the renovation in ways that conformed with the blogger's personal tastes.

The news reports, as they expressed some of the key tendencies we observed in the material, convinced us that spaces such as lobbies and corridors – the common places – are the essential sites of the enactment of the *obshcheye*, and they are significant in a number of ways. First, there is no established relationship between *obshcheye* and ownership. The corridors are difficult to locate in property terms: as a rule, they are divided equally among all property owners in the building. Still, the ownership of communal spaces, customarily incorrectly attributed by their occupants to 'the state', is often simply unknown to them.[3] Second, the common spaces of blocks of flats in Russian cities formally designated as 'places for common use', *mesta obshchego pol'zovaniya* (*места общего пользования*), are a fragile social reality: hanging a picture of one's own creation in a communal space may lead it to disintegrate. Disentangling the *obshcheye* of the corridor from the question of ownership without it ever losing the power to collectivize makes it a productive entry point into the world of collective things and collective concerns. How is the *obshcheye* of the corridor organized and in what ways is it defined?

Nash: The *obshcheye* that we share

The corridors in Placid Hollow are long and monotonous, lined with doors and painted in neutral colours. Each corridor begins at the lift shaft and stretches a good 35 metres, until it ends at a blind wall. The lift, the rubbish chute next to it, and sometimes the stairs form a centre, from which two, in places four, corridors radiate out. When just built, the corridor in a place like Placid Hallow gives the impression of anonymity in an institutional space (Figure 3). It is a perfectly *obshcheye* corridor according to housing law: its square metres are equally distributed to and owned by all of the occupants of a given tower.[4]

Figure 3. The *obshcheye* corridor in Placid Hollow.

There is a widespread practice dating back to the Soviet times of transforming these long corridors by partitioning them into smaller, but still shared, units. The partitioning is done by residents living on the same floor with the help of doors and locks. A new wall is built at the beginning of the corridor, close to the lift and the landing of the stairs, and a door with a lock is installed (see plan in Figure 4). An enclosure is made – a new corridor uniting six to eight flats and their occupants.

Out of this enclosure emerges a new social ontology: *nash* (наш) – our – corridor. It relates to, yet is different from, a simply *obshcheye* – common – corridor. Below is a post on the VK group page for Placid Hollow from one resident to another. We kept the original tenor in the translation in order to convey its didactic, instructive intention:

Aleksandr, the enclosure of the inter-unit hallway does not fall under 'structural alteration' or 'the forcible alienation of the communal property' – read carefully the code and keep the definitions clear. Therefore, consultation [regarding the enclosure] is only required among the occupants of the immediately affected units. The managing companies, as well as the occupants themselves,

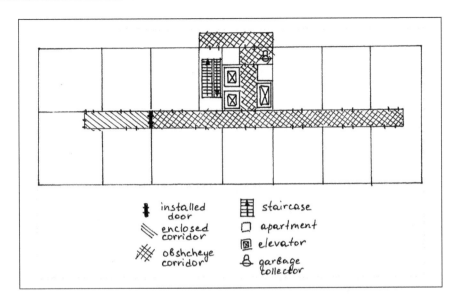

Figure 4. Plan of a typical floor with the enclosure in Placid Hollow.

see the real advantages of such enclosure: in the enclosed corridor no one steals fire extinguishers, hides dope behind the electric junction box, shoves in unwanted advertisements, consumes alcohol or urinates; it stays clean and orderly; the neighbours are in close touch with one another.

The post makes clear that the decision to enclose or not belongs to a small group, those who live in immediate proximity to one another, sharing the floor. Legal status of the corridor's portion has not changed: nominally the space remains communal, that is, the property of all residents of the tower. Access to it, however, is drastically reduced by the enclosure to only 20 to 50 residents. De facto, the enclosure infringes on the rights of access and use of those who do not live on that floor, or cannot be part of the enclosure (most often because of the physical layout of the hallway). Yet, no one objects, everyone seems to have a stake in the game, and so it rolls on. The contingency of events in the corridor (hiding dope, turning it into a public toilet) is minimized, and the atmosphere is rendered more pleasant. The enclosed space is common in a new way: from the abstractly 'everyone's', it is turned into something that is concretely 'ours'. Let us stay a little bit longer with this event.

Using dictionaries and a reference system called 'The National Corpus of the Russian Language', sociolinguist Kapitolina Fedorova demonstrates a change in the meaning of the lexeme *obshcheye* (Fedorova, 2011). She shows that the word has shifted towards greater abstraction and lost its specific group referent. Today, *obshcheye* is something that mediates between different actors and connects them as a group. It also stands for an 'abstract' or 'general' category of things: *obshcheye smysl* (общий смысл) – the general meaning, and *obshcheye termin* (общий термин) – the abstract notion. The lexeme containing *obshch-*, Fedorova argues, is in the process of being de-semanticized, that is, reduced in meaning.

Figure 5. A communal shelf marked with green tape. Someone left some food and a note that these were the ingredients for a pilaf, in order to protect them from being taken by any individual. The plan was to cook pilaf for all the tenants.

Our material, though echoing Fedorova's main point, goes further. Fedorova places two diverging meanings of *obshcheye* in a linear progression in which the concrete is superseded by the abstract over the course of a century. In our findings, by contrast, both meanings coexist and overlap, and it is this overlap that destabilizes the word's meaning. An example from our second location, Agora, illustrates this point.

At Agora, many spaces and things are shared. The kitchen, for example, has a special *obshcheye polka (общая полка)*, a communal shelf, demarcated by green tape (as the example in Figure 5). Consequently, everything that is placed on it is *obshcheye*, that is, communal. A conflict erupted when one tenant, driven by the desire to treat her co-residents, made a pie and placed it on the green shelf, and another, without consultation, ate the pie, all himself. The upset cook, when interviewed, explained to Liubov that in the way she thinks of it, *obshcheye* means shared, and accordingly, everyone has the right to enjoy a piece of her pie. The transgressor defended himself by pointing out that what ends up on the green shelf becomes *obshcheye*, and as such, belongs to no one in particular, but is available for complete appropriation (which he performed by eating it all).

In places such as Placid Hollow where collectivism is not an agreed-upon organizing principle, the work of separating 'no one's' from 'ours' is done by physical means – a partition wall augmented by a collective agreement. A post on a VK forum pertaining to no communal setting in particular but addressing the *obshcheye* in general thus formulates the point: 'Nothing in the obshcheye corridor is yours. It's OBSHCHEYE. Which means, no one's. One's OWN things are kept in one's OWN flat.' The physical enclosure changes the semiotics of the hallway and transforms it into a corridor 'shared by all parties involved':

> According to our common agreement, the corridor is closed off and all neighbours can keep their belongings in it: strollers, bicycles . . . This was the very idea behind the enclosure. It is more convenient to keep such items in the corridor than the flat. Even in our spacious three bedroom [flat], a stroller is a nuisance.

The physical enclosure provided by the door, the lock and the partition wall has its linguistic counterpart: the pronoun *nash* (*наш*) – ours. *Nash* reduces the scale of the collective, signals a proprietary relation between the subject and the object, and introduces an emotional intimacy to it: *nash* corridor is closer than *obshcheye* corridor. A combination, *nash obshcheye* corridor, is also possible and when used, mobilizes proprietary emotions even more towards a greater sense of responsibility and collective care, '*This is nash obshcheye corridor! Let's keep it clean together!*' Given the unstable nature of *obshcheye*, both the physical and the linguistic enclosures – the partition and the word *nash* – ease the tension between *obshcheye* as 'no one's' and as 'belonging to everyone'. The exact meaning with which *obshcheye* is endowed determines action in, as well as towards, the common space of the corridor: its cleaning, its upkeep, noise and smell control, and much more. We might say, then, that the word and the wall order the commons, and that the central issue here is to prevent it from sliding into no one's concern.

Kommunalka: The *obshcheye* we no longer want

If *nash* stabilizes *obshcheye* as a positive category, *kommunalka* (*коммуналка*) and *obshchaga* (*общага*) signify the poignancy of its negative pole. Svetlana Boym summarized the core of the *kommunalka* in her seminal work, 'The archaeology of banality: A Soviet home':

> Kommunalka – a term of endearment and deprecation – was a result of the post-revolutionary expropriation and resettlement of private apartments in the urban centers; it consists of the individual or family rooms (neither living rooms, bedrooms, nor studies, but all-purpose rooms that can perform any function) and 'places of communal use', a euphemistic expression for a shared bathroom, corridor and kitchen that usually serves as the neighbours' battleground. Here one encounters endless schedules of 'communal duties', and endless scolding from fellow neighbours. (1994, p. 266).

In his study of communal flats anthropologist Ili'ya Utekhin describes one populated by as many as 56 people (Utekhin, 2004). *Obshchaga* is also a moniker; it refers to *obshchezhitiye* (*общежитие*) – literally, 'common living': the dormitory-style housing that not only colleges and universities but also factories and enterprises provided for their employees in the Soviet period. The shortage of housing was one of the most enduring and profound crises of the Soviet Union (Boym, 1994; Gerasimova, 2002; Harris, 2013; Zavisca, 2012), and as *kommunalka* and *obshchaga* were the Soviet state's responses to it, both have negative associations: both stand for imposed-from-above commonality.

No longer much of a reality, *kommunalka* today signals 'a nostalgic ruin of Soviet civilization' (Boym, 1994, p. 266), and occupies a special fictional place in oral accounts of Soviet life. The discourses that Liubov recorded in Placid Hollow and Agora are no exception. The imagery of *kommunalka* and *obshchaga* proliferate on group pages and serve as regular points of comparison.[5] Their use in the two settings is different, however. In Placid Hollow, the references are all about the materiality of the corridor and its aesthetics. Items of personal use that are kept there elicit a major discursive nod. Pictures of spaces cluttered with bulky trunks, bicycles, footwear and unwanted furniture are posted on the group wall to shame those who exceed a 'reasonable' number of items stored in the *obshcheye* corridor or leave them in a state of disrepair, dirty, etc. Clutter is essential to *kommunalka*, and *kommunalka* is ubiquitous in Placid Hollow residents' discourse, 'For some reason, what I see [in the photograph] is a kommunalka somewhere in the city centre.'[6]

Object-ness is a key aspect of *kommunalka* imagery. Here is an exchange that illustrates this: 'And where is the ubiquitous entresol?? Where is the rusted sleigh hung on a nail? Where are the countless skis that don't match in size?', mockingly enquires one group member. '[Emoji 'smile'] A sleigh, skis and felt boots [valenki] combined, and you have a complete set! [emoji 'smile'].' The exchange triggers another post: 'Hang the laundry to dry too . . . surely the place is too small already.' This is not a random exercise in wit, but an act of disciplining, since the thread appeared in response to a post about a cluttered corridor. This is to suggest that *kommunalka* actually polices, by the way of mockery, shared space, preventing it from falling into two extremes: becoming *obshcheye* as in 'no one's' by virtue of neighbours dumping their unwanted stuff there, or 'privatized' by being occupied with objects.[7]

The spectre of *kommunalka* haunts Agora as well, but in a different way. To begin with, Agora shares many of the physical qualities of a *kommunalka*: it actually was one in the past, before being purchased by a private individual, renovated, and rented out to Agorians. The corridor here is long – more than 20 metres – dark, and with signs of decay: poor electrical wiring, cracked walls, worn-out hardwood floors and exposed plumbing (Figure 6). The walls, painted off-white, are decorated with paintings and drawings left or made by previous residents. The collection is random and feels crowded. Doors to individually occupied – private – rooms have no locks or even latches. The rooms are supposed to be accessible. There is an old wardrobe and a clothes rail in the corridor plus a few bicycles. A newspaper article describes Agora's interior as 'a pile of recycled objects', some of which were found in 'a nearby skip'. The place as a whole, the journalist notes, is in the state 'of the perpetual fixing' ('My zhivem v kvartire-obshchestvennom prostranstve', 2017). The appearance of Agora's communal corridor is not that different from that of a *kommunalka*: in interviews with Liubov, Agorians describe a *kommunalka* as a space filled with useless things, with dim lighting and shabby shared facilities. Yet, Agora is no *kommunalka*, and one resident even called it an 'anti-*kommunalka*'. Where does the difference lie?

> I believe that it is not so important how new and aesthetically pleasing a given space is. More important is how much love and energy has been invested in it. And 'cosy' is not when the renovation is up-to-date, but when the space is filled with friendship, trust, and care about the

Figure 6. *Obshcheye* corridor in Agora. The walls have been painted by the tenants. The ceiling lights do not work. Personal belongings (bike, clothes and laundry) are stored outside the rooms.

common space. One day, we may all buy our own private studios where everything will be new and up-to-snuff, but somewhere in that new kitchen we will still have a part of the wall on which each guest, each friend will leave something – a tag, a note, a drawing; and in this something will live the outlandish and unrestrained spirit of Agora.

This VK post written by a young female resident frames the material reality of Agora away from the *kommunalka*, while acknowledging its physical resemblance. It is not the materiality – 'the shell' – she says, but the spirit that makes the difference. In Agora, all the residents are single (couples are not admitted), tend to work for creative or not-for-profit organizations, or they freelance. Agorians are between 25 and 40 years of age, travel frequently, and accept as a norm free access to nearly all spaces in the flat, including their own rooms. Agora is a place of organized art events and public debates, often political, and when those take place, the largest room is open to the public. The physical reality of Agora displays a similarity to that of a *kommunalka* without being identical to it.

Agorians insist that their community's genealogy is very different from that of a *kommunalka*. The founder of another communal place in Moscow expressed this well in an interview:

> Every time one says 'obshchezhitiye' or 'kommunalka', [one sees] a cockroach cross the wall, food disappearing from the fridge, drying laundry hanging in the smoke-filled corridor, and the alcoholic neighbour cursing his life. It seems time is needed to update and change the meaning of 'communal flat'. 'Koliving' on the other hand, is a new word with a not entirely clear meaning, but with a very clear idea: a life together. ('Kto stroit v Moskve. . .', 2018)

The disjuncture between Agora and the *kommunalka* is underscored further by the words Agorians use to describe them. Whereas Agora has a 'worn-out cosiness', they told Liubov, the *kommunalka* is outright 'sordid', and while Agora is an 'authentic commune', a *kommunalka* is a motley assortment of involuntary occupants. If in a *kommunalka* 'people are forced to leave with each other, in Agora we are happy to interact'; if *kommunalka* imposes endless schedules on its residents of communal duties, Agora 'is a magnet for people with shared interests', for whom cleaning is 'a work of love', work 'that can be collectively forgotten and equally collectively and suddenly remembered'. Most importantly, identifying with co-living and opposing the *kommunalka* positions Agora not as a reproduction of something from the past, not a nostalgic regression into a Soviet order of things, but as a progressively political social innovation.

So-obshchestvo: Communicating, 'hanging out' and creating the *obshcheye*

Is there a positive term Agorians use to define their sociality, and if so, what is it? Recall Svetlana Boym's apt description of the *kommunalka* in which the corridor figures as 'the neighbours' battleground'. In Agora, the corridor is defined first and furthermost as a space for '*obshcheniye*' (*общение*). *Obshcheniye*, noun, and *obshchat'sya (общаться)*, verb, run parallel to English, where 'communication' overlaps in meaning with commune and communion. However, as Fedorova reminds us, the Russian word also stands for 'being in relation to someone', or 'to have a community of interlocutors'. 'With whom do you usually *obshchaesh'sya*?' is a question about one's social circle.

In Agora, both semantic meanings of *obshcheniye* are at work, and both the corridor and the kitchen play an essential role as places where *obshcheniye* takes place. For example, 'stepping into the corridor, stepping into the obshcheye space, means a transition from the state of privacy to the state "I am ready to obshchatsya – to interact!"', one of the Agorians told Liubov. 'If I want to *po-obshchat'sya* with someone, I go to the kitchen; if I want to *po-obshchat'sya* and no one is in the kitchen, I simply sit in the kitchen, read a book and wait', another told her. *Obshcheniye* does not have a purpose other than that of socializing together; it is about 'hanging out' and 'being engaged'.

While *obshcheniye* may not be utilitarian, it is nevertheless productive. Not sure what to call it, an Agorian thus formulated this point for Liubov:

> I think in a kommunalka, well, you have no bonus, no added value to living with someone else . . . You live there because you have to, and people there are just a nuisance to you. But here,

well, you like the people, you talk to them, you have a good time with them, the talk is interesting . . . So, this is something added, some additional social space, a value.

This 'something added' is what Agora is as an organizational form: it is '*so-obshchestvo*'. Related to '*obshchestvo*' – 'society' – '*so-obshchestvo*' may be equated with 'community' in English, though it is smaller and more particular in terms of the identity of its members. 'We are a so-obshchestvo of friends, we have nothing to mete out among ourselves, we are ready to assist each other, ready to give and to receive, in other words, we always live in close touch.' This is how Agorians define themselves. However, whereas 'community' shares its morphology with 'common', *so-obshchestvo* stands in between, and takes its meaning from both, *obshchestvo*, society, and '*obshchast'sya*', to communicate, to engage. It is not a coincidence that in the quote above, a resident spoke of conversing and having 'an interesting talk' as generative of sociality. *Obshcheniye* is the added value.

In Agora, *so-obshchestvo* is inseparable from *obshcheniye*, engagement; and engagement is dependent upon the corridor and the kitchen, as common – *obshcheye* – spaces. It is this particular kind of interlocking of words and spaces that makes Agora an *anti-kommunalka* – not merely different, but opposed to the communal flat – and that constitutes it as a collective predicated on engagement and interaction. Translating this into the language of the commons, we might say that 'the resource' is social engagement, and its by-product is *so-obshchestvo*.

Discussion and conclusions

Our article began with the observation that words which becomes terms are part of the making of generalized model-systems. We took as an example 'the commons' – a term which commands attention and is on the rise as a privileged object of research. Yet, a review of relevant literature revealed that, first, the word has been 'stretched' across different phenomena and lost its specificity (De Moor, 2011), and second, the differentiation between its scholarly and everyday uses has been vague. Critics note the term's blind spots – is it about property relations or social imaginaries, management or affection? They question its 'vagueness' (Wagner & Talakai, 2007) and internal incoherence.

Treating concepts as sensitizing devices, we have proposed what we consider a good counterexample: the Russian-language category of *obshcheye*. As people go about making a life together – by being 'neighbours', 'owners', 'good citizens', 'co-residents', or simply 'us' – they name things and they act, and their words, practices and locations mesh. *Obshcheye*, with its enormously rich social history and strong cultural presence, is productive for thinking through the semantic, social and affective dimensions of life in common and giving these dimensions a theoretical significance. What we ethnographically reconstructed by following some key meaning-generating practices is a patchwork of adjectives, pronouns and nouns. They all are associated, but in any given context only a limited number of terms are drawn from this larger network. These properties take meaning – and make sense – only here-and-now and in connection with specific concerns and practices. *Kommunalka* is a type of domestic space, but also a social imaginary pertaining to Soviet history; *so-obshchestvo* is an emergent form of sociality based on a

Figure 7. *Obshcheye's* semantic network.

consistency of practices: communication and interaction; and *nash* is a zone within the *obshcheye* for which everyone cares, in contrast to that other *obshcheye* which evokes no such feeling. Semantic connectedness within *obshcheye* exists but is not characterized by coherence. It is instead achieved through material mediation in practice and has a strong affective dimension. *Obshcheye* is a semantic web with a patchwork character, but the fact it is a patchwork is not an epistemic problem. It is an asset: the selection of notions that form the network is expressive of specific concerns, and, as such, an important analytical tool. We visualize this semantic network in Figure 7.

Nash, kommunalka (interchangeable with *obshchaga*), and *so-obshchestvo* are three semantic nodes around which clusters of relations form.[8] The relations are of resemblance and opposition organized around a set of concerns: care, access, sociability and attachment. Very rarely, if at all, is there any concern with ownership. The positive and the negative characteristics are co-present and co-constitutive of each other. This relational sociology of *obshcheye* is hardly surprising, but its implications for thinking about terms and their relationships with model-systems may be not be immediately obvious. *Obshcheye* is a hybrid and the Russian language makes this immediately apparent. The hybrid composite of *obshcheye* also casts doubt upon the coherence of taxonomies of 'collective' or 'common'. Allow us to explain.

We take 'concern' to signify a matter of importance; it is a focused interest but may also be a locus of concentrated anxiety. Mieke Bal, influenced by Isabelle Stengers, wrote that 'the role of concepts is *to focus interest*': 'de facto, concepts organise a group of phenomena, define the relevant questions to be addressed to them, and determine the meaning that can be given to observations regarding the phenomena' (Bal & Marx-Macdonald, 2002, p. 31). Our research into the communal life in a Russian city yielded not one, but at least three phenomena pertaining to collectivity, tied by vectors of tension and generating words and emotions. They tune us into a wide set of concerns – with time (not wanting to be 'Soviet'), ownership (worrying about what is 'no one's'), affective connectivity (one sits and waits for a conversation), and the act of caring for people and for spaces. Each word and each relationship in the semantic network we drew reflects what is important to residents of The Hollow and Agorians as they go about ordering their lives together. The anxiety of the dissolution of a common place like the corridor into no one's *obshcheye* motivates residents of Placid Hollow, who became neighbours as a result of purchasing a property. These are people who, on a relatively arbitrary basis, reach out, stay in touch and coordinate how they will manage their corridor. Belonging, reciprocity and boundaries are of paramount importance here. In Placid Hollow, residents actively prevent the dissolution of the commons by imposing *nash* on the shared space and policing it with *kommunalka*. Words and images here bind and discipline. Members of the *so-obshchestvo* in Agora ascribe importance to and form matters of concern differently. Agorians are small in number and have control over whom to admit to their community. For them, what is important is the engagement itself, their interactions, communication and reciprocal care. The *obshcheye* of *so-obshchestvo* resists social atomization by propagating empathy as a building block for greater solidarity. Agorians also use the imagery of *kommunalka*, but not as a defence of privacy and order. Committed to the idea of progressive social innovation, members of the *so-obshchestvo* separate themselves from the involuntary commonality of *kommunalka*. The commons as a term could plausibly be applied to the range of spaces, rights and emotions that we discussed as *obshcheye* here, but it would not allow us to learn what is salient for each of these here-and-now, and how local history affects what is most immediately relevant.

Let us be clear: our proposition is not to replace 'commons' with '*obshcheye*'; this would reproduce model-centrism by privileging a particular reality. Instead, our proposal is to employ local linguistic repertoires and deploy those discoveries to move away from centring any particular reality as 'model' in social research. Concerns, rather than concepts, appear to us as more productive points of departure, and semantic networks accommodate this task better than singular concepts.

Acknowledgements

We would like to thank Andrew Barry, Nancy Ries, John Law, Annemarie Mol, Diana West and the members of Culture Club of the Department of Sociology at the University of Amsterdam for their thorough and thoughtful feedback on the earlier drafts of this article; and Helen Faller for her careful work with the English language in which this article is written.

Funding

The authors received no financial support for the research, authorship, and/or publication of this article.

Notes

1. *Obshcheye*, which translates either as 'common' or 'shared' in English, shares its root with *obshchestvennoye* (общественное), but the meaning of the latter in English is much closer to 'public' than to 'common'. Both differ from *kommunal'noye* (коммунальное, communal) which in Russian in one sense denotes a loathed type of housing (*kommunalka*), in a second applies to the utilities sector – *kommunal'noje khozyajstvo* (коммунальное хозяйство) – and in still another evolves into *kommuna* (коммуна) – the commune, a new and celebrated type of collective living. The addition of the possessive pronoun *nash* (наш, ours) fragments the semantic field of *obshchee* even further.

2.   As Russian grammar is notoriously complicated, and adjectives like *obshcheye* tend to change significantly depending on gender and inclination, we decided to use a single form of *obshcheye* to facilitate reading familiarity and ease, even though often such use is grammatically incorrect.
3.   Both area names are pseudonyms.
4.   It is difficult to say with any certainty how many residents may have rights of ownership over corridors, landings, lobbies, and other such spaces. Our own observations suggest that in a smaller tower of 300 units, there can be as few as 300 owners, assuming that each apartment belongs to single person (which is not always the case). But in other instances, such as three towers united by a shared base two storey high in the same Placid Hollow complex, there can be as many as 3,575 apartments, suggesting at least the same number of owners.
5.   Neither institution has completely vanished from post-socialist landscape; communal flats and dormitories still exist in St. Petersburg today. However, it is not these 'actually existing' places that excite the imagination of our interlocutors, but preconceived imaginaries, if not outright stereotypes.
6.   Since the historic centre of St. Petersburg became prime real estate more than a decade ago, all *kommunalkas* worth anything have been bought by Russia's new rich, and those that remain communal property are believed to be beyond redemption (or renovation).
7.   Another important aspect of the use of the *kommunalka* and especially *obshchaga* is to signal social mobility. The move to a privately owned flat for personal use is for many a move up the social ladder. By accusing neighbours of reproducing the material order of communal living, and therefore belonging to the outdated 'communal culture', new homeowners jealously guard their social advancement.
8.   It is important to note that the words that make up the semantic web of *obshcheye* are not cognates in a linguistic sense. Nor should the organizational structure of the semantic web we reconstructed here be treated as constant and universally applicable. Different contexts – different convergences of space, practices, and language – will generate different networks of meaning in need of being studied.

References

Abbott, A. (1988). *The system of professions*. University of Chicago Press.
Bakker, K. (2007). The 'commons' versus the 'commodity': Alter-globalization, anti-privatization and the human right to water in the global south. *Antipode, 39*(3), 430–455.
Bal, M., & Marx-Macdonald, S. (2002). *Travelling concepts in the humanities: A rough guide*. University of Toronto Press.
Benkler, Y. (2004). Sharing nicely: On shareable goods and the emergence of sharing as a modality of economic production. *The Yale Law Journal, 114*(2), 273–358.
Boym, S. (1994). The archeology of banality: The Soviet home. *Public Culture, 6*(2), 263–292.
Brednikova, O., & Zaporozhets, O. (2016). Veter, ustalost' i romantika nochi (ob osobennostyah novykh zhilykh massivov) [Wind, fatigue, and romanticism of the night: on the peculiarities of the new housing construction]. *Laboratorium: Russian Review of Social Research, 2*, 103–119.
Buchli, V. (1999). *An archaeology of socialism: The Narkomfin communal house*. Berg Publishers.
Caffentzis, G., & Federici, S. (2014). Commons against and beyond capitalism. *Community Development Journal, 49*(Suppl. 1), i92–i105.
Chatterton, P. (2010). Seeking the urban common: Furthering the debate on spatial justice. *City, 14*(6), 625–628.
De Moor, T. (2011). From common pastures to global commons: A historical perspective on interdisciplinary approaches to commons. *Natures Sciences Sociétés, 19*(4), 422–431.

Fedorova, K. (2011). Obshchestvo: mezhdu vsem i nichem [Society: caught between everything and nothing]. In *Ot obshchestvennogo k publichnomu* [How does civic activism fail?] (pp. 13–68). EUSP Press.

Gerasimova, E. (2002). Public privacy in the Soviet communal apartment. In D. Crowley & S. E. Reid (Eds.), *Socialist spaces: Sites of everyday life in the Eastern bloc* (pp. 207–230). Berg.

Gopalo, O. (2018, December 20). 'Postroy svoy dom i delay, chto khochesh'': sosedi izurodovali kartiny rostovchanina, prevrativshego pod"yezd v Tret'yakovku ['Build your own house and do whatever you want there!' Neighbours vandalized art works of a Rostov resident, who transformed their lobby into Tret'yakov museum]. *Komsomol'skaya Pravda*. www.rostov. kp.ru/daily/26923.4/3970405/ (accessed 17 December 2019).

Hardin, G. (1968). The tragedy of the commons. *Science, 162*(3859), 1243–1248.

Harris, S. E. (2013). *Communism on tomorrow street: Mass housing and everyday life after Stalin.* Woodrow Wilson Center Press.

Harvey, D. (2012). *Rebel cities: From the right to the city to the urban revolution.* Verso Books.

Hess, C. (2008, July 14–18). *Mapping the new commons.* Paper presented at Governing Shared Resources: Connecting Local Experience to Global Challenges, the 12th Biennial Conference of the International Association for the Study of the Commons, University of Gloucestershire, Cheltenham. http://dlc.dlib.indiana.edu/dlc/bitstream/handle/10535/304/ Mapping_the_NewCommons.pdf (accessed 16 May 2019).

Hirt, S. (2012). *Iron curtains: Gates, suburbs and privatization of space in the post-socialist city* (Vol. 27). John Wiley & Sons.

Knorr-Cetina, K. (1981). *The manufacture of knowledge: An essay on the constructivist and contextual nature of science.* Pergamon Press.

Krause, M. (2016). 'Western hegemony' in the social sciences: Fields and model systems. *The Sociological Review, 64*(2), 194–211.

Kto stroit v Moskve kolivingi s komnatami za 50 tysyach rubley [Who builds in Moscow co-living with the rent 50,000 rub per room?] (2018, March 6). *The Village.* www.the-village.ru/village/business/new-biz/304395-kolivium (accessed 16 May 2019).

Kuttler, T., & Jain, A. (2015). Defending space in a changing urban landscape – a study on urban commons in Hyderabad, India. In M. Dellenbaugh, M. Kip, M. Bieniok, A. K. Müller & M. Schwegmann (Eds.), *Urban commons: Moving beyond state and market* (pp. 72–90). Birkhäuser.

Lewin, M. (1990). The obshchina and the village. In R. Bartlett (Ed.), *Land commune and peasant community in Russia* (pp. 20–35). Palgrave Macmillan.

Mann, A., & Mol, A. (2019). Talking pleasures, writing dialects. outlining research on Schmecka. *Ethnos, 84*(5), 772–788.

Mironov, B. (1985). The Russian peasant commune after the reforms of the 1860s. *Slavic Review, 44*(3), 438–467.

My zhivem v kvartire-obshchestvennom prostranstve [We live in apartment-public-space] (2017, March 17). *The Village.* www.the-village.ru/village/people/experience/258534-kubometr (accessed 16 May 2019).

Obshchezhitiye XXI veka. (2018, November 7). TV official page on VK.com. https://vk.com/ video-148235461_456247754 (accessed 16 May 2019).

Ostrom, E. (1990). *Governing the commons. The evolution of institutions for collective action.* Cambridge University Press.

Park, R. E., Burgess, F. W., & MacKenzie, R. D. (1925). *The city.* University of Chicago Press.

Paxson, M. (2005). *Solovyovo: The story of memory in a Russian village.* Indiana University Press.

Shevchenko, O. (2008). *Crisis and the everyday in postsocialist Moscow.* Indiana University Press.

Thompson, E. P. (1963). *The making of the English working class.* Victor Golancz.

Utekhin, I. (2004). *Ocherki kommunal'nogo byta* [Essays on communal life]. OGI.

Utekhin, I. (2018). Suspicion and mistrust in neighbour relations. In F. Mühlfried (Ed.), *Mistrust: Ethnographic approximations* (pp. 201–217). transcript Verlag.

Vaccaro, I., & Beltran, O. (2019). What do we mean by 'the commons?' An examination of conceptual blurring over time. *Human Ecology, 47*, 331–340.

Wagner, J. R., Berge, E., Brara, R., Bruns, B., Caton, S. C., Donahue, J., . . . Swyngedouw, E. (2012). Water and the commons imaginary. *Current Anthropology, 53*(5), 617–641.

Wagner, J., & Talakai, M. (2007). Customs, commons, property, and ecology: Case studies from Oceania. *Human Organization, 66*(1), 1–10.

Zavisca, J. R. (2012). *Housing the new Russia*. Cornell University Press.

Author biographies

Liubov Chernysheva is a PhD candidate at the Amsterdam Institute for Social Science Research (University of Amsterdam, the Netherland). Her PhD thesis focuses on the life-in-common in a post-socialist city. She studies the practices of sharing, governing and digitally mediating everyday realities in different forms of neighbour relations and housing. Liubov is currently involved in the international research project Estates After Transition (supported by ERA.Net RUS Plus and RFBR) studying recent urbanization processes in post-socialist housing estates in St. Petersburg, Russia. She is also a part of a research team that studies urban space contestation in big Russian cities and mechanisms of interests coordination in the urban development processes (supported by the Russian Science Foundation grant).

Olga Sezneva (Ph.D., New York University, 2005) is a scholar, educator, writer and art curator. She teaches urban sociology at the University of Amsterdam. Her research on cities and memory, media piracy, and spacial justice has appeared in international journals *Environment and Planning D, Journal of Urban History, Poetics* and *Critical Historical Studies*. Olga is also a member of the international artists collective Moving Matters Travelling Workshop, where she does poetic performance art. She co-supervises (with Prof. Olav Velthuis) Liubov Chernysheva's dissertation.

War and balance: Following *shi* and rebalancing militant English-language knowing apparatuses

The Sociological Review Monographs
2020, Vol. 68(2) 81–95
© The Author(s) 2020
Article reuse guidelines:
sagepub.com/journals-permissions
DOI: 10.1177/0038026120905475
journals.sagepub.com/home/sor

Wen-yuan Lin

國立清華大學, Guólì Qīng-Huá DàXué, [National Tsing-Hua University], Taiwan/R.O.C

Abstract

English language and its warlike knowing apparatuses dominate global academic practice, including the repertoire of critique in social sciences. But what might be done about this? The paradox is that if we fight this, we simply rehearse the same logic of antagonism. This article tries to avoid this bind, experimenting instead with an alternative apparatus – an approach that values the art of balancing. In presenting this approach, *shi-as-reasoning* (shì, 勢), I take inspiration from Dr Hsu, a Chinese medical (CM) doctor in Taiwan, who avoids fighting viruses while treating patients with SARS in biomedically dominated clinics, and who publishes his work in English-language biomedical research journals. In doing so, he balances among the complexities of *shi* in the body of diseased patients, possible herbal interventions (decoctions), the contexts of CM practices in Taiwan, and English-language dominated biomedical research. Since this article describes Dr Hsu's practices in English, it makes use of elements taken from the material semiotics of social science, Dr Hsu's accounts of CM, and the logic of the non-antagonistic interplay between *yin* and *yang*. Following the lead of Dr Hsu, it thus suggests that a *shi*-inflected-reasoning might help to rebalance a situation that is imbalanced as a result of the domination of English in academia.

Keywords

Chinese medicine, English-language knowing apparatus, SARS, *shi*-as-reasoning, yin and yang

> It matters what thoughts think thoughts. It matters what knowledges know knowledges. It matters what relations relate relations. It matters what worlds world worlds. It matters what stories tell stories. (Haraway, 2016, p. 35)

Corresponding author:
Wen-yuan Lin, National Tsing-Hua University, Center for General Education, No. 101, Section 2, Kuang-Fu Road, Hsinchu, 30013, Taiwan/R.O.C.
Email: wylin1@mx.nthu.edu.tw

Transplanting terms

'Might it help to transplant terms rather than translate them?' asks Annemarie Mol, considering how this might be done in practice on English (Mol, 2014, p. 111). She suggests that:

> English travels globally. But for all that, it is not a universal language. Facing this may yet increase the chance that we/they come to engage in serious long-distance conversations. Messing up their/our languages may be a part of this. (Mol, 2014, p. 108)

In order to achieve this, she resists the widespread model of the academic fight (Tannen, 1998), and recommends transplanting rather than translating terms, because the former makes differences matter while the latter conceals these. The term she transplants is *lekker*, a Dutch word that cannot be directly translated into English where, in different contexts it roughly means 'nice', 'delicious' or 'pleasant'. Following *lekker* around nursing homes and dietary practices in the Netherlands and re-articulating these in English, Mol shifts the conceptual boundaries of care, bodily pleasure, and we/they distinctions in her translations. Instead of fighting English she diffracts it, and re-tells its theoretical repertoires with *lekker*. '[T]here is', she writes, 'no such thing as a meta-theory . . . all we have is infra-theory, travelling and transforming along with the words in which it is articulated' (Mol, 2014, p. 108). Thus, transplanting *lekker* enacts an alternative knowing apparatus that is about connecting as well as breaking worlds in the Dutch and English languages.

How does this inform the art of academic practices? 'Argument', Lakoff and Johnson (1980, p. 4) observe, 'is war.' They add that '[t]his metaphor is reflected in our everyday language by a wide variety of expressions.' For instance (their examples): 'Your claims are *indefensible*.' 'He *shot down* all of my arguments.' 'I've *never won* an argument with him.' 'Our' in their phrase 'our everyday language' means (American) English speakers. But as authors such as Latour (1988), Serres (2008) and Mol (2014) have noted, in the West more generally the *fight* has been the dominant metaphor for handling intellectual difference. Such is its epistemic habitus: academic critique works by dividing, conquering and fighting. And as the English language has grown in academic significance, so too has its warlike knowing apparatus.

What might be done about this? The paradox is obvious: those who fight it, simply rehearse the same logic of antagonism. In this article, like Mol, I try to avoid this bind, but in a slightly different way, by experimenting with an alternative apparatus – an approach that avoids antagonism because instead it values *balancing*. I do this by drawing on the practices of Dr Hsu, a Taiwanese Chinese medical (CM) practitioner, as he intervened in the SARS (severe acute respiratory syndrome) epidemic not by fighting the virus directly, but rather by using various balancing strategies. After presenting an account of his strategies, I use these to re-articulate the character of criticism.

As I do this, I wrestle with two difficulties. First, CM is its own world with its own particular histories, classics, modes of training and apprenticeship, institutions and vocabularies. Translation of my fieldwork into English is difficult because the realities being manipulated in CM are far removed from most English-language forms of common sense. Second, CM is also a world in which there are huge differences between different traditions and practices. While biomedicine is not a monolith either, CM is heterogeneous in a way which means that it does not cohere in a manner that accords with most 'Western' idealizations of scientific knowledge. It does not assume that there is such a thing as universal good knowledge that can be generalized and applied regardless of context. Instead, at least very often, its practitioners imagine (again to put it briefly) that what they know is situated and context specific rather than being of general validity or applicability (see Lai & Farquhar, this volume). With these difficulties in mind, I want to insist that this article is not about 'CM in general' (whatever that might mean), but about Dr Hsu's SARS-relevant practices. And as I describe those practices, I will inevitably be using English terms that offer only approximate translations of Dr Hsu's Chinese descriptions.

In what follows, two of these terms are crucial: *qi* (qì, 氣), and the term that interests me most, *shi*-as-reasoning (shì, 勢). Here is the approximate logic. Like many CM practitioners, Dr Hsu takes medical problems to be the expression of *qi* that is *out of balance*. *Qi* can be unsatisfactorily translated as flows of energy (Unschuld, 1987). In this understanding intervention becomes a matter of balancing or rebalancing those flows of energy. So in the case of SARS (I will describe this more fully below) Dr Hsu's strategy was not to attack the virus. Instead, he sought to intervene in the flows of various forms of out-of-balance *qi* or energy and rebalance these in order to effect a cure. This is where the second term, *shi*, kicks in. As with *qi*, the word *shi* cannot easily be translated into English. Roughly, however, it means 'power' or 'tendency'. When it refers to the transformation of things or situations, it applies both to movement or change, and to the situation itself. In particular, it describes the *inclination or propensity of things* (Jullien, 1995, p. 291, n.1). Sinologist François Jullien has written at book length about the transformation of *shi* in a series of fields (including Chinese classical painting, political strategy and historiography), but has found it impossible to exhaust the senses of the term. He has also observed that while *shi* does not figure as a major concept in Chinese thinking, it remains a disconcerting word 'torn between points of view that are apparently too divergent', but yet 'with an illuminating logic' (Jullien, 1995, pp. 12–13). And that 'illuminating logic'? He suggests that this is a specific way of reasoning in which we 'open ourselves to . . . immanent force and learn to seize it' (p. 13). Following this prompt, I try to show how Dr Hsu tinkered with *shi* – a sense of how things are going or unfolding – to restore balance in diagnosis, the design of medication, and in writing papers in English for the biomedically dominated medical profession.

Before I move on, I need to flag up a few more warnings. First, CM is not only about *shi* or balancing. As Dr Hsu knows well, other strategies, including strategies for fighting diseases, are to be found in CM's copious principles of treatment (Lin, 2017). Indeed, he also uses some of these alternatives himself. Second, though Dr Hsu tends to argue that biomedicine is about fighting disease, as I noted above, biomedicine is also complex and multiple in practice (Mol, 2002), so here I am describing his understanding of biomedicine in the context of SARS, rather than offering my own analysis of biomedicine. Third, though I cannot explore this in the present article, it is also important to note that contemporary CM is not autonomous, and its shape is partly the consequence of long-term historical entanglement with biomedicine both institutionally (so, for instance, biomedicine dominates healthcare in Taiwan) and in how it understands itself, its diagnoses, and its forms of treatment (Zhan, 2009).

Coping with *shi* in the clinic and in research

SARS came to Taiwan in March, 2003. The hospital Dr Hsu served in at that time soon found itself admitting patients. The SARS coronavirus was not identified until mid-April 2003 and, even worse, biomedicine had – and still has – no effective cure. Some biomedical doctors were reluctant to care for hospitalised patients. Being doubly-licensed in biomedicine and CM, Dr Hsu had practised biomedicine for ten years and had started the CM department in his hospital only three years earlier. He volunteered to work with SARS patients, and designed a CM clinical study. 'This,' he said in interview, 'was an opportunity. If biomedicine could have helped, there would have been no room for CM. . . . At that point, I had just finished my Masters' degree and planned to do a PhD. I thought this was an unusual chance. . . . I was curious about such a mysterious epidemic and . . . how much CM could do about it. . . . I needed to see patients in person.[1]

Dr Hsu's intervention was a product of contingency. Despite the fact that CM has coexisted with biomedicine in Taiwan since the nineteenth century, it is unusual for CM and biomedicine to work closely together, and it is even more unusual to find a doubly-licensed doctor transferring from biomedicine to CM. Moreover, as he notes, Dr Hsu only had the opportunity because it was clear that biomedicine could do little for SARS patients.

Dr Hsu' strategy was to handle the situation from the perspectives of both CM and biomedicine. On the one hand, he studied CM classics and designed a new form of medication (in CM this is known as a 'decoction'[2]), based on information collected from patients. On the other hand, his Masters' study on the integration of CM and biomedicine taught him the need to verify the effectiveness of CM in a manner recognizable to proponents of biomedical science.

Before SARS came to Taiwan, like most CM practitioners, Dr Hsu had started by studying classic texts in CM. In his case he had surveyed those of a particular approach, the 'warm disease' school.[3] This had led him to devise a decoction for hospital staff to help them resist infection. After SARS arrived, he drew on this background to design a new form of medication, True-gone[4] decoction (TGD), first for staff and then for patients. At the same time, in order to verify TGD's efficacy he designed a randomized, double-blind, controlled pilot study. The findings were exciting. According to one of the English-language publications:

All enrolled patients received routine western-medicine treatment. Patients were randomly allocated to one of the three supplementary treatment groups. . . . Chest X-ray was done every 1 or 2 days for every patient. . . . Patients from . . . TGD . . . took less days before showing improvement (6.7 ± 1.8) compared with placebo group (11.2 ± 4.9), which showed statistical significance ($P=0.04$) (Hsu et al., 2008, p. 355).

The study only claimed to prove that the length of hospitalization for non-critically ill patients was reduced for those who took the decoction (Hsu et al., 2008, p. 360), but there were no SARS deaths or new infections in Dr Hsu's hospital during the epidemic.

A CM clinical trial on SARS patients like this is rare. Dr Hsu is proud of it but still not entirely satisfied with it. Perhaps unsurprisingly, the problem turned around questions of translation. '[It is] like teaching overseas students. . . . Many things were lost . . . [when they were put into] English. It is very difficult [to express these in English]. But you have to cope with that . . .'. So what is lost? This can be checked by comparing Dr Hsu's Chinese and English-language papers. The latter takes the typical scientific format conventional in biomedicine and applies this to CM research. Starting with a short introduction, the design of the experiment is described, and data and statistical analysis follow, and it concludes with a discussion and an account of the limitations of the study. By contrast, most of the Chinese papers start by discussing excerpts from CM classics, followed by outlining approaches and principles for diagnosis and treatment derived from those classics, before moving on to explain the design of TGD and concluding with its effects on patients.

So what is being transplanted from English into CM in the English-language papers? Clinically, there are biomedical examinations (X-ray and laboratory tests) and forms of treatment, the randomized controlled application of CM medication, and a biochemical explanation of the efficacy of CM ingredients. In addition, however, the trial itself introduces a very specific understanding of the world and knowledge that is foreign to many CM approaches. First, the design and the execution of the trial assume a naturalistic ontology, a self-evident 'out-there' objective world that works with universal mechanisms (Descola, 2013). Second, the scientific methodology of randomized, double-blind, controlled study is assumed to be a procedure that will uncover those mechanisms. And third, quantitative statistical verification is taken as substantial proof of sound knowledge.

This tells us that what concerns Dr Hsu is not simply an issue of language or translation (though this is real enough), but also what we might think of as a particular knowing apparatus that is being carried in this scientific version of the English language.[5] This apparatus, composed of a specific worldview, ontology and epistemology, also implies institutional conventions that guarantee the sound scientific production of knowledge, often in the form of disciplinary knowledge – much current CM academic research included. Dr Hsu observes that this entails specific ways of arguing and criticizing that are foreign to the CM approaches to which he is committed:

> The [academic and biomedical] systems come from the West, and we [followers of traditional approaches] must adapt [to them] if we are to find a way of getting into them. . . . In order to publish in SCI [science citation index] journals, you have to follow [scientific protocols] to make it solid and defensible . . . while dropping what you cannot explain clearly [such as *shi* and the design of TGD] . . . or . . . the reviewers will attack the paper . . . and you end up in the mud, fighting, and don't get through . . .

The lesson is this. Though these typically take themselves to be objective and neutral, English-language scientific (and more generally academic) practices are imagined and work through particular tropes and metaphors including warlike forms of language. Indeed, as I noted above, making an argument is often taken to be like preparing for war (Haraway, 1991; Lakoff & Johnson, 1980). Thus Dr Hsu has to *solidify* his position in order to *defend* his arguments from *attacks* by reviewers and their criticisms who might otherwise *destroy* those arguments. And these tropes are not simply a matter of literary style. They are embedded in biomedical practice too. The SARS guidelines from the Taiwan Center for Disease Control advises the use of anti-viral drugs and steroids for treatment. The thinking is that the immune system guards the body by fighting the invasive organisms (Martin, 1994). Therefore, anti-viral drugs are intended to *kill* the virus, but since the immune system is also taken to *fight* the invasive virus to the point of over-reaction, steroids are used to *suppress* the immune system which might otherwise *destroy* the body (Hsu et al., 2008, p. 357).

Diagnosing the *shi* of SARS in patients

So a warlike knowing apparatus inflects ways of treating SARS patients in biomedicine, as well as the search for truth in scientific research and the style of academic debate. However, Dr Hsu's strategy for handling this is to try to avoid fighting. Though he talks little of the tropes embedded in what he says or does, the way in which he talks is suggestive. He says, for instance, that he 'followed', 'adapted to' and 'coped with' circumstances. These terms suggest that an alternative knowing apparatus may be at work. He also writes about *shi* in his Chinese papers, and in interviews he often used phrases such as 'following the *shi* [of something]'. So what is the 'illuminating logic' of *shi* in his practice? How does he 'open . . . [himself] to . . . immanent force and learn to seize it'? (Jullien, 1995, p. 13) The answer comes in three parts.

First, he uses *shi*-as-reasoning to apprehend the dynamics at work in the situation, such as *qi*. This means that when he worked on SARS he did so in ways that were quite unlike his understanding of the logic of biomedicine. His object was not to identify the character of the virus and the mechanism of infection, in the hope of being able to prescribe a specific drug. Instead he looked at SARS with *qi* in mind. Clinically, *qi* can be understood as flows of energy along meridians (jīng luò, 經絡) that in Chinese medicine are understood to run in and through the body. These flows create *shi*; that is, they create various propensities, possibilities, and likely changes. If there is disease, then these flows of *qi* are blocked, or become unbalanced and disturbed, which means that they create unusual *shi*. Thinking in this way, Dr Hsu notes that 'the major issue . . . is that the *shi* [of the disease] (bìng shì, 病勢) shifts rapidly'. He writes in a Chinese paper:

> In *On Plague* (瘟疫論) 'When a disease spreads around a whole area, all the households suffer from the same disease. It is [caused by] the mixed *qi* (zá qì, 雜氣) that circulates at the time and causes disease. . . . As a particular *qi* goes into particular visceral systems (zàng fǔ, 臟腑) and meridians and develops into a particular disease, [when mixed *qi* is prevalent] it follows that people have the same disease . . . .' (何彥頤 et al., 2003, p. 26)

The specificities here do not all matter. But what is important is that though *On Plague* is a classic CM text written in the mid-seventeenth century, it is relevant to Dr Hsu's contemporary practice because it tells him that the wellbeing of people depends on the balance of *qi*. The *qi* is right when it circulates properly among what Chinese calls the 'ten-thousand things' (wàn wù, 萬物), which means everything in the world, and it does this in the right order at the right time. Against this, 'mixed *qi*' is evil since it does not 'match . . . the season', so when it rises, the body is overwhelmed and becomes imbalanced.

So *shi* is a way of apprehending the circumstances of disease. Second, however, it is also a way of understanding how things (and their *qi*) change. So, for instance, in one Chinese paper Dr Hsu describes how the shifting *shi* of SARS unfolds and how the body is disturbed.[6] In particular, he explains how the *shi* (of evil *qi*) disturbs different parts of the body and causes various forms of imbalance (for instance, obstructing a particular meridian leads to lack of appetite). The point is that in a world of *qi*, each part of the body resonates with the *qi* of specific meridians. Evil *qi* causes various problems because it disrupts the balance between those meridians. Confronted by so many problems, in the context of SARS Dr Hsu had to choose the best diagnostic techniques to determine the pattern of *shi* and so devise appropriate treatment.

These dynamics can be illustrated if we think about the reasoning indexed by the *tai chi* symbol (see below). This is a way of imagining the endless possibilities of the minimalist interplay between *yin* and *yang*. Thus while *yin* and *yang* are primarily in opposition, their dispositions are fluid, and the various relational configurations and their patterning and unfolding explicate various propensities. So *yin* and *yang* are not only in contrast with each other, but are also mutually dependent, in tension and included in each other, and at the same time they are in a dynamic and reciprocally transforming balance of constantly changing movement (王秀, 2011, pp. 32–37). The interplay of *yin* and *yang* is central to many CM classics, and for Dr Hsu their dynamics are at work in the relations between right *qi* and evil *qi*. This tells him that the relations between these two are complex, constantly shifting and contextual. Drawing on this reasoning with biomedicine in mind, Dr Hsu therefore specifies the *shi* of SARS by exploring how a-virus-in-a-specific-condition-(evil *qi*)-affects-a-particular-patient's-body-(right *qi*)-in-a-specific-situation. (The hyphens are deliberate. They are a way of insisting that these relations and whatever makes them up are all on the move together.)

So this is a way of apprehending circumstances and how they will change, but (third point) this means that it is necessary to follow *shi* closely. Indeed, CM has developed many approaches for detecting and anticipating the ways *shi* shifts and transforms. Each approach has its specific focus and techniques, and each implies a different way of thinking about treatment (Farquhar, 1994). For Dr Hsu, the point is to work out which approach to draw on. It is to determine whether the current *shi* of a disease resembles the way of reasoning and the *shi* described in a specific approach.[7] This implies the need for close observation. So, for instance, early clinical observations led him to an approach called four sectors (wèi qì yíng xiě, 衛氣營血)[8] analysis which assumes that *shi* progresses through four stages or sectors. But this conclusion was not completely clear, and caused him anxiety and concern, not only because other CM doctors thought differently, but also because he could not find the initial stage that would allow him to confirm this diagnosis. Looking into this carefully, he says that:

> One night, I asked one patient for the full details [of the progress of the disease], then I asked many [patients], and I found that . . . progress in the initial stage (sector of *wei*) was so rapid that it was over before they were admitted to hospital . . . [the *shi* of SARS] is very different from the description in the classics, but it still followed the progression [they describe].

This was a success that rested, as I have just noted, on careful observation. As a result his diagnosis was confirmed, and strategies for what was to become a successful medical intervention were suggested.

Manoeuvring *shi* in and with a decoction

So what did Dr Hsu actually do in practice? 'At the beginning [of SARS], many people used those anti-virus medications.'[9] Against this, he judged that to fight was not to make good use of CM. Arguably, in thinking this he was following an approach which teaches him that in complex cases fighting disease directly does not work because it does not take the *shi*-of-disease-in-the-patient's-body-as-a-whole into consideration (馬光亞, 2011). Instead, and in this tradition, he planned a form of treatment with many issues in mind which he specified, tried to evaluate, and used when tinkering with the various *shi* at work.

In a detailed account of his strategy he explains that while SARS is a kind of heat, he does not simply repress it with cold medication. This is not only because 'strong cold' fighting 'strong heat' hurts the body more, but also because cold medication leads the *shi* to close the exterior of the body and prevent evil *qi* from departing. So though there is still some conflict, fighting and repressing only imbalance disease *shi* further. Instead Dr Hsu intervened by following, diverting and reducing disease *shi* without directly confronting it. The details cannot be explored here, but he carefully devised a series of treatment principles for rebalancing that include 'cool acrid exterior-resolving', 'heat-clearing and toxin-resolving', 'dispersing liver' and 'harmonizing the stomach'.[10]

But how to achieve this? The answer to this question leads us to the *shi* of medication (yào shì, 藥勢). Some CM approaches use specific herbs to treat a particular disease directly – an approach similar to the pattern common in biomedicine (Unschuld, 1987). But Dr Hsu worked indirectly by determining the therapeutic priorities and arranging an appropriate combination of herbs. Here he used the art of formulary design. This is complex in practice, but it works by combining four principles or functions called the 'sovereign' (jūn, 君), the 'minister' (chén, 臣), the 'assistant' (zuǒ, 佐) and the 'courier' (shǐ, 使). We may think of these as roles or functions or ways of thinking about how different medications work together in combination. So the sovereign is responsible for handling the major or most urgent problem, while the minister addresses secondary issues in order to support the work of the sovereign. Alongside these, the assistant tackles more general issues and sometimes restrains or balances the effects of the sovereign and the minister, while the courier usually harmonizes the combination and leads the combination of medication to the best place for it to work. This is complex. So, for instance, this is what Dr Hsu says about the TGD decoction:

> It was urgent to clear the heat, I used large portion of *Shi Gao* (shí gāo, 石膏, *Gypsum fibrosum*) as the sovereign. . . . *Fang Fong* (fáng fēng, 防風, *Siler divaricatum*) . . . also helped in clearing the heat. Then patients also had serious diarrhoea, so *Zhi Zi* (zhī zi, 栀子, *Gardeniae jasminoides*) and *Huang Gin* (huáng qín, 黃芩, *Scutellaria baicalensis*) . . . were working on the stomach and spleen, together they were ministering to improve the stagnation of *qi* in the stomach and the spleen [meridian]. . . . *Chai Hu* (chái hú, 柴胡, *Bupleurum chinense*) for dispersing liver [meridian] . . . and *Ban Xia* (bàn xià, 半夏, *Pinellia ternate*) for stomach . . . were the assistants. . . . *Huo Xiang* (huòxiāng, 霍香, *Agastache rugose*) and *Jie Geng* (jié gěng, 桔梗, *Platycodon grandiflorum*) were couriers. . . . the former played the role of reversing courier (fǎn shǐ, 反使) that prevented the visible (virus) and invisible (horror and anxiety) evil from going further, and the latter (tended to go up and) lead the medication to the lung [meridian].

The details are again not important in the present context, but what is significant is the general strategy. Some thoughts on this. Reading what he says literally, we might think that he was designing TGD as if he were deploying an army. So *Shi Gao*, a 'cold medication' which is the sovereign, is aimed at the patients' fever, the most urgent problem in the situation. It seems that a war metaphor is at work here. Indeed, it is said in CM that 'prescribing a formula is like deploying an army' and one famous doctor even claimed that the 13 chapters of Sun Tzu's classic, *The Art of Warfare*, exhaust the strategies of treatment (清·徐大椿, 1978). But if we want to understand Dr Hsu's approach this is misleading. First, the use of a military metaphor does not necessarily imply conflict. Indeed, Sun Tzu does not have much to say about fighting. He writes that when planning the attack 'to win a hundred victories in a hundred battles is not the highest excellence; the highest excellence is to subdue the enemy's army without fighting at all' (Sun Tzu, 1994, p. 111). He tells his readers that the wise general is one who 'seek[s] victory from *shi* and does not demand it from his men' (Sun Tzu, 1994, p. 120) and the chapters of *The Art of Warfare* describe ways of achieving victory with the least effort by detecting and manipulating the *shi* of warfare (Law & Lin, 2018).

This leads us to a second question. What does 'prescribing a formula is like deploying an army' mean? The answer takes us to the combination of herbs in the prescription. In the famous *Compendium of Materia Medica* (first published in 1596 CE) everything is classified in terms of its properties and its taste (xìng wèi, 性味) (Unschuld, 1986). For instance, Dr Hsu explains that *Shi Gao* is cold in inclination and can be used for clearing heat, *Chai Hu* is for dispersing the liver, and *Zhi Zi* for harmonizing the stomach and spleen. However, to put it like this is also misleading. This is because in the world of *shi*, things are not first immobilized before being set into motion and changed under the impetus of causal factors. Instead, as I have noted above, everything is in motion and in changing relations with everything else. Since the diseased body reflects imbalanced *shi*, the formulation of medication is designed to mobilize the various contextually-bound medicinal inclinations into the *shi* of TGD as a whole.

To think about this it helps to return to the *tai chi* illustration and imagine that *yin* symbolizes the evil *qi* of SARS while *yang* the right *qi* of medication. Imbalanced *shi* manifests itself differently in different situations and stages of the disease (*yin*), and also in different patients' bodies. This means that medication has to be arranged in different ways in order to achieve rebalance. Practically, this is the reasoning that underpins the composition of herbs and their effects in the relational configurations of a decoction. To put it differently, herbs have inclinations not in and of themselves but in the metamorphoses that take place between the endlessly many things that in Chinese understandings make up the world (Nappi, 2009) – that is, they reflect or form a part of *shi*. So they do not work exactly in the same way all the time, but have different effects in different compositions when arranged in different prescriptions, so their combination (the sovereign, minister, assistant and courier logic that I touched on above) is also a matter of balancing them well in each specific treatment. This is also why each decoction has (a) specific courier(s), for instance *Huo Xiang* and *Jie Geng* in TGD, that will lead the *qi* of the medication to work at the proper place.

Being a *shi*-following courier

The argument is thus that each moment of movement in the body and each formulation is different. The decoction as a whole is designed to manipulate the biased *shi* of herbs to rebalance *shi* of disease. It is the *imbalances* in the *shi* of these movements and formulations that form the focus of CM diagnosis and intervention. To be clear, let me reiterate that what I have described is just an example from a specific CM approach. There is no single 'Chinese' world of *shi*: as I noted above, there are many different versions of CM. Neither, again to be clear, are there two separate and coherent worlds, with Chinese medicine on the one hand and biomedicine on the other. As I noted earlier, though the academic English-language knowing apparatuses may think of themselves as enacting a single 'one-world world' (Law, 2015), they also generate different practices and realities which interact and overlap in a range of ways (Mol, 2002). That said, the CM/biomedicine distinction is important too. For Dr Hsu's work on SARS, as we have seen, English-language academic apparatuses have been transplanted into CM. But how might we reverse the direction of travel? How might we transplant *shi* back into English-language academic apparatuses in social science, as this article has sought to do?

One way is to think simultaneously, as many CM approaches do, about the 'social' and the 'medical'.[11] Here Dr Hsu's SARS strategy is suggestive. For instance, in 2003, around the world there was talk of 'fighting SARS', and similar language turned up in Taiwan, with talk in government and hospitals and wider society again of 'fighting SARS' (kàng shà, 抗煞) with praise for 'SARS fighting heroes'. Dr Hsu thought about what was happening, using *shi*-as-reasoning and the method of formulary design:

> For the patients, . . . I think good quarantine practices were the sovereign. . . . Although the orthodox treatment was biomedicine . . ., our TGD . . . helped our staff to care for the patients without worrying about infection, and that is minister. . . . And the courier, I think it was the good will of everybody. Having good will made [medical] people willing to do their job, and then . . . people will follow.

There is nothing here about *fighting* SARS. It is about gently and very slightly moving things forward by shifting *shi* both 'medically' and 'socially'. CM doctors using this approach often talk in this way. Talking about the denigration of CM in the late nineteenth century one wrote:

> In a long-lasting and severe situation (*shi*), if you dramatically change how people are used to being, they will be suspicious and afraid. So now I give gentle advice and I negotiate with my readers. (清·唐宗海, no date)

Dr Hsu similarly follows the *shi* of the situation to reflect on the 'social' and the 'linguistic' as well as the 'clinical'. Commenting on how he presented the case in English, he says:

> Of course, I was a fresh CM practitioner at that time and I was not in the position to write in the way I liked . . ., I am senior now . . . maybe it would be different if I have to do it again . . .

Nevertheless, Dr Hsu managed to negotiate between the two worlds. He not only wrote papers in both English and Chinese, but also explained his four sectors analysis and the effect of TGD in relation to the biomedical account of the clinical progression of SARS (Hsu et al., 2008) and designed a questionnaire for standardizing his diagnosis and analysis in the Chinese papers (許中華 et al., 2004). But this is also a strategy for imagining and practising CM:

> The differences between various situations are not [a problem to do with this] point and [that] point. . . . you have to take the whole into account, and that is what I say about *shi*. This is difficult to 'teach'. . . .You have to see the condition, then . . . some students start to observe more deeply, and then . . . [t]hey will apprehend and experience many things [in *shi*] gradually . . .

In contrast to a strategy that emphasizes the necessity for action that is direct and explicit, to follow *shi* is to know differences without necessarily challenging and working with the separations implied in an analytical approach. Apprehending and balancing means attending to very many subtleties. Whether it be manoeuvring between the crises of SARS patients and his decoctions, the direct approach of biomedicine and the strategies of CM, the conventions of English-language academic writing and those of writing in Chinese, or indeed, the differences between CM approaches, Dr Hsu attended to their subtleties in all of these contexts. His *shi*-as-reasoning practices were not about fighting between opposites, but rather about tinkering, following and manoeuvring differences that were also mutually dependent, in tension and included in each other. They were about sensing and working within an ever changing, dynamic and reciprocally transforming balance of constantly changing movement.

Here I do not seek to mobilize *shi*-as-reasoning to criticize warlike knowing apparatuses. To do so would be to rehearse a logic of antagonism. Instead, I offer a lesson for as and when this might be helpful. As I try to show in this hybrid account that draws from both the material semiotics of social science, the logic of *yin* and *yang*, and CM in Dr Hsu's accounts and practices, he does not enter into controversies about whether SARS is caused by a virus, about biomedicine as against CM approaches, or about forms of academic convention. Instead he seeks ways of nudging imbalances between the various *shi*, even in cases of conflict. Borrowing from the prescription metaphor, this is how Dr Hsu works as a creative and complementary series of couriers for shifting the tensions between these differences in different situations. And that is the lesson. Instead of waging endless war, Dr Hsu seeks ways of rebalancing warlike inclinations and imbalances.

Rebalancing the antagonistic critical agenda

How does this help us in social science? Is there a 'critical' agenda for alternative worlds implied in *shi*-as-reasoning? What is imbalanced in English-language dominated social science? And how might this be rebalanced? Drawing from Dr Hsu's practices, I conclude with some brief suggestions.

First, there is the issue of *what it is to be critical*. 'Criticism' has itself been critiqued (Latour, 2004). But the issue is: does critique necessarily imply something akin to fighting, to war, and the hope of victory or the fear of defeat? Or might this be re-imagined? Confronted by warlike knowing apparatuses of various kinds, as we have seen Dr Hsu neither fights nor marginalizes himself. Instead he follows the complexities of *shi* of the situation and plays the role of the 'courier'. As with the *yin–yang* dynamic of *tai chi* reasoning, as he treats patients and publishes research he finds ways of rebalancing by loosening the tropes and the practices of antagonism. Here, then, is the first thought. If we draw on *shi*-as-reasoning then what it is to be critical might not imply conflict, but instead suggests *strategies of loosening and rebalancing*. And it might also suggest the need for the kinds of flexibilities implied by the dynamics of the *tai chi* symbol. The thought, then, is that in this alternative version of criticism, tactics and strategies would never be fixed because there are no universal solutions. Instead, these would become subtle and fluid.

Second, we have learned that in each imbalanced situation there are ever so many issues or problems tangled together. So Dr Hsu does not diagnose a particular problem. He does not home in on language, biomedical domination, or academic publishing. Instead he recognizes that all of these are present, and that what I have called the English-language knowing apparatus is just one part of this. This means he does not identify a root cause for any imbalance, and neither does he use CM resources as a remedy to counter that root cause. To do so would be to reproduce the practices of war-as-conflict (such as identifying and killing the SARS coronavirus) and *shi*-as-reasoning would have been lost. The implication is that if we want to alter English-language domination and its infra-theoretical baggage, importing *shi* (or any other knowing apparatus) by itself will not work. Likewise, neither will it work to simply use *shi*-as-reasoning to criticize chronic and pervasive conceptual domination. Instead, a sensibility to *shi* and balancing suggests that it would be useful to reach out for and follow the complexities of conceptual clashes and then work by nudging a way through their frictions (Tsing, 2005).

Third, as a part of this it would be wise to think about the role of the *courier*. In Dr Hsu's prescription this is important because it moves the *shi* of disease and medication forward with the least possible effort. We saw this for TGD as a treatment, but the argument applies elsewhere, too. For instance, in his interviews with me Dr Hsu sought to guide me to the alternative knowing apparatus of *shi*. Understanding that I am exploring CM from a social science perspective he said, '[y]our work might lead non-CM people to understand and help to change the situation'. In all of these contexts he worked – and works – as the courier to help shift imbalanced situations.

Finally, what I have described above suggests that it might be wise to change the way we imagine knowledge from the very beginning. Perhaps, drawing on *shi*-as-reasoning, knowledge of something might be understood as knowing the propensities of things. And then, if we turn this logic round and apply it to social science, we might think of the latter as imbalanced as a result of the *shi* of English-language domination. Indeed, we might think of rebalancing this by rethinking the interferences between languages with their infra-theories and their knowing apparatuses (Lin, 2017). Many, including the contributors to the present volume, have sought to do this.[12] But each language is different. Each has its own propensities, biases and inclinations. However, if we think of this in a CM-inflected way, each language can also be understood as a potential courier rather than a bearer of ultimate truth. Each, that is, allows us to tell different theoretical and critical stories of the thinkable and the unthinkable. And so it is with this article. This has been a proposition about what *shi* might add to English, but in presenting this I have mixed elements taken from (English-language-dominated) material semiotics of social science, the logic of the non-antagonistic interplay between *yin* and *yang*, and Dr Hsu's CM approach to rebalancing. These are the configurations that this article has carried into English-language social science. My hope is that this might count as a contribution towards rebalancing rather than a step in yet another critical war.

Funding

The author declared receipt of the following financial support for the research, authorship, and/or publication of this article: The author received grant support from the Ministry of Science and Technology, Taiwan/R.O.C. for the research reported in this paper.

Notes

1. Dr Hsu is one of the CM practitioners I interviewed in Taiwan. The descriptions without citations in this article are from my fieldnotes.
2. A form of CM medication made by cooking herbs in a specific combination.
3. This is one of the major CM approaches developed around the seventeenth century, and it is used in particular in treating plagues.
4. True-gone is in the form of a soup cooked from a combination of herbs prescribed by a CM doctor. The name True-gone is similar to the pronunciation of Chinese 除根 (chú gēn; 除 means eradicate and 根 means root). Together they mean eradicate the root of SARS.
5. I am not suggesting that the English-language science is unique in this respect. But in the context of biomedicine it is dominant, at least for a CM practitioner such as Dr Hsu.
6. Dr Hsu writes: '[According to the patients' symptoms] [t]he disease is caused by hot and warm toxic evil [*qi*] (wēn rè dú xié, 溫熱毒邪) invasion. The external evil stagnates and obstructs meridians, so the body and head ache. The guarding *qi* (wèi qì, 衛氣) fights the evil *qi*, so the patient feels cold and has fever. The hot and warm toxic evil invades the lung [meridian] so the patient coughs and has a sore throat. It stagnates and obstructs the *qi* of the liver [meridian] and thus the stomach and spleen (pí wèi, 脾胃) do not work well and the patient has symptoms including feeling like vomiting, a dry and bitter mouth, lack of appetite or diarrhea' (何彥頤 et al., 2003, p. 23). Here, the relations between the *qi* of visceral systems correlate with the dynamics of the five phases (wǔ xíng, 五行) dynamics: wood (mù, 木; liver), fire (huǒ, 火;

heart), earth (tǔ, 土; spleen and stomach), metal (jīn, 金; lung) and water (shuǐ, 水; kidney) (Wiseman & Ellis, 1995, pp. 7–12). As earth *qi* goes to wood in order to nourish it, when wood (liver) *qi* is obstructed the earth (spleen and stomach) *qi* becomes stagnated.

7. Dr Hsu writes: 'different theories explain the development of disease and classify the ways disease transforms and shifts differently. Taking three burners (sān jiāo, 三焦) pattern differentiation for instance, the early stage of this [SARS] disease [can be regarded as] mainly about the upper and the middle burners, . . . but it is not plausible when it comes to the lower burners in the later stage. Some scholars use damp-warm . . . differentiation, but most of them cannot explain the full course [of the disease], and most of them are only [using] theoretical deliberation without clinical experience' (許中華 et al., 2004, p. 72).

8. The progression in the four sectors approach: first stage in the *wei* (wèi fēn, 衛分) sector, second in the *qi* sector (qì fēn, 氣分), and third and fourth stages in the sectors of *ying* (yíng fēn, 營分) and *xie* (xiě fēn, 血分).

9. Such as Lonicera and Forsythia Powder (yín qiào sǎn, 銀翹散) for heat-clearing toxin-resolving (qīng rè jiě dú, 清熱解毒).

10. Dr Hsu wrote: 'As Zhang shugu (章虛谷) says: "In the beginning [of disease], using cool acrid [medication] to resolve the exterior, not the congealing cold as it might retain the evil . . ." Thus, "we cannot use cold congealing [medication] for heat-clearing toxin-resolving. . . . We focused on cool acrid exterior-resolving (xīn liáng jiě biǎo, 辛涼解表), heat-clearing and toxin-resolving, and dispersing the liver (shū gān, 疏肝) and harmonizing the stomach (hé wèi, 和胃). We must also take care of the condition of the *qi* of the stomach in order to ensure the effect" ' (何彥頤 et al., 2003, p. 23).

11. In inverted commas because this division makes little sense in CM. I appreciate that much contemporary academic work, for instance in Science and Technology Studies (STS) works in a similar manner.

12. Mol's suggestions about *lekker* and the argument of this article join a long line of suggestions from authors such as Verran (2001), who writes about Yoruba numbering, Strathern (1991), who describes and transplants Hagen reasoning to rethink the European division between nature and culture, and de la Cadena (2010), who similarly subverts this division by drawing the indigenous Ecuadorian commitment to *Pachamama*.

References

de la Cadena, M. (2010). Indigenous cosmopolitics in the Andes: Conceptual reflections beyond 'politics'. *Cultural Anthropology, 25*, 334–370.

Descola, P. (2013). *Beyond nature and culture.* The University of Chicago Press.

Farquhar, J. (1994). *Knowing practice: The clinical encounter of Chinese medicine.* Westview Press.

Haraway, D. (1991). *Simians, cyborg, and women: The reinvention of nature.* Routledge.

Haraway, D. (2016). *Staying with the trouble: Making kin in the Chthulecene.* Duke University Press.

Hsu, C.-H., Hwang, K.-C., Chao, C.-L., Chang, S. G. N., Lin, J.-G., Ho, M.-S., Chang, H.-H., Kao, S.-T., Chen, Y.-M., & Chou, P. (2008). An evaluation of the additive effect of natural herbal medicine on SARS or SARS-like infectious disease in 2003: A randomized, double-blind, and controlled pilot study. *Evidence-Based Complementary and Alternative Medicine, 5*, 355–362.

Jullien, F. (1995). *The propensity of things: Toward a history of efficacy in China.* Zone Books.

Lakoff, G., & Johnson, M. (1980). *Metaphors we live by.* The University of Chicago Press.

Latour, B. (1988). The enlightenment without the critique: An introduction to Michel Serres' philosophy. In A. P. Griffiths (Ed.), *Contemporary French philosophy* (pp. 83–98). Cambridge University Press.

Latour, B. (2004). Why has critique run out of steam? From matters of fact to matters of concern. *Critical Inquiry, 30,* 225–248.

Law, J. (2015). What's wrong with a one-world world. *Distinktion: Journal of Social Theory, 16,* 126–139.

Law, J., & Lin, W.-Y. (2018). Tidescapes: Notes on a shi(勢)-inflected social science. *Journal of World Philosophies, 3,* 1–16.

Lin, W.-Y. (2017). Shi (勢), STS and theory: Or what can we learn from Chinese medicine? *Science, Technology & Human Values, 42,* 405–428.

Martin, E. (1994). *Flexible bodies: Tracking immunity in American culture – From the days of polio to the age of AIDS.* Beacon Press.

Mol, A. (2002). *The body multiple: Ontology in medical practice.* Duke University Press.

Mol, A. (2014). Language trails: 'Lekker' and its pleasures. *Theory, Culture & Society, 31,* 93–119.

Nappi, C. S. (2009). *The monkey and the inkpot: Natural history and its transformations in early modern China.* Harvard University Press.

Serres, M. (2008). *The five senses: A philosophy of mingled bodies (I).* Continuum.

Strathern, M. (1991). *Partial connection.* Rowman and Littlefield.

Sun Tzu (1994). *Sun Tzu: Art of war.* Westview Press.

Tannen, D. (1998). *The argument culture: Stopping America's war of words.* Ballantine.

Tsing, A. (2005). *Friction: An ethnography of global connection.* Princeton University Press.

Unschuld, P. U. (1986). *Medicine in China: A history of pharmaceutics.* University of California Press.

Unschuld, P. U. (1987). Traditional Chinese medicine: Some historical and epistemological reflections. *Social Science & Medicine, 24,* 1023–1029.

Verran, H. (2001). *Science and an African logic.* The University of Chicago Press.

Wiseman, N., & Ellis, A. (1995). *Fundamentals of Chinese medicine.* Paradigm.

Zhan, M. (2009). *Other-worldly: Making Chinese medicine through transnational frames.* Duke University Press.

王秀 (ed.) (2011). *中醫基礎："十一五" 國家重點圖書出版規劃項目,* 中國江蘇省: 江蘇科學技術出版社.

何彥頤, 陳建中, 謝抒玲 & 許中華 (2003). 從SARS來襲談時疫防治之道. *中國中醫臨床醫學雜誌,* 9(3), 25–27.

何彥頤, 陳建中, 謝抒玲 & 許中華 (2003). '嚴重急性呼吸道症候(SARS)之中醫診治與臨床實例.' *中國中醫臨床醫學雜誌,* 9(3), 22(3), 22–24.

馬光亞 (2011). *台北臨床三十年,* 台北, 知音.

清·唐宗海 (no date). *勸讀十則* https://zh.wikisource.org/zh-hant/%E5%8B%B8%E8%AE%80%E5%8D%81%E5%89%87.

清·徐大椿 (1978). *醫學源流論,* 臺北市, 臺灣商務.

許中華, 陳建中, 何彥頤, 謝抒玲 & 王繼榮 (2003). 嚴重急性呼吸道症候群(SARS)中西結合觀. *北縣中醫會刊雜誌,* 6(3), 81–85.

許中華, 黃焜璋, 趙崇良, 林昭庚, 周碧瑟 & SARS研究小組 (2004). 從衛、氣、營、血辨證分析SARS疾病傳變台灣本土證型分析（台北醫院病例）. *臺灣中醫醫學雜誌,* 3(1), 68–80.

Author biography

Wen-yuan Lin is Professor at the National Tsing Hua University. He is a sociologist and a STS practitioner by training. He uses STS material semiotic approaches to explore the politics of emerging alternative knowledge spaces in technological and medical practices. He is the author of 看不見的行動能力：從行動者網絡到位移理論 (*Invisible Agency: A Displacement Theory for Subalterns*) (Academia Sinica Press, 2014).

Búskomor politics: Practising critique in the ruins of liberal democracy

The Sociological Review Monographs
2020, Vol. 68(2) 96–108
© The Author(s) 2020
Article reuse guidelines:
sagepub.com/journals-permissions
DOI: 10.1177/0038026120905476
journals.sagepub.com/home/sor

Endre Dányi

Universität der Bundeswehr München [Bundeswehr University Munich], Germany

Abstract

How to engage with the recent crisis of liberal democracy in a politically productive manner? Using the example of Hungary, the first part of this article contrasts two empirical strategies. The first takes inspiration from Science and Technology Studies (STS) and explores the conditions of critique within the architecture and infrastructure of liberal democracy. The second empirical strategy turns to a novel by László Krasznahorkai and a film by Béla Tarr, and engages with the problem of critique through *búskomorság*. This common Hungarian word refers to a sad-sombre sentiment that is both collective and thoroughly political. The second part of the article focuses on an exhibition created by Béla Tarr that combined these two empirical strategies in a generative way. With the help of the exhibition and recent empirical examples, the article outlines what could be called *búskomor politics* – a set of critical practices that take place not so much within the architecture and the infrastructure of liberal democracy as amid its ruins.

Keywords

critique, democracy, Hungary, melancholy, resistance

Introduction

After decades of demanding democratisation, more participation and a closer involvement of 'the people' in decision-making, social scientists are now confronted with a series of developments where 'the people' are claimed to be undermining the values and institutions of liberal democracy. The most obvious examples are the rise of populist movements in Eastern and Western Europe, the Brexit referendum in the UK, the election of Donald Trump as US President and Jair Bolsonaro as President of Brazil, but the list can be easily extended (Müller, 2016). It is possible to argue that these and similar developments are the effects of

Corresponding author:

Endre Dányi, Faculty of Social Sciences, Bundeswehr University Munich, Werner-Heisenberg-Weg 39, Neubiberg, 85577, Germany.
Email: e.danyi@unibw.de

processes *external* to democratic politics, such as growing inequality or the disintegration of collective identity (Fukuyama, 2018). However, there are also good reasons to believe that they are the direct consequences of the *internal* workings of democratic politics, which tends to produce its own crises on a regular basis (see Mouffe, 2000; Rancière, 1999; Schmitt, 1988). If the latter is correct, then there is a renewed urgency for social scientists to critically engage with liberal democracy as a political reality – and to do so empirically.

In this article, I present two strategies that show how this might be done through the example of Hungary – a country that in the 1990s and 2000s was regarded as an exemplary case of successful democratisation, but that in the past 10 years has become a forerunner of right-wing populism. The first empirical strategy takes inspiration from Science and Technology Studies (STS) and explores the conditions of critique within the architecture and infrastructure of liberal democracy. Paying close attention to the nuts and bolts of modernity is a common move in STS: it renders visible the hidden politics of seemingly apolitical processes, especially in the contexts of knowledge making, state building and international development (see Barry, 2013; Bowker & Star, 1999; Harvey et al., 2016,;von Schnitzler, 2016), and by doing so opens up alternatives. This empirical strategy is also useful when it comes to the analysis of the normal operation of democratic institutions, but the recent crisis of liberal democracy poses a serious challenge for STS's own understanding of politics.

This is where the second empirical strategy becomes important. It turns to a novel by László Krasznahorkai and a film by Béla Tarr, and engages with the problem of critique through *búskomorság*. This is an everyday Hungarian word that comes close to 'melancholy' but has a somewhat different connotation: it refers to a sad-sombre sentiment that is both collective and thoroughly political. In the final part of the article, I focus on an exhibition created by Béla Tarr that combined these two empirical strategies in a generative way. With the help of the exhibition, I outline what could be called *búskomor politics* – a set of critical practices that take place not so much within the architecture and the infrastructure of liberal democracy as amid its ruins.

In political analysis an interest in ruins is of course not new. In the 19th century, crumbling castles and palaces played an important role in the discursive and material construction of national pasts (Hobsbawm & Ranger, 1983), while in the 20th century sites of unprecedented devastation were used to memorialise the horrors of Nazism and Stalinism (Gafijczuk & Sayer, 2013; Huyssen, 2003). More recently, there have been several attempts to reconceptualise ruins as traces of ongoing processes – economic and ecological ruinations – inherent to the workings of liberalism (Povinelli, 2016; Stoler, 2013; Tsing, 2015; Tsing et al., 2017). Mindful of these works, I consider this article as a double intervention that uses *búskomorság* to highlight how attention to ruination can inform political analysis and that, using my recent empirical work on a hunger strike, a harm reduction programme and a counter-parliamentary ceremony, indicates how such an analysis might help us rethink the practice of critique in ruinous times.

Democracy in place

In social and political theory, liberal democracy tends to be treated as *an abstract model of governance* where political power is placeless (Lefort, 1988). And yet liberal democracies the world over boast spectacular buildings that constitute both the literal and the figurative conditions of possibility for democratic politics. What could we learn about liberal democracy as a particular political reality if we analysed it through its 'proper place'?

This question was the starting point of my Lancaster-based PhD research. It was inspired by STS, particularly laboratory studies (Knorr-Cetina, 1981; Latour & Woolgar, 1986; Law, 1994; Lynch, 1997). In one way or another, these works spoke against the idea that scientific knowledge is a matter of free-floating ideas by examining the locations and socio-material practices that allow for experimental science (Livingstone, 2003). They did so not in order to discredit experimental science, but to contest particular techno-political imaginaries associated with it. I sought to use this empirical strategy to analyse democratic politics in Hungary, which after 1989 went through an intense – and by all external measures, successful – period of democratisation.[1] During my ethnographic research in Budapest between 2006 and 2010, I examined how liberal democracy had been established as a distinct techno-political imaginary that was considered to have no alternatives (Dányi, 2012).

The central object of my research was the Hungarian parliament building: a grand neo-Gothic palace on the east bank of the Danube. At the time of its construction in the late 19th century, it was the largest parliament building in the world, with two symmetrical houses and an impressive cupola hall in the middle. Drawing on laboratory studies, I decided to use the building – its architecture and infrastructure – as a methodological guide to my fieldwork (Dányi, 2015; see also Latour & Weibel, 2005). This allowed me to see not only a gradual unfolding of parliamentary history, punctuated by failed revolutions, but also a wide range of material entities that 'make up' contemporary democratic politics, from symbolic artefacts (flags, statues, coats-of-arms) through documents and their apparatuses (bills, voting machines and the National Assembly's Information System) to the physical bodies of elected politicians.

The actual and virtual walls of the parliament building kept these otherwise incommensurable entities together, giving the impression of a singular model of governance. However, the shift of attention from political ideas to the 'stuff of politics' (Braun & Whatmore, 2010) helped to reveal that democratic politics consists of *multiple modes of doing* (Law, 2002; Mol, 2002) that hang together in tension. Take, for example, the transfer of the Holy Crown – the ultimate symbol of the thousand-year-old Hungarian state – from the National Museum to the cupola hall of the parliament building. In the controversy around this, two ways of defining 'the people' clashed: one that understands the political community in terms of rights and obligations (as defined in the Constitution), and another one that emphasises a sense of belonging (supposedly aroused by the royal jewels). Similarly, it appeared that due to the way the legislative process worked, the Parliament actively contributed to restricting 'the political' to public debates about well-defined problems, while all kinds of other decisions were delegated to the realm of 'the technical'. Finally, shadowing a Member of Parliament as he moved from faction meetings to TV studios, from street demonstrations to charity events, from parliamentary debates to informal discussions with members of his party, suggested that 'politics' was conceptualised less in terms of representation (of the general will) than as an ongoing sales operation in a market of competing worldviews (socialist, conservative, liberal, green and so on).

These insights pointed beyond the actual objects of my ethnographic research. If 'the people' could be constituted in terms of either rights and obligations or a sense of belonging, if problems were handled as either political or technical, and if political practice was torn between representation and marketing, then there was a possibility of articulating alternatives *within* liberal democracy. One way of understanding 'the people' might be strengthened over the other, one way of relating to problems might be fostered at the cost of another, and different worldviews might coexist in ways that do not take the form of a market. As the research I had conducted from the academic distance of Lancaster began to articulate tensions within liberal political practices, it also began to open up new ways of being a Hungarian citizen. I no longer had to submit myself to the predetermined terms of democratic politics; I could address those terms, doubt them, put them into motion, stage them differently. While alternatives to liberal democracy were not on the horizon, taking on this intricate type of political subjectivity allowed for a particular form of critique (Foucault, 1997).

In political analyses, normative considerations tend to precede empirical work, or altogether bypass it as unnecessary. But if critique was to work with multiple modes of doing and explore the tensions between different socio-material arrangements from within, then it could not start out from external norms. Instead, it had to carefully attune to contrasting normativities at stake in the practices at hand.[2] For me, this meant that critique came to depend on detailed empirical analyses of peoples, problems and worldviews as the central terms of liberal democracy. But at the same time, attending to differences *within* suggested that there were always alternatives. Hence, there was always a possibility for improvement – an insight that imbued my project with a sense of pragmatist optimism.

A storm is coming

After my fieldwork in Budapest, I moved from Lancaster to Berlin to write up my PhD thesis. I did notice a few unnerving signs along the way: the governing socialist-liberal coalition had split up over a failed healthcare reform; the global financial crisis in 2008 hit Hungary hard; and right-wing populists were on the rise, holding mass rallies across the country. Still, the 2010 general election came to me as a shock. It brought a landslide victory for the conservative Fidesz (with a two-thirds majority in the new National Assembly), and the far-right Jobbik entered parliament as the third largest party. The day after the election, the German political magazine *Der Spiegel* illustrated its report on the election with a dreary image, showing the parliament building in Budapest under dark clouds and amid lightning. A storm was coming.

More than eight years and two election cycles later, the storm is still raging. It is systematically ruining the architecture and infrastructure of liberal democracy. Viktor Orbán's government has unilaterally rewritten the Constitution, filled the Constitutional Court and other independent institutions with politically loyal figures, reduced the size and the political importance of the National Assembly, remodelled the parliament building and the square in front of it, modified the election law, and curtailed press freedom and the freedom of academic research. It has also legitimated a quasi-fascist worldview through a series of media campaigns and government policies.

A clear example of the latter is the Hungarian government's response to the European refugee crisis, materialised in the erection of a razor-wire barrier on the border with Serbia and Croatia. The initial part of the barrier was built in 2015, and since then it has been extended and strengthened several times. This means that undocumented migrants fleeing from the Middle East and North Africa through the Balkan route to the European Union are forced to turn back or spend an indefinite period waiting in makeshift transit zones, often in inhumane conditions (De Genova, 2017). The significance of the erection of the razor-wire barrier points beyond the refugee crisis: it stands in stark contrast with Hungary's active participation in the dismantling of the Iron Curtain on the border with Austria in 1989. Political analysts, who took the latter to be a triumph of liberal democracy, often refer to the former as the symbol of 'illiberal democracy' (Puddington, 2017; about the term, see Zakaria, 1997).

As I was witnessing these and similar events, obsessively reading the news, talking to friends and family, regularly visiting Budapest, I found myself losing my hard-earned pragmatist optimism. That the empirical material of my thesis was becoming outdated was one thing: ethnography, after all, is always 'untimely' (Rabinow et al., 2008). But what was I supposed to do with my STS-inspired critique 'from within'? How was it possible to relate to ruination as a researcher-citizen? The liberal/illiberal dichotomy, however evocative, was not very helpful: after all, Viktor Orbán and Fidesz are not the opposites of liberalism, but its very products.[3] How then to get a better analytical grip on what was going on, not only in Hungary, but also in other countries in Europe, North and South America and elsewhere?

The Melancholy of Resistance

One possible answer to the above question is to shift from pragmatist optimism to *búskomorság*. This commonly used Hungarian word (pronounced approximately as *boosh-ko-more-shaag*) refers to a combination of sadness and sombreness.[4] It comes close to the English word 'melancholy' but has other theoretical and political connotations. While in Sigmund Freud's (2005) work melancholy is defined as a pathological form of mourning, *búskomorság* denotes a collective sentiment, rather than an individual disposition. And while in Walter Benjamin's (1994, 2003) writings, or in recent interpretations thereof (Brown, 1999; Traverso, 2017), melancholy is associated with the impossibility of critique, *búskomorság* is inextricably linked with stubborn forms of resistance.[5]

I began to think about the political purchase of this sentiment through László Krasznahorkai's novel *The Melancholy of Resistance*, and Béla Tarr's *Werckmeister Harmonies*, which is a film based on the middle chapter of the novel. Krasznahorkai and Tarr are undoubtedly the masters of *búskomorság* (Kovács, 2013), and I feel that researcher-citizens like myself can learn a lot from their 'búskomor politics' as ruinous storms keep raging across the globe. I am not out to argue that the STS-inspired empirical strategy concerned with materialities and differences-within has expired or lost its value. Instead, I turn to Krasznahorkai and Tarr's works and techniques of storytelling because, in addition, there is an urgent need for modes – and moods – of doing that help us make sense of situations in which pragmatist optimism is no longer adequate.

Krasznahorkai's *The Melancholy of Resistance* was first published in Hungarian in the tumultuous year of 1989. (The English version was published in 1998 and received the International Man Booker Prize in 2015.) The story is situated in the eastern part of Hungary, in a small and sleepy town, where extraordinary things begin to happen after a travelling circus arrives and sets up camp in the main square. The key attraction of the circus is the carcass of an enormous whale, 'the largest whale in the world', carried around in a massive truck. The leaflets advertising the circus programme also mention a performance by 'the Prince' – a mysterious figure whose speeches stir anxiety and unrest wherever the circus goes.

What happens in the town in Krasznahorkai's novel has happened in other towns as well. Shortly after the arrival of the circus, groups of suspicious-looking men appear in the main square. They position themselves around the whale in ominous silence. Rumours about the fast-approaching apocalypse spread across the town. Around sunset, after an undecipherable speech by the Prince, the crowd sets off to systematically vandalise the town. It burns down the cinema, breaks the doors and windows of several houses, terrorises residents throughout the night. Early in the morning a handful of men break into a local hospital and start to ruin the equipment and beat up defenceless patients. Then, all of a sudden, as if someone had pulled the plug, the riot comes to a halt. The crowd scatters and the military arrive with several armoured vehicles and a tank to 'restore order'.

Although *The Melancholy of Resistance* was written before the fall of the Berlin Wall and the collapse of the Soviet Union, it is possible to read it as a story about the democratisation of Central and Eastern Europe. The circus – the democratic spectacle – travels from one place to the next, carrying the whale along with it as the Leviathan, the symbol of sovereignty (Shapiro, 2016).[6] The whale is already dead, but that seems to be the smaller concern. The bigger concern is that for its operation the circus depends on the Prince – a demagogue who knows how to work the crowds much better than any circus director.

Werckmeister Harmonies

A decade after the publication of *The Melancholy of Resistance*, Krasznahorkai rewrote the middle chapter as a script for Béla Tarr's film *Werckmeister Harmonies* (2000). Both the book and the film narrate the arrival of the circus and the unfolding of the riot through the interplay among three main characters: Valuska, the local postman, Mr Eszter, a public intellectual, and Mrs Eszter, his estranged wife, who has been the driving force behind the organisation of a new movement called 'A Tidy Yard, An Orderly House'. In my reading, these characters are the respective embodiments of three understandings of political order: celestial harmony, enlightened rationality and brute force.

The film begins with a scene in the pub: around closing time, a handful of regulars persuade Valuska to choreograph a total eclipse of the Sun using several drunks as cosmic entities. Valuska instructs three men to play the parts of the Sun, the Earth and the Moon, and makes them rotate around each other in an orderly fashion. Meanwhile, he describes what happens during an eclipse. First, the air gets colder, then the sky darkens, the dogs begin to howl, the birds withdraw to their nests, and finally there is complete silence. 'Are the hills going to march off? Will heaven fall upon us? Will the ground open under our feet? We don't know.' After a while, Valuska reassures everyone that there is no need to be afraid. All is not over, because sooner or later the Moon swims away, the sunlight returns, and warmth floods the Earth again. The hopeful – one could say pragmatist optimistic – performance peaks with everyone in the pub blissfully orbiting around each other, celebrating that the total eclipse of the Sun is over.

The scenes that follow show that in addition to delivering mail and newspapers, Valuska also works as a caretaker at the house of Mr Eszter, helping out with menial tasks. Mr Eszter himself is a gloomy philosopher who has spent the past couple of years at home, withdrawn from public life. He passes the day sitting at his piano, delivering lectures on the nature of order to either Valuska or his voice recorder. From one of these lectures we learn that Mr Eszter's normative critique is concerned with Western harmony. He takes this to originate with Andreas Werckmeister – a baroque composer and music theorist. Werckmeister's writings had a strong influence on Johann Sebastian Bach, especially those that related harmony to the movements of the planets. Mr Eszter is convinced that Werckmeister's intervention was a disastrous error, which can only be remedied by developing an entirely new theory of tuning.[7]

The circus is already in town when Mr Eszter's daily routine is interrupted by his estranged wife. Together with her lover, the police chief, Mrs Eszter has organised a movement – 'A Tidy Yard, An Orderly House' – in order to establish a new order in town. Using Valuska as a messenger, she asks Mr Eszter to do her a last favour, visit a list of prominent residents and generate public support for the initiative. Reluctantly, Mr Eszter complies, while hoping to soon return home and complete his theory of tuning. What he does not know is that his errand is part of a devious plot. Mrs Eszter uses the riot that follows the Prince's speech as an excuse to seize power, eliminating everyone who is in her way, including her husband and Valuska. Early next day, when the riot is over, we see her making arrangements with the military officers by the tank. They regard her as the only person around who can be entrusted with running such a crazy town.

In Krasznahorkai's book the perspective shifts between Valuska, Mr Eszter and Mrs Eszter. Tarr's film, by contrast, concentrates almost entirely on Valuska. He is presented as an angelic figure, a messenger (Serres, 2009) who affects all those whom he visits, even if he is not fully aware of the contents of the messages he brings them. We see him choreographing the local drunks in the pub; we register his astonishment as the circus arrives in the middle of the night; we share his awe of the whale, which he visits on several occasions; we follow him as he confusedly finds himself in the middle of the mob; and through his eyes we witness the senseless destruction of the hospital. Finally, we see him getting arrested for his 'involvement in the riot' by the military and – due to the scheming of Mrs Eszter – being confined to the local mental hospital. One of the last scenes of the film shows Valuska sitting on the edge of his hospital bed, staring ahead in silence. His only visitor is Mr Eszter, who has been kicked out of his house by his former wife and the police chief. Mr Eszter now lives in the summer kitchen with his piano, that he finally managed to retune. He invites Valuska to move in with him once he is released. Valuska does not react. Both he and Mr Eszter know that his release is unlikely to happen anytime soon.

Till the end of the world

The very last scene of *Werckmeister Harmonies* shows Mr Eszter walking across the town square after visiting Valuska in the mental hospital. He comes across the enormous body of the whale, which lies amid the ruins of the circus. Just as the Hungarian parliament building on the east bank of the Danube, the whale had been celebrated as the largest of its kind. But despite – or maybe because of – its enormous size, it proved to be defenceless when attacked by the mob stirred up by the Prince. In the end, the mob, as Jacques Rancière writes in his book on Tarr's cinema, was not able to achieve its goal – it did not destroy everything utterly. What it did destroy, however, is 'the possibility of having the vision, in one's mind and in one's eyes, of a harmonious order other than the simple order of the police' (Rancière, 2015, p. 60). This is a *búskomor* realisation, which sinks in slowly – as if the whole purpose of the film was to bring the viewer to this unmistakable affective state.

So, where do we go from here? What are the conditions of possibility for critique in situations where the prospect of the harmonious order called liberal democracy is shattered into pieces? Are researcher-citizens, such as myself, condemned to choose between the compromised existence of public intellectuals, like Mr Eszter, confined to the summer kitchen of his former home, and the broken, disillusioned silence of Valuska?

Béla Tarr's response to current political events, and especially to the way the Hungarian government handled the European refugee crisis, suggests otherwise. In 2016, after the first wave of refugees went through Hungary, Tarr wrote a public call for solidarity, which was read out during a large demonstration in front of the Hungarian parliament building. After a few hours, the demonstration was over. It hardly had an impact on the legislature controlled by Fidesz, but Tarr's *búskomorság* did not stop there. It continued to grow and in early 2017 materialised in an exhibition at the EYE Filmmuseum in Amsterdam.[8]

The exhibition, titled *Till the End of the World*, combined installation art with snippets from Tarr's films. Upon entering the exhibition space, visitors had to walk past a replica of the Hungarian–Serbian border, which consisted of the infamous razor-wire barrier, a no-man's land of scorched grass, and several news photographs taken during the refugee crisis. All the materials were STS-compatible, but what they made visible and tangible were not so much the political architecture and infrastructure of a member state of the European Union as the ruins of a borderless Europe as a distinct techno-political imaginary (Guldemond, 2017). After 1989, this techno-political imaginary had been a central component of political transformations on both sides of the Iron Curtain. Here were its remains: it had been shattered into pieces, with no alternatives in sight.

After the border crossing, the visitors were led through several rooms featuring iconic objects and scenes from Tarr's films: a life-size naked tree in the middle of a relentless storm; an empty kitchen table; homeless men queuing for a meal; a crowd of elderly people huddled together under a roof waiting for the rain to stop; drunkards from the opening scene of *Werckmeister Harmonies* enacting the total eclipse of the Sun. Within the context of the exhibition, these objects and people had more to do with each other than with the films they had been taken from: together they became the documentation of fragmented lives amid ruination.[9] The scenes were quasi-ethnographic depictions of *búskomorság*, as they simultaneously invoked a sense of disillusionment and the need to carry on, no matter what.

The final room of the exhibition was titled 'Muhamed'. It was the projection of an 11-minute long shot of a young boy playing the accordion. The shot began with a close-up of the boy's face, then the camera slowly zoomed out and the environment – a shopping centre – became visible. While playing, the boy kept looking at us with serious distrust in his eyes. Who exactly is this 'us' that he was looking at? Within the exhibition space, the visitors were not interpellated as members of specific nation states, diligent experts in solving social problems, or representatives of particular worldviews. Instead, they found themselves, willingly or unwillingly, implicated in modes of doing allowed for by ruined institutions and imaginaries associated with post-Cold War democratic politics.

Conclusion: búskomor politics

On the way out from the exhibition I was overcome by a strong sense of familiarity: with *Till the End of the World* Tarr had given shape to the very space I have been trying to navigate since the end of my fieldwork in Budapest. He had used *búskomorság* to draw attention to ruination as a political process – a process that continues to destroy the possibility of a harmonious order 'other than the simple order of the police'. At the same time, he also demonstrated the critical potential of this sentiment. In my reading, *búskomor politics* denotes multiple modes of doing that take place within the cracks of liberal democracy, that seem 'impossible' from the perspective of political institutions, but that irritate the latter's terms in generative ways.

In the past six or seven years, in various collaborative research projects I have concentrated on three such modes of doing. The first was a hunger strike that took place in Brussels in 2012 and involved 23 refugees from North Africa and the Middle East (Abrahamsson & Dányi, 2019). Without any documents (see M'charek, this volume), the refugees had no chance of obtaining residency permits in Belgium; without residency permits they had no chance of starting their tormented lives anew. The hunger strike was their last resort; a desperate attempt to make their impossible situation public. According to the logic of sovereignty, which constantly distinguishes 'us' from 'them', the *sans-papiers* did not belong to the Belgian people and therefore had no political agency. At the same time, the alliances that emerged between the hunger strikers, medical experts and political activists redefined – if only temporarily – what it entails to act politically. Instead of speaking on behalf of anyone, a handful of doctors and activists helped to create and maintain a space for the refugees' silence, thereby allowing political agency to develop on site.

The second mode of doing that exemplifies *búskomor politics* is associated with the regulation of intravenous drug use in Lisbon (Dányi, 2018). Unlike most countries in Europe, in Portugal the consumption of harmful substances is not illegal. What makes the Portuguese drug policy unique, however, is not simply decriminalisation; it is the realisation that insofar as drug use constitutes a problem, it cannot be solved through legislation alone. In fact, looking for solutions might not be the most productive way of engaging with it at all. This is, at least, what I learned from social workers affiliated with a harm reduction programme I visited in 2015. Through their everyday care work they showed that while drug use as a problem is unlikely to ever disappear, it is possible – and indeed necessary – to distinguish between better and worse ways of living with it.

Finally, the third mode of doing I encountered during fieldwork in a Yolngu community in the Northern Territory in Australia in 2016 (Dányi & Spencer, 2020). This Indigenous community, like many others in the Northern Territory, was badly affected when the Australian government decided to solve various problems – including drug use and domestic violence – by sending in medical staff escorted by the military. The Northern Territory Emergency Response (also known as 'the Intervention') disregarded all local and regional authority structures, triggering memories of a colonial past when Indigenous people had not been recognised as political entities at all. As a form of protest, the Yolngu organised a ceremony, a counter-parliament based on ancient law, to highlight the multiplicity of legal-political traditions within a seemingly singular nation state. By doing so, they also contested the idea that democratic politics is necessarily organised around different views of the same world. It is high time, they suggested, that we sensitise ourselves to forms of politics that recognise different worlds as well.

Although these modes of doing are quite dissimilar, as instances of *búskomor politics* they share several important characteristics. In a liberal democratic context, they seem apolitical because they do not share the central terms of institutional democratic politics. They resist the idea that 'people' can only be defined along an 'us'/'them' distinction, they challenge the conviction that all problems can be dealt with through legislation, and they insist that politics happens as much across worlds as within them. These modes of doing refuse to organise themselves into a harmonious order; they do not offer redemption or tell about a future where all is well. And yet they are determined to identify – even create – practical differences between bad and worse. A critique informed by *búskomor politics* is to engage with these and similar modes of doing on their terms, learn from them, and give them space amid the ruins of liberal democracy.

Acknowledgements

I am deeply grateful to Nida Alahmad, Rohullah Amin, Elaine Gan, Bernd Herzogenrath, Teresa Koloma-Beck, Christoph Michels, Janie Ondracek, Yannik Porsché, Sebastian Ureta, Peter Wehling, Katharina Wuropulos and Tobias Wille for their helpful comments on earlier versions of this text, to Gergely Mohácsi, Olga Sezneva and the anonymous reviewers of *The Sociological Review* for their careful suggestions, and to John Law and Annemarie Mol for their editorial guidance and intellectual companionship throughout the years.

Funding

The author received no financial support for the research, authorship, and/or publication of this article.

Notes

1. The country joined NATO in 1999 and the European Union in 2004.
2. On this understanding of critique, see Boltanski (2011) and Latour (2004).
3. Until 2000, Fidesz was member of the Liberal International, the world federation of liberal parties – for a while, Viktor Orbán was Vice Chair of the organisation.

4. This move resonates with recent discussions in STS about 'styles of knowing' (Lai & Farquhar, this volume) and the 'politics of how' (Law & Joks, 2019).
5. For a general overview of melancholy in Western thought, see Clair (2005), Földényi (2016) and Lepenies (1969). *Búskomorság* resonates strongly with other vernacular versions of melancholy, for example with *saudade* (Magalhaes, this volume), *toska* and *hüzün* (Bowring, 2008).
6. The cover of the English edition heralds Krasznahorkai's book as 'a mitteleuropean *Moby Dick*'. Melville's classic novel has often been discussed as an early critique of capitalism (see, for example, Deleuze & Guattari, 1987). Unfortunately, a closer comparison of the two works – and the two whales – are beyond the scope of this text.
7. The absurdity of such an undertaking is nicely illustrated by Antoine Hennion's (2016) discussion of the relationship between truth and performance in baroque music – see also Kwa (2002).
8. More information about the exhibition is available on the Filmmuseum's website (www.eye-film.nl/en/exhibition/b%C3%A9la-tarr) and its official video of the event, which contains an interview with Tarr (https://youtu.be/SUv1qSqkpMc).
9. For a discussion of Béla Tarr's last film, *The Turin Horse*, as an analysis of human existence amid the ruins of modernity see Ginn (2015) and Latour (2013) – and Viveiros de Castro and Danowski's (2018) commentary on the latter.

References

Abrahamsson, S., & Dányi, E. (2019). Becoming stronger by becoming weaker: The hunger strike as a mode of doing politics. *Journal of International Relations and Development*, *22*(4): 882–898.

Barry, A. (2013). *Material politics: Disputes along the pipeline*. John Wiley & Sons.

Benjamin, W. (1994). Left-wing melancholy. In A. Kaes, M. Jay & E. Dimendberg (Eds.), *The Weimar Republic sourcebook* (pp. 304–306). University of California Press.

Benjamin, W. (2003). *The origin of German tragic drama*. Verso.

Boltanski, L. (2011). *On critique*. Polity.

Bowker, G. C., & Star, S. L. (1999). *Sorting things out: Classification and its consequences*. MIT Press.

Bowring, J. (2008). *A field guide to melancholy*. Oldcastle Books.

Braun, B., & Whatmore, S. (2010). *Political matter: Technoscience, democracy, and public life*. University of Minnesota Press.

Brown, W. (1999). Resisting left melancholy. *Boundary 2*, *26*(3), 19–27.

Clair, J. (2005). *Mélancolie: Génie et folie en Occident*. Gallimard.

Dányi, E. (2012). *Parliament politics: A material-semiotic analysis of liberal democracy* (PhD thesis). Department of Sociology, Lancaster University.

Dányi, E. (2015). The parliament as a high-political programme. In A. Müller & W. Reichmann (Eds.), *Architecture, materiality and society: Connecting sociology of architecture with science and technology studies* (pp. 99–118). Palgrave Macmillan.

Dányi, E. (2018). Good treason: Following actor-network theory to the realm of drug policy. In T. Berger & A. Esguerra (Eds.), *World politics in translation: Power, relationality and difference in global cooperation* (pp. 25–38). Routledge.

Dányi, E., & Spencer, M. (2020). Un/common grounds: Tracing politics across worlds. *Social Studies of Science*, forthcoming.

De Genova, N. (2017). *The borders of 'Europe': Autonomy of migration, tactics of bordering*. Duke University Press.

Deleuze, G., & Guattari, F. (1987). *A thousand plateaus.* University of Minnesota Press.

Földényi, L. (2016). *Melancholy.* Yale University Press.

Foucault, M. (1997). What is critique? In S. Lotringer (Ed.), *The politics of truth* (pp. 41–81). Semiotext(e).

Freud, S. (2005). *On murder, mourning and melancholia.* Penguin.

Fukuyama, F. (2018). *Identity: The demand for dignity and the politics of resentment.* Farrar, Straus & Giroux.

Gafijczuk, D., & Sayer, D. (2013). *The inhabited ruins of Central Europe: Re-imagining space, history and memory.* Palgrave Macmillan.

Ginn, F. (2015). When horses won't eat: Apocalypse and the anthropocene. *Annals of the Association of American Geographers, 105*(2): 351–359.

Guldemond, J. (2017). *Béla Tarr: Till the end of the world.* EYE Filmmuseum.

Harvey, P., Jensen, C. B., & Morita, A. (2016). *Infrastructures and social complexity.* New York: Routledge.

Hennion, A. (2016). Fallacy of the work, truth of the performance: What makes music baroque: Historical authenticity or ontological plurality? In J. Law & E. Ruppert (Eds.), *Modes of knowing: Resources from the baroque* (pp. 84–114). Mattering Press.

Hobsbawm, E., & Ranger, T. (1983). *The invention of tradition.* Cambridge University Press.

Huyssen, A. (2003). *Present pasts: Urban palimpsests and the politics of memory.* Stanford University Press.

Knorr-Cetina, K. (1981). *The manufacture of knowledge.* Pergamon.

Kovács, A. B. (2013). *The cinema of Béla Tarr: The circle closes.* Columbia University Press.

Krasznahorkai, L. (1998). *The melancholy of resistance* (G. Szirtes, Trans.). Tuskar Rock Press.

Kwa, C. (2002). Romantic and baroque conceptions of complex wholes in the sciences. In J. Law & A. Mol (Eds.), *Complexities: Social studies of knowledge practices* (pp. 23–52). Duke University Press.

Latour, B. (2004). Why has critique run out of steam? From matters of fact to matters of concern. *Critical Inquiry, 30*(2): 225–248.

Latour, B. (2013). *Facing Gaia: A new enquiry into natural religion.* Gifford Lectures, Edinburgh.

Latour, B., & Weibel, P. (2005). *Making things public: Atmospheres of democracy.* MIT Press.

Latour, B., & Woolgar, S. (1986). *Laboratory life: The construction of scientific facts.* Princeton University Press.

Law, J. (2002). *Aircraft stories: Decentering the object in technoscience.* Duke University Press.

Law, J. (1994). *Organizing modernity.* Wiley-Blackwell.

Law, J., & Joks, S. (2019). Indigeneity, science, and difference: Notes on the politics of how. *Science, Technology, & Human Values, 44*(3), 424–447.

Lefort, C. (1988). *Democracy and political theory.* Polity.

Lepenies, W. (1969). *Melancholie und Gesellschaft.* Suhrkamp.

Livingstone, D. N. (2003). *Putting science in its place.* University of Chicago Press.

Lynch, M. (1997). *Scientific practice and ordinary action: Ethnomethodology and social studies of science.* Cambridge University Press.

Mol, A. (2002). *The body multiple: Ontology in medical practice.* Duke University Press.

Mouffe, C. (2000) *The democratic paradox.* Verso.

Müller, J.-W. (2016). *What is populism?* University of Pennsylvania Press.

Povinelli, E. A. (2016). *Geontologies: A requiem to late liberalism.* Duke University Press.

Puddington, A. (2017). *Breaking down democracy: Goals, strategies, and methods of modern authoritarians.* Freedom House. https://freedomhouse.org/sites/default/files/June2017_FH_Report_Breaking_Down_Democracy.pdf (accessed 19 October 2019).

Rabinow, P., Marcus, G. E., Faubion, J., & Rees, T. (2008). *Designs for an anthropology of the contemporary*. Duke University Press.

Rancière, J. (1999). *Disagreement: Politics and philosophy*. University of Minnesota Press.

Rancière, J. (2015). *Béla Tarr, the time after*. University of Minnesota Press.

Schmitt, C. (1988). *The crisis of parliamentary democracy*. MIT Press.

Serres, M. (2009). *Angels: A modern myth*. Flammarion-Pere Castor.

Shapiro, M. J. (2016). 'The light of reason': Reading the Leviathan with 'The Werckmeister harmonies'. *Political Theory*, *45*(3), 385–415.

Stoler, A. L. (2013). *Imperial debris: On ruins and ruination*. Duke University Press.

Traverso, E. (2017). *Left-wing melancholia: Marxism, history, and memory*. Columbia University Press.

Tsing, A. L. (2015). *The mushroom at the end of the world*. Princeton University Press.

Tsing, A. L., Bubandt, N., Swanson, H. A., & Gan, E. (2017). *Arts of living on a damaged planet*. University of Minnesota Press.

Viveiros de Castro, E., & Danowski, D. (2018). Humans and terrans in the Gaia war. In M. de la Cadena & M. Blaser (Eds.), *A world of many worlds* (pp. 172–203). Duke University Press.

von Schnitzler, A. (2016). *Democracy's infrastructure*. Princeton University Press.

Zakaria, F. (1997). The rise of illiberal democracy. *Foreign Affairs*, *76*(6), 22–43.

Author biography

Endre Dányi is Visiting Professor for the Sociology of Globalisation at the Bundeswehr University in Munich, Research Fellow at the Goethe University in Frankfurt am Main, and University Fellow at the Charles Darwin University in Darwin, Australia. Inspired by STS, his PhD was a material-semiotic analysis of liberal democracy. In his Habilitation, Endre is looking at specific situations where democratic politics breaks down or reaches its limits. In addition to teaching and research, he is co-founder and co-editor of Mattering Press – an Open Access book publisher that specialises in STS.

The Sociological Review Monographs
2020, Vol. 68(2) 109–124
© The Author(s) 2020
Article reuse guidelines:
sagepub.com/journals-permissions
DOI: 10.1177/0038026120905477
journals.sagepub.com/home/sor

In Colombia some cows have *raza*, others also have breed: Maintaining the presence of the translation offers analytical possibilities

Marisol de la Cadena
Department of Anthropology, University of California-Davis, USA

Santiago Martínez Medina
Instituto de Investigación de Recursos Biológicos Alexander von Humboldt [Alexander von Humboldt Biological Resources Research Institute], Colombia

Abstract
This article is about cows in Colombia, the practices that make them different. Although our main concern is not the difference among breeds, we pay crucial attention to the word breed which, in its exclusive animal-use, does not exist in Spanish. Its translation becomes *raza*, a word that is also used to classify humans and therefore easily translates into English as 'race'. Maintaining these differences in analytical sight, we follow the practices that make *res* and *ejemplar* – two types of bovines. Untranslatable to English, *res* refers to an ordinary cow or bull; the second one indicates an exemplary bovine, even a prized one. The practices that make these animals are different. We explain how making *res* does not meet the requirements of breed, while making *ejemplar* does; consequently, while the latter has breed, a *res* has a slippery *raza*, one that, difficult to pin down, transgresses the firmness of breeds. Thus, *raza* can be different from breed, and surprisingly, it is also different from 'race' in English: the slippery quality of *raza* also surfaces when talking about people, at least in Colombia and Peru, the countries of origin of the authors of this article. If classified, their *raza* may shift from 'white' to 'mestizo' (not white) depending on the eyes of the beholder – like *res*!

Keywords
artificial insemination, breed, cow-making practices, race, *raza*

Corresponding author:
Marisol de la Cadena, Department of Anthropology, University of California-Davis, One Shields Ave, Davis, CA 95616, USA.
Email: mdelac@ucdavis.edu

This article is on 'cow-making' in Colombia. Growing out of joint ethnography, it imagines 'cow' (or rather *res*) as a complex entity that weaves innumerable non-humans together with human beings in mutual life-shaping conditions. In this way of thinking, 'cow-making' in Colombia becomes the convergence of multispecies material-semiotic assemblages.[1] At the same time, the article is also about language, language differences, and the uses of language by the authors.

We are both anthropologists. Santiago (also a physician) was born and works in Colombia while Marisol is a Peruvian who reads and writes Spanish but lives most of her life in English. Santiago works and writes mostly in Spanish, but also reads and writes English. This shows in our collaboration: working together we tend towards more Spanish, but we also routinely use both languages, even in the same sentence. We may use English to clarify what we have said in Spanish and, of course, the opposite also happens. Our practice (of which we are usually oblivious) fractalizes English and Spanish as they entangle and affect one another in our work. This gets more complex when we consider the idiomatic heterogeneity of Spanish (*español* for Santiago, but *castellano* for Marisol).[2] Variations proliferate in our fieldwork (Marisol sometimes needs Santiago to 'interpret' what is being said in the field), but though 'working between languages' frequently leads to uncertainty, it is also ethnographically enriching. So our fieldwork diaries are in Spanish and English, as were the early drafts of this article. Pushed into English at a late stage, we came to realize that we would not have written the same article in Spanish. At the same time, the tensions between the language of fieldwork and that of (the final version of) writing has also been productive. Indeed, in one sense we follow Walter Benjamin's (1968) call for the language of the original to inflect the language of the translation.

These complexities noted, our focus is ethnographic: our concern is with human–cow relations in Colombia. Crucial to the practices in our field are the words: *res, ejemplar* and *raza*. None of these three terms finds easy translation into English. *Res* and *ejemplar* refer to different types of cows in Colombian bovine idiom.[3] *Res* is something like a 'common bovine', an animal that is not outstanding or remarkable, while *ejemplar* is a bovine of excellence, an 'exemplary' creature. In the pages that follow we start by looking at these words and the practices that make each of these entities. Then we turn to '*raza*', a word that both overlaps with and differs from the English word 'breed' into which it is usually translated. The bumps that make '*raza*' and 'breed' different from, yet translatable into, each other allow us to conclude with a brief discussion of *raza* as a multispecies category: a Colombian bovine idiom that overlaps and is different from breed, *and* a nation-building category that classifies humans that is built historically on a tension between biology and culture.

Res

Res is one of our favourite Colombian bovine idioms; it is also an ordinary Spanish word. The *Diccionario de la Real Academia de la Lengua Española* (an authority similar to the *Oxford English Dictionary*), defines *res* as 'four-legged animal belonging to certain domestic species, like bovine cattle, sheep etc, or wild ones such as deer, boar, etc.' (*'animal cuadrúpedo de ciertas especies domésticas, como del ganado vacuno, lanar, etc., o de los salvajes, como venados, jabalíes, etc.'*). It also specifies that in certain Latin American countries, Colombia among them, *res* is synonymous of *'animal vacuno'* or 'bovine animal'.[4] So in Colombian bovine idiom, *res* may be used to refer to bovines disregarding age and sex: cow/*vaca*, bull/*toro*, steer/*novillo*, heifer/*novilla*, calf (male and female, *ternero* and *ternera*, respectively), they can all be called a *'grupo de reses'*, a group of *reses*. *Res* can also be used to refer to any bovine disregarding its phenotypical characteristics.

In the singular, the word *res* (in its reference to bovine) does not travel into English. In English, 'cattle' is always plural[5] and it does not distinguish between animals in terms of breeds, sexes, or age – indeed it can also be translated to Spanish as *ganado*. Both words, 'res' and 'cattle', have implications of ownership: they refer to property in the relations between human and animal.

In addition to definitions, words and things become through material-semiotic ecologies of practices. To illustrate what we mean, we offer a fieldwork entry narrating some cow-making practices that include people, animals and things (corrals, trucks, ropes, prods, money) and work to make *res* and *reses*. We draw the entry from our visit to the *feria de ganado* – the local term for a cattle market or cattle fair – in a town near Bogotá called Zipaquirá where we went with our friend Eduardo, a cattle merchant, whose small plots of land are next to the house where we stay when we are doing fieldwork in the area. This is from Santiago's field notebook:

> The person in charge of the animals is a young tough-looking guy. He holds a long thin stick with a leather string that works as a handle; called a *bordón*, the stick is a commonly used tool when working with cattle and sold at the *ferias*. Two other guys help the first one and we are attracted by their constant movement, their loud voices and also by the way they handle a group of ten animals of heterogeneous colour and size. They are moving them from a larger corral – where they have been with other cattle – to one that is smaller from where the animals will board a truck (or more realistically, the men will have to make them board the truck.) At the same time Marisol is recording the scene with her cell phone.

> I approach the metal fence to listen and get a better look at what they are doing. The tough-looking young guy yells that I should be careful: the *res* can hit me – *la res te puede golpear*, he tells me. I take the opportunity to ask what they are doing. He answers 'these reses are going to the *matadero*', the slaughterhouse; they need to get them into the truck. We then see the men walk behind the *reses*, raise their open arms and wave forward with their hands; they also push them and poke them with the *bordón*. It is not easy task; while the majority reluctantly walk into the truck, not all *reses* collaborate, some turn back into the corral as the truck gets full.

Here age, size, or type is irrelevant. The man uses the word *res* (singular) to warn Santiago, and says they are 'taking reses (plural) to the slaughterhouse'. He disregards the animals' sex, except for a bull that was tethered to make loading easier and prevent him from harming the others. Their breeds were disregarded notwithstanding their heterogeneity; a *matarife* (almost literally: one who makes kill) had bought the lot and was taking them to be transformed into *carne de res* to be sold in small butchers in nearby towns.

Ejemplar

If the Feria de Zipaquirá is populated by *reses* and humans, this is not the case of some other *ferias de ganado*. These may be populated by expensive animals, their owners, and representatives of cutting-edge cattle industry equipment. So not all 'cow-making' practices make *reses*. We ask a female veterinarian about *res* and the cattle fair she attends in Bogotá:

> It does not make any sense to say, 'I am going to show one or two reses at AgroExpo.' She adds very emphatically: 'Those are not *reses*!! What we say is we are going to take x number of *ejemplares* to the Fair.' [She grimaces with disgust at the thought, and maybe even at our question, as she mockingly imitates someone saying:] 'I am going to show three *reses* at AgroExpo' *'Llamar reses al buen ganado es un insulto.'* It is an insult to refer to good cattle as *reses*.

AgroExpo is the most important cattle fair (*feria ganadera*) in Colombia. It happens every second year and convenes the most important associations of cattle breeders (*asociaciones de criadores de ganado*) as well as representatives of every imaginable cattle industry product. Animals are purportedly the main exhibit and (it seemed to us) in constant competition. This is implicit as they are shown in corrals that display the name of *the finca* (ranch)[6] they belong to, and it is explicit in the arenas where (not infrequently international) judges choose champions. Winning a championship at AgroExpo is a big feat for the breeder–animal couple. Like entering the national Cattle Hall of Fame, it grants prestige, and with this the possibility of becoming a supplier of breeding stock, most usually semen, but embryos as well. And this is why, as our veterinarian friend told us, AgroExpo is not a place to find *reses* – at all! What we find there is *ejemplares*: 'exemplar/s' would be a literal translation (as the reader correctly suspects). It indicates that the cow or bull is the best of its breed (which includes its productive purpose: milk or beef) at its specific reproductive stage (adult male or female, heifer or steer, female or male calf). An *ejemplar* does not simply belong to a breed. It *exemplifies* the breed and it is thus more than the animal itself: it is a successful multispecies biocapitalist conglomerate, an economic, scientific, political and reproductive vital entity, the gathering of distributed heterogeneous practices.[7] In short, the difference between AgroExpo and the market in Zipaquirá could hardly be greater. At AgroExpo there is no crowding or prodding. Instead the place of the *ejemplar* is in AgroExpo's manicured arena where, along with its trainer (both stern and pampering), it is paraded before the judges. Two different worlds.

The different lives of cows: *ejemplares* are registered information, *reses* are only known by their owners

The life of an *ejemplar* begins at a ranch, where soon after birth it is marked with an identifying number on an ear tag – a common biopolitical practice for monitoring cattle health. However, when it comes to the *ejemplar*, this number is special for it will eventually be connected to a considerable amount of valuable data; usually known as pedigree, it includes the *ejemplar*'s ancestry, birthdate, his and his descent's productive and reproductive features. Registered in an *asociación de criadores* (a breeders' association) he becomes a documented animal, a member of the *raza*-breed he represents.[8] If the animal is exceptional this bull will continue his life as a commercial breeder, spending days at a 'semen collection centre'. There his semen is extracted, analysed for quality, marked with his name, date of collection and then frozen to be conserved in straws or *pajillas de semen* (literally 'straws with semen').[9] He becomes the ancestor of entire populations that can trace their lineage to his famous name.[10] These kinds of bulls, producers of semen biologically known and commercially handled, populate cattle catalogues replete with the hereditary information supposedly carried in every semen straw that buyers look at when they are selecting the right bull for their cows.

The productive and reproductive success of their hereditary composition adds to the value attached to their names. At the same time, the price of their semen – the vital substance and the subject of scientific inspection and economic speculation – may vary in the course of their lifetime. This is because their names also carry with them the names of their owners, and their historical *criadores*, breeders, and their success in championships adds to the socio-economic and bio-prestige of the *finca* that made them. Against this, an animal whose genealogy – and productive and reproductive information – is not known cannot be registered; its *raza* is not certified even if the animal fulfils the appropriate phenotypic characteristics. The *raza* of an *ejemplar*, in English its *breed*, depends on an extensive administrative apparatus. As a data generation practice, then, the registration of *ejemplares* is necessary to turn particular bulls into specific biocapitalist entities and their semen into a commodity. And because the *certified* reproductive substance also guarantees a considerable rate of success in impregnation, by purchasing it the idea that buyers are also acquiring an *ejemplar*'s offspring is not far-fetched. The *ejemplar* is itself a market of futures.

Now let us go back to Zipaquirá, the rural town fair we visited near Bogotá. Here, as we noted, most *reses* are on their way to the slaughterhouse. The sex of these animals is unimportant, they are *reses*, immediate objects of monetary transaction. When a buyer asks, *cuánto por esta res?* How much for this *res*? the seller is not offended. In these small *ferias*, the cattle whose immediate fate is not the *matadero* are usually cows – female bovines. Bought by peasants for reproduction, such cows will probably get pregnant (via insemination) throughout the course of their lives and produce milk for their calves, for the family, and for sale. Eventually, albeit a lot later, they too will be taken to the *matadero*, the final destination of the *res*. Lack of pasture, an endemic condition in these farms, currently intensifying due to the frequency of drought or excessive rain caused by climate change, seems to be shortening the life of *reses*, and consequently, increasing their numbers at the slaughterhouse.[11]

The qualities and defects of *reses* are known to their individual owner, and unlike *ejemplares*, they do not belong to a lineage; their name (they usually have one) is only known in the small farm where they live. The origin of the *res* is usually unknown. With some luck someone may recall who the mother was, while lost in memory will be the source of the semen with which the latter was inseminated. This animal may be marked by phenotype that while marking *raza*, does not translate into breed.[12]

When *raza* does not translate into breed: making cows with slippery phenotypes

If the *raza* of an *ejemplar* may be translated into the English word 'breed', this is not the case for the *raza* of *res*. So much we learned when watching a small herd in the *altiplano* of Cundinamarca while talking to Rosalba, Eduardo's wife. She raises cattle, *res*, but does not necessarily breed them. Marisol asks Rosalba to identify the *razas* in the herd.

R.   [This] one is a *barcina*, she is *la más criolla*, the most creole. Some people call them *montañeras, indias, aindiadas* – they are from 'out there', they have never been inseminated, *nunca han tenido cruces*, they have never been crossed. They maintain the line. They are not domesticated.

Q.   And the ones closer to us?

R.   The third one is a mix, *como con jersey*, like with a jersey mix, it is lighter . . . The others are *normandos*, Normande. *Tienen pinta de normandos*, they look sort of Normande. That cow is Normande because she has almost no horns, her horns are not long.

Q.   And those smaller ones?

R.   Mmmm that first calf, is also sort of a Normande, but it should have more freckles . . . it is more like with Holstein, but it also looks Normande. It is neither Normande, nor with black [spots] like Holstein – it can be both: a Normande of Holstein. The other one is Holstein with Ayrshire; but [also] neither because Holstein is white and Ayrshire is red – this one is neither one, but it is both.

All of the cows we are looking at are mixed, but there are some whose mixtures are lost in time and/or not the result of insemination, like the *barcina* in Rosalba's description which, she tells us, has never been inseminated. She describes this condition as 'having never been crossed' and therefore being '*más criolla*, less mixed' by which she means (implicitly, it became explicit after we ask) 'with commercial breeds'. *Barcina* describes a colour (brown-reddish) but the cow could share this with other cows, and this is therefore insufficient to mark her *raza*. She is a '*más criolla*' because Rosalba knows the cow's origins: she came from 'out there', a *montañera*, 'from the mountains', a hillbilly, or 'like an Indian', *aindiada* as Rosalba puts it. All these features indicate that the reddish cow we are looking at 'has not been domesticated', by which Rosalba means that it is not the result of insemination and therefore, it or she is *more criolla* – more creole – which means 'more pure' in our friend's bovine idiom.[13] Perhaps *menos* [less] *criolla* would be the result of insemination, therefore less pure and somewhat domesticated. It becomes clear that every cow in the herd is mixed, and that what went into the mix is unclear.

It is self-evident that Rosalba knows about cows and distinguishes their phenotypic qualities. These, however, are not revealed in recorded data, and neither are they simply displayed by the cow. Rather, Rosalba discerns the marking features of cows through evaluations of her own. But what is most noteworthy about this is that these have *no pretence of stability*. She may embark in discussions with Eduardo, her husband, or with her neighbour, the owner of the cows, to decide the *raza* of a particular cow. But what is decided at one moment may be different later. In Rosalba's practice the animals' *raza* is variable and, albeit within limits, the criteria she uses to identify *raza* are also flexible. That flexibility marks the difference between the *raza* that Rosalba is concerned with and the *breed* that depends on singular, clear-cut and stable, administration.

In Rosalba's practice – a practice she shares with her neighbour and her husband – the *raza* of the cow she describes is not a mixture of well-circumscribed breeds. Instead, *raza* shifts and mixtures are guessed at with more or less probability.[14] Yet records are kept: Rosalba may remember the *raza* – in the sense of breed – of the semen she used to inseminate her cows even after she sells them. The name of the bull it belonged to may be relevant or not. Rosalba's cows are uncertain mixes, *cruces* whose compositions are unknown in the way required by breeding associations. Nevertheless, the practice of artificial insemination in these farms does more than reproduce *reses*. Through it, commercial *raza*-breeding meets *raza* in the making of lineage-less animals whose reproduction, in turn, increases the demand for the industrially produced semen straws created by commercial *raza*-breeds.[15]

Raza meets breed as commercial language: making better cows

So, what more can be said about the encounter between *raza* and breed? Consider the following:

> Simmental is a good *raza*-breed to cross with the Brahman/Cebu *razas*-breeds because it increases the yield of both meat and milk. . . . The well-known characteristics of the Brahman/Cebu such as resistance to heat, to parasites, their grazing ability, and calving ease complement with the qualities that *la raza Simmental*/the Simmental breed offers, such as their fertility, longevity, milking qualities, early sexual maturity, maternal excellence, fast growth and high-quality meat thus increasing and potentializing the production of these two *raza*-breeds.[16]

This, taken from a Colombian webpage, is strikingly similar to the description of Simbrah cattle in a US based webpage.[17] *Raza* from the first is equivalent to 'breed' in the second; *hacer raza* Simbrah would find translation as 'breeding Simbrah', a process that requires careful in-farm registration of the genealogical mix until the combined right proportion of Simmental and Brahman obtains Simbrah, a different breed that is also described as 'synthetic' in Colombia (a word that is also used in English). In the process of this particular kind of breeding, offspring are obtained that cannot be identified as Simbrah. When they have 50% of each (Simmental and Brahman) they are called F1. Others are a mixture of the two breeds in percentages that do not find a name in *raza*-breed nomenclature,[18] though when these animals participate in the reproductive genealogical progression towards Simbrah, their information is recorded to calculate their percentage contribution to the process that will eventually result in the 'synthesis' that is this breed.[19]

Crossbreeding does not simply produce new synthetic breeds.[20] Though it sounds oxymoronic, it may also produce a '*pure* crossbred animal'. The quote that follows is an explanation of how this works from our fieldwork in Bogotá.

If I mix two animals of different *razas*-breed the result of the first *cruce* is registered as an F1; if I continue with the same two breeds, the second one is registered as 3/4; the third one is registered as 7/8; the next one will be registered as 15/16. Finally, the result of the next crossbreeding will be an animal known as *puro por cruzamiento* or 'pure after crossbreeding'.

Crossbreeding requires that each of the two *razas*-breeds that participate in the reproduction be treated as a unit. At each moment of crossbreeding that unit is divided by two so that the fractions of each breed in the next generation can be calculated. Making *raza*-breed through crossbreeding makes animals whose genetic characteristics are followed and certified so that they can be used to design an animal that reflects the specific productive and reproductive objectives of the breeder, the *criador*. Thus, registered animals are also used in long-term designs to improve herds via crossbreeding.

Gilberto, a good friend and a wise and caring veterinarian, explains how he used *cruces* (crossing breeds) to improve the milk quality on a dairy farm. Milk of good quality, he says, is free of microbes (it is clean) and has a specific protein/fat composition. The first requirement can be achieved with hygiene and health controls. But to improve milk composition he has, in his words, to *meter raza* or introduce different *razas*-breeds to the herd.

> Here you see cows of different *razas*-breeds. [He points at the animals to show their varied heights, weights, colours, face shape, shape of udders, their height from the ground, the shape of their legs and hooves.] We have handled this herd genetically to improve the quality of the milk. When I started working on this farm, the herd was mostly Holstein and a few Simmental; I started to mix them with diverse *razas*-breeds: Jersey, Brown Swiss, Montbeliarde. I got Parhol [not a *raza*-breed, but a well-known Brown-Swiss and Holstein mix] and Montbeliarde-with-Holstein which I then mixed with Holstein again. Now we get more and better milk.

Borrowing Santiago's fieldwork dairy, he sketches his explanation of how he organizes this crossbreeding. He uses the *finca*'s records, which include genealogical information that goes deep back into the history of the farm. Then he studies catalogues to choose the semen he will buy, taking into consideration the characteristics of *each cow* in the farm's milking herd. He remembers each of them individually, but if he has any doubts he consults the carefully kept records. This programme connects data across farms with the catalogue of the company that sells the semen which is the bull's only until it has been extracted. This practice is impossible without records.

The result of this crossbreeding to improve the herd is not an *ejemplar*, but *neither is it a res*. What is being made are *vacas*, cows: productive animals '*con información*', with information, whose genetic composition is known. However, the purpose of such information is not the production of a commodity (like the embryos or sperm of *ejemplares*) but to improve the productive capacity (of cows and milk). These are profit-making cows whose breeds can be identified. Some may be referred to as *animales de raza* and like the families that may own them, this phrase might translate as 'well-bred'. Yet, our veterinarian friend talks about these animals in a way that would be insulting to the families he works for. He explains that being the result of mixtures, these animals are registered as '*animal mestizo con tipo racial predominante*', a *mestizo* animal with a predominant breed type. The nuance has to do with *raza*. This Spanish word is used to classify not only animals but also humans in ways that no longer feel comfortable for the seemingly English equivalent word 'race'. The conclusion is that while '*meter raza*' (introducing different *razas*-breeds to the herd) translates as 'breeding', it means more. For this term is not just about cattle. It also absorbs local idioms to do with nation building and this calls for attention to human 'race/s'. But since '*meter raza*' is at the same time intertwined with international practices of breeding (and the information and records that go with those practices), making '*animales de raza*' is also part of a worldwide market-oriented conversation.

Using semen straws to produce *reses*

We are in Chocontá, a small rural town where we learn about peasant cow-making as we visit with one of the local veterinarians, Dr Rodríguez:

> . . . there have been too many bad experiences with black Holstein. I rarely sell that semen. They eat too much, they are too delicate [prone to disease], the rate of successful insemination is low: they calf every two or three years! And then, it takes too long for the calf to be independent. The best-selling semen straws are Normande and Jersey – people cross Jersey with Holstein.[21] People also like Normande: those cows easily get pregnant at insemination, every year! It works like clockwork, it is dual purpose, and it acclimatizes well here; when the cow is small, I recommend Jersey, otherwise during labour the calf, and even the cow may die.

When his clients seek advice he asks: 'What is your cow like? Is it sort of Normande? Is it small?' He does not ask for the breed. When he says 'sort of Normande' he wants to know the size and productive purpose of the cow: 'sort of Normande' may include other *razas*, and precision is irrelevant. The characteristic he thinks his clients should look for is *facilidad de parto* (or ease of calving), for the main goal is successful reproduction. Then, once he has sorted out what the client wants, he goes to the catalogue and looks at the bulls with all their information about genealogy. But he doesn't really need detailed information. He is only after 'basic' productive features.

> I need a milk producer, that calves easily, and one that makes daughters because that is what people want. We also check that it is not white. The catalogue has all the information about the bull, it is the history of the bull.

In short, he converts (translates!) the information about commercial *raza*-breed into the capacities of those local cows and the productive needs of their owners. And it is here that *raza* both meets and escapes 'breed' in the commercial sense of the term. This is because the semen in the straws he sells certifies a bull that exemplifies a breed, for example a Jersey. Yet, the offspring will never rise to the standards of their paternal exemplary origin. Instead, they will be 'cows' or 'bulls' – they will be *res*. They will labour on a peasant farm, and the commodities they produce will not be registered in meticulously kept data files that are scientific or quasi-scientific and that serve the reproduction of their lineage. Instead, their milk, meat and hides will go to local markets to be sold for money to sustain the family.[22]

Criar and *crianza*: living with cows . . .

We learn, then, that in Chocontá, *pajillas* (semen straws) participate in the reproduction of *reses* – or cows that will become such – without necessarily translating peasant house-holds into profit-making endeavours. Indeed, in a peasant context the homogenizing ten-dency of commercial breeds to improve herds (in order to increase profits) is being diverted into making cows with a slippery *raza* in order to assure a better life for the peas-ant human–animal family. We spent several cold and rainy days with Daniela. Like Rosalba she lives in Chocontá and manages a herd of perhaps 12 cows (five or six may be her sister's, the rest are hers), four of which are milking.[23] The cows graze in three hec-tares of very poor pasture – the landscape is hilly all around. She uses artificial insemina-tion and borrows a bull only when this fails. We asked her what she looks for in a semen straw, and her answer was: strong legs because the cows have to climb a lot, and good milk production. She remembers the name of the bull (definitely an *ejemplar*) whose semen she used to impregnate each of her cows because it is bad reproductive practice to impregnate a daughter with her father's semen – but the *raza* of the cows is slippery: they have names, and a sort of approximate *raza*. Daniela does not 'improve her herd' in order to increase profitability: her cows may eventually become *carne de res*, beef. But mean-while she lives with them and vice versa. The money she gets by selling their milk is also for the cows, for their food, which then leads to more milk, which represents more money both for the cows and the family. Ultimately, they all eat with the money obtained from the cows and, to be sure, from Daniela's work.[24] Her way of 'making cows' is a far cry from that practised in commercial breeding. Instead she would describe her practice as *criar vacas*, a phrase that moves to English as 'rearing cows' but also as raising them, as in a multispecies family. Here again, then, there are bumps in translation, and those bumps continue to make us think. So, for instance, speakers of the Colombian bovine idiom who understand English would frown if we were to translate Daniela's practices of '*criar*' as 'breeding', while they would approve of translating *Asociación de Criadores de Holstein* as 'Holstein Breeders Association'. There is a fork in the translation here that ties to dif-ferent practices because *criar reses* (peasant *vacas*, cows that will eventually become *reses*) does not require practices to improve the breed of the herd. Practices of *crianza* may make (slippery) *raza* on the peasant farm, and breeds (that demand stability) as they are taken on by member of an *asociación de criadores*.[25]

Jonat, a Simbrah *ejemplar* bull in the semen-collection centre, illustrates a case of *crianza* that translates into English as 'commercial breeding'. After a successful perfor-mance at AgroExpo, we met Jonat at the cattle ranch owned by Don Raúl; at AgroExpo, he was referred to as Jonat's *propietario y criador*. The phrase comfortably moves to English as 'owner and breeder'. Imagined long before his birth, Don Raúl designed Jonat during a laborious 10-year experimental process in which he impregnated the best of his own Simmental cows with the semen of Brahman, Simbrah or Simmental bulls, until he finally obtained the bull that satisfied the qualities he was looking for. Jonat has become perhaps the most important of Don Raúl's biocapitalist assets, his semen a commodity widely sold in straws for artificial insemination coveted as good breeding material. Don Raúl invests money in Jonat, keenly marketing the bull's reproductive potential and genetic capacities, and providing him with comfort and care, for both commercial and non-commercial reasons. The bovine idiom *propietario y criador* emphasizes Don Raúl's importance in Jonat's life and radiates (to a possible market audience as well) the feelings of pride and care that attach Don Raúl to the bull's genetic qualities which he, Don Raúl, considers to be not only his property, but also his own achievement.

Despite the differences, Don Raúl's farm also resembles that of Daniela: there is care. When we met Jonat we also met Ricki, a worker on the farm. He was involved in the process of designing the genetic mixture that finally yielded Jonat, but now he attends to the bull's everyday wellbeing. He visits the pasture where Jonat grazes every day, provides him with water and salt, and looks after that major and crucial exhibition feature of *ejemplares*, his bodily form. They know one another in ways that allow Ricki to swiftly handle Jonat's huge body. They travel together to cattle fairs, share days and nights, and at the AgroExpo Ricki sleeps, eats and takes baths with Jonat. They even catch the same diseases. Ricki may also act as an intermediary between potential buyers of Jonat's semen straws and Don Raúl, but he is also deeply attached to Jonat. He missed him when the bull was at the semen collection centre, and cheerfully sent us a voice message when Jonat returned to the ranch. '*Volvió el hombre*', he said, 'the man is back'.

Crianza links to both *raza*/'breed' and slippery 'race'. It links people who would not otherwise be together. But in both cases, in addition it connects animals and humans in practices of care comprising intimacy and *cariño*, a deep feeling of attachment coupled with generosity that 'affect' only superficially translates. *Crianza* is embedded in diverse ways of multispecies togetherness.

Conclusion

In this article we have explored a series of Colombian bovine idioms. Drawing on our fieldwork on 'making cow', we have shown how the practices for doing this vary from location to location. There are places – the AgroExpo is one example – in which a bio-commercial logic of breeding dominates. Here animals are bred as *ejemplares*, exemplary animals, that will become tomorrow's suppliers of semen for those who wish to improve their herds. Stability here is crucial: in these practices what we have called the '*raza*-breed' is held in place, and as a part of this, information is crucial. Each animal – and each semen straw – comes with a long genealogy. The value of the animal resides in this combination: a biological form that is carefully maintained goes together with information about the breeding that produced the animal.

This is *raza* in one form. Alongside this, peasant farmers also practise *raza*, but in a different way. So, for instance, we showed that Rosalba's cows are mixed as to their *raza*. Some are the product of artificial insemination, and some (those that have not been 'domesticated', are more *criolla*, 'more creole') are not. They also have different *looks*, and as she describes their colour and size Rosalba uses the language of breeds (Normande, Holstein) even though these are animals without a recorded lineage. But what is even more striking is that the names that she uses to describe a particular cow shift. A 'bit of Normande' does not necessarily remain a 'bit of Normande' but may become something else instead. If the *raza* of *ejemplares* is all about stability, in the context of peasant farming flexibility stands out as crucial. This has to do with local concerns. Peasants want their cows to do well in a specific setting. So, as we saw, Daniela is hoping for cows that will thrive on her poor hilly pasture, *res* with strong legs and good milk production, cows that are productive. She remembers who parented her cows but does not hold on to information about their long-term genealogy and is not invested in certification. On the small farm, the, cows are not *ejemplares* but rather *res* and this comes with a different investment in what it means to have a *raza*.

So peasant *raza* is unlike commercial *raza*-breed. At the same time, these two worlds intersect. Peasant farmers may want to use commercial semen straws to improve the productivity of their animals and this helps to feed biocommerce. This logic was described to us by the veterinarian Gilberto. He worked with genetic information for farmers who wanted to improve the milk production of their herds. The resulting cows came with genetic information about their lineage, and hence are neither *ejemplares* nor *res*. Instead they counted as *vacas*. The intersection of the two worlds also goes in the other direction: some of the practices of human–animal care that characterize peasant farming may also be found in the high-tech biocommercial and competitive world of the *ejemplares*.

What are the lessons from all this for the trials and tribulations of writing in English? As we observed at the outset, our materials are in Spanish, our thinking, talking and writing is in both Spanish and in English, and this final text is in English (and has been revised by an editor). The bumps that we encountered along the way we have used as ethnographic and analytical opportunities. For out of the many bovine idioms at work in Colombian farming practices only a few map onto the categories embedded in the English languages. Trying to write about the other 'untranslatable' ways of organizing human–animal relations in English helps to rob everything that might seem self-evident in any particular bovine idiom of any self-evidence. 'Breed' is not the same as *raza*. There are overlaps, but also gaps between the two words and the work they do. Trying to articulate in English what *raza* is in commercial breeding practices and what it is in peasant farming helped us with our analysis of 'cow-making' in Colombia.

But there are lessons for English as well. And these do not just have to do with cows, but also with humans. Historically, as many authors have noted, terms of classification, such as *raza* and breed, have been used to describe both humans and non-human animals.[26] However, in English 'race' and 'breed' have been pried apart. Race came to be used for irreducible and unalterable human difference, while breed mostly came to apply to animals. As a part of this, race became a contested term, while breed became a commercial matter. The term 'breeding', interestingly, still applies to both, implying acquired and long-term improvement, cultural in the case of people, and genetic in the case of animals. However, and by contrast, in the Spanish of contemporary Latin American there is no word for the modern notion of 'breed' other than *raza*. This means that in the region *raza* is used to talk about both animals and people. And as we were analysing *raza* in the context of cow-making it struck us that this has different meanings. It may be fixed, as it is in commercial breeding and its genealogical databases, or it may be variable, as it is in most peasant practices. And what, then, about the humans? Historically, Latin American elites have often had 'brown skin'. (Both of your authors fall into this category.) Unlike Anglo-American practices of race where skin colour was taken as a sign of 'race' that is obvious to the eye, in Latin American, to the disconcertment of at least some Europeans and Americans,[27] the *raza* of elites has been certified by lineage of blood or university titles rather than skin colour. And the mechanism at work in creating those elites, then, is not unlike that of *raza* in the sense of 'breed': it depends on paperwork.[28] Perhaps this is an insight that might be transferred from Spanish to English?

There are complications to this argument that take us beyond the scope of this article. But the point that we want to end with is that bovine idioms and human idioms are not just linked because both may be the object of similar categorizations. Added to this, bovines and humans come together in human–animal practices, and the humble *res* and the arrogant *ejemplar* partake of – and strengthen – the status and the conditions of their owners. In the absence of a certified breed a *res* would be socially out of place in AgroExpo, while an *ejemplar*, an animal whose breed is certified, does not belong in the small town cattle fair of Zipaquirá. 'Out of placeness' is indexed by either having or lacking breed certification. But the people involved also similarly either belong or not. When visiting AgroExpo, Eduardo gets lost and wanders round its edges marvelling what he sees. The reverse is also the case. In small town cattle markets, owners of *ejemplares* are equally at a loss, and the semen of their prize bulls would not find a buyer because it is not obviously better than that of other bulls. In short, the making of *res* and *ejemplar* also makes social place and it may extend to the humans doing the making. Some are well bred while others – those lacking the certification of lineage – are not.

Funding

The authors declared receipt of the following financial support for the research, authorship, and/or publication of this article: Marisol de la Cadena received funding from the UC Davis New Research Initiatives for research on this paper.

Notes

1. That cow-making material semiotic assemblages are different and differentiated goes without saying (about material-semiotic assemblages see Law, 2019). About 'cow' as an object of history see Erica Fudge (2017).

2. Our English is not the same either and we both relate to it, our second language, differently as well. About the geopolitics of 'bad spoken languages' see Rodriguez Medina (2019).

3. 'Bovine idiom' is a notion coined by Evans Pritchard; it comprised an elaborate vocabulary he considered necessary to understand the social life of the human group he was studying (called Nuer) and was used to talk about the cattle and herds they owned (Evans Pritchard, 1940, p. 19). Analogously, we use 'bovine idiom' to name those cattle-related vocabularies and practices following which enables us to explore sections of the dense material-semiotic grids of cow-making in Colombia.

4. There is a slight translation bump here which we are not opening to discussion: we have translated *vacuno* as bovine, although the word is composed of *vaca*/cow plus the suffix *uno*/ish. So 'cowish' would be a 'literalized' way of writing what *vacuno* means.

5. Cattle is a *plural tantum* (plural only in Latin) according to the online *Oxford Dictionaries*: https://blog.oxforddictionaries.com/2015/05/18/12-nouns-that-are-always-plurals/

6. *Finca* is an interesting word in Colombian Spanish: it can name from a wealthy ranch to a small peasant farm.

7. Very briefly, we conceptualize the biocapitalist material-semiotic practices of cattle reproduction as the entanglement of the sciences of (animal) life and political economic regimes to produce life-generating substances as 'objects' (semen straws, frozen embryos), commodities (obtained/

expropriated from animals) to be sold, speculated with, and valorized in a capitalist market. This form of biocapitalism may partially displace the reproductive role of animal sex and replace it with diverse human and non-human intra-related practices for the production of animal life. An important consequence of this is that the reproduction and production of life become the same overlapping event (see Franklin, 2006; Franklin & Lock, 2003; Helmreich, 2008; Sunder Rajan, 2006). For a history of artificial insemination see Clarke (2007) and Franklin (2007).

8. *Ejemplares* are the result of practices of scientific breeding, about which Haraway says 'the breeding system that evolved with the data-keeping system was called scientific breeding, and in myriad ways this paper-plus flesh system is behind the histories of eugenics and genetics, as well as other sciences (and politics) of animal and human reproduction' (Haraway, 2008, p. 53).

9. In this article we focus on semen straws; we have yet to follow embryo transfer of fertilized oocytes, another important commodity that circulates in the biocapitalist market of cattle reproduction. As embryo donators cows can also be *ejemplares* but their number is proportionately smaller. The speed at which they become ready for this biotechnology is lower than that of bulls becoming bio-economically proven as 'good' sperm producers.

10. See www.calciolandia.com/animais/visualizar/a7368-radar-dos-pocoes

11. The number of *reses* arriving at the slaughterhouse has increased, we were told on one of our visits to the facility; we have witnessed this growth as well as the consequent private investment to technically accelerate the dismembering process by enlarging the corrals, refrigerating, and delivery zones.

12. English-speaking scholars have written prolifically on 'breed'. See for example Harriet Ritvo (1992, 1995, 1997), Sarah Franklin (2007), Haraway (2003) and Gabriel Rosenberg (2017). Yet, as we discuss in the next section, some practices of '*raza*' also escape much of the history and practice of breed.

13. Here, 'pure' means *without* artificial insemination; intriguingly this idiom implicitly makes a difference between 'natural reproduction' (as in a cow impregnated by a bull) and human intervention in cattle reproduction, precisely as in 'artificial insemination'. About '*razas criollas*' see Gallini (2005).

14. Cristina Grasseni (2005, 2007a) talks about the relevance of vision for cattle farmers; Rosalba's vision is indeed trained and Grasseni would call it 'skilled' – yet '*res*' makes difficult the standardization of vision, and rather requires for it to be a hybrid skill: included in it would be a shared conversation about what is seen.

15. Working in European farms, Grasseni has described how applied locally reproductive technologies, including artificial insemination, 'provide ample scope for local negotiations, resistance and conflict' (Grasseni, 2007b, p. 496).

16. See https://asosimmentalcolombia-com.jimdo.com/raza-1/raza-simbrah/

17. See www.thecattlesite.com/breeds/beef/90/simbrah/

18. Even so, these animals are not *reses*; their individual and genealogical information – owner, number, sex, ancestral breed combination, productive and reproductive qualities and other characteristics – is fully registered in the pertinent breeders' association.

19. This may be what gives them their name in Spanish: *razas sintéticas*; the phrase translates to English most usually as 'composite' but they are also called 'synthetic' and 'hybrid'. See www.thecattlesite.com/breeds/beef/80/composite/ (accessed 7 October 2019).

20. In this process 'breed' is the unit to track what is being mixed. The production of synthetic breeds entails the calculation of proportions of the different breeds that will eventually make a single animal. To track what is being mixed, each breed is represented as a unit; from this process a hybrid synthetic bull results that is considered a new breed. Paradoxically to lay ears, crossbreeding produces a breed that is 'pure', yet this breed does not imply the purity of lack of mixture.

21. Normande is promoted locally by AsoNormando, the national association. They have a rural extension service to extend the market for the bull semen they produce at locally affordable prices.
22. What circulates in the sperm straw is, in a sense, placeless breed; after successful artificial insemination, it becomes placed, emerging through local animal epigenetics
23. That the size of the herd is unclear (to us) tells of Daniela's homestead: of course, she knows how many animals she has, but this number is not something she cares much about.
24. Daniela and her cows work together and for each other, to sustain their mutually dependent lives. On collaboration and work among farmers and their animals see Porcher and Schmitt (2012) and Porcher (2015, 2017).
25. Commercial semen straws are common to both; yet they may be differently entangled as they emerge from *crianza* that translates as 'breeding' and from *crianza* that does not.
26. The scholarly literature – both on race and breed – has already asserted the connections between race (and racism) and animal breeding as modern practice (Derry et al., 2018; Franklin, 2006). On human breed and breeding (as in 'well-bred') see Edwards (2000). In Latin America, the interrelated divergence between human *raza* (and race) and animal and human breed is replete with a long history of complexities for which this article is not the place. But see Ginzburg (2017) for the etymology of early modern human–animal *raza* and its connection with breeding.
27. In 1912, in the highland city of Cuzco, Peru, an English professor at the local university and the leader of the first urban census of the city, commenting on the accuracy of the data, complained that brown-skinned 'mestizos' tried 'to be included as white' (Giesecke, 1913, as cited in de la Cadena, 2005). This was not without precedent: when in 1846 the geographer Johan Jakob Von Tschudi visited Lima he had a similar complaint: the elites, he said 'self-identify as "whites" and confront Indians with superiority. Nothing can be more flattering than to ask them if they are Spanish, a question that they answer affirmatively, even as all their features are obviously indigenous' (von Tschudi, 1966, as cited in de la Cadena, 2005).
28. On differences between *raza* in Latin America and race in the US, see de la Cadena (2005). For differences among different Latin American countries, see Wade et al. (2014).

References

Benjamin, W. (1968). *Illuminations* (H. Arendt, Ed., H. Zohn, Trans.). Brace and World.

Clarke, A. E. (2007). Reflections on the reproductive sciences in agriculture in the UK and US, ca. 1900–2000. *Studies in History and Philosophy of Biological and Biomedical Sciences, 38*(2), 316–339.

De la Cadena, M. (2005). Are mestizo hybrids? The conceptual politics of Andean identities. *Journal of Latin American Studies, 37*(2), 259–284.

Derry, M., Haraway, D., Landry, D., Ritvo, H., & Swart, S. (2018). *Humanimalia* roundtable on breed. *Humanimalia, 10*(1), 5–26.

Edwards, J. (2000). *Born and bred: Idioms of kinship and new reproductive technologies in England*. Oxford University Press.

Evans-Pritchard, E. E. (1940). *The Nuer: A description of the modes of livelihood and political institutions of a Nilotic people*. Clarendon Press.

Franklin, S. (2006). Bio-economies: Biowealth from the inside out. *Development, 49*(4), 97–101.

Franklin, S. (2007). *Dolly mixtures: The remaking of genealogy*. Duke University Press.

Franklin, S., & Lock, M. (2003). Animation and cessation. In S. Franklin & M. Lock (Eds.), *Remaking life and death: Toward an anthropology of the biosciences* (pp. 3–22). SAR Press.

Fudge, E. (2017). What was it like to be a cow? History and animal studies. In L. Kalof (Ed.), *The Oxford handbook of animal studies*. Oxford University Press.

Gallini, S. (2005). El Atila del Ganges en la ganadería colombiana [The Attila of the Ganges in the Colombian cattle ranching industry]. *Nómadas, 22,* 186–197.

Ginzburg, C. (2017). Conjunctive anomalies: A reflection on werewolves.*Revista de Estudios Sociales, 60,* 110–118.

Grasseni, C. (2005). Designer cows: The practice of cattle breeding between skill and standardization. *Society & Animals, 13*(1), 33–49.

Grasseni, C. (2007a). Good looking: Learning to be a cattle breeder. In C. Grasseni (Ed.), *Skilled visions: Between apprenticeship and standards* (pp. 45–66). Berghahn Books.

Grasseni, C. (2007b). Managing cows: An ethnography of breeding practices and uses of reproductive technology in contemporary dairy farming in Lombardy (Italy). *Studies in History and Philosophy of Biological and Biomedical Sciences, 38*(2), 488–510.

Haraway, D. J. (2003). *The companion species manifesto: Dogs, people, and significant otherness.* Prickly Paradigm Press.

Haraway, D. J. (2008). *When species meet.* University of Minnesota Press.

Helmreich, S. (2008). Species of biocapital. *Science as Culture, 17*(4), 463–478.

Law, J. (2019). *Material semiotics.* www.heterogeneities.net/publications/Law2019MaterialSemi otics.pdf (accessed 12 May 2019).

Porcher, J. (2015). Animal work. In L. Kalof (Ed.), *The Oxford handbook of animal studies.* Oxford University Press.

Porcher, J. (2017). *The ethics of animal labor: A collaborative utopia.* Palgrave Macmillan.

Porcher, J., & Schmitt, T. (2012). Dairy cows: Workers in the shadows? *Society & Animals, 20,* 39–60.

Ritvo, H. (1992). Race, breed, and myths of origin: Chillingham cattle as Ancient Britons. *Representations, 39,* 1–22.

Ritvo, H. (1995). Possessing Mother Nature: Genetic capital in eighteenth-century Britain. In J. Brewer & S. Staves (Eds.), *Early modern conceptions of property* (pp. 413–426). Routledge.

Ritvo, H. (1997). *The platypus and the mermaid and other figments of the classifying imagination.* Harvard University Press.

Rodriguez Medina, L. (2019). A geopolitics of bad English. *Tapuya: Latin American Science, Technology and Society, 2*(1), 1–7.

Rosenberg, G. (2017). Breeds and breeding. In J. Salazar Parreñas (Ed.), *Gender: Animals* (pp. 229–246). Macmillan.

Sunder Rajan, K. (2006). *Biocapital: The constitution of postgenomic life.* Duke University Press.

Wade, P., López Beltrán, C., Restrepo, E., & Ventura Santos, R. (Eds.). (2014). *Mestizo genomics: Race mixture, nation, and science in Latin America.* Duke University Press.

Author biographies

Marisol de la Cadena is a Peruvian scholar. She teaches anthropology at the University of California-Davis. Her latest publications are *Earth Beings: Ecologies of Practice across Andean Worlds* (Duke University Press, 2015) and *A World of Many Worlds* co-edited with Mario Blaser (Duke University Press, 2018). She currently works with Santiago Martínez Medina on practices of cow-making in Colombia.

Santiago Martínez Medina is a Colombian anthropologist and physician. He works at Instituto de Investigación de Recursos Biológicos Alexander von Humboldt, Bogotá, Colombia. His latest publication is 'Corpo-real ethnographies: bodies, dissection planes, and cutting. Ethnography from the anatomy laboratory and public morgues in Colombia' (with Julia Morales-Fontanilla, *Tapuya: Latin American Science, Technology and Society*, 2019). He currently works with Marisol de la Cadena on practices of cow-making in Colombia.

Not quite clean: Trailing *schoon* and its resonances

The Sociological Review Monographs
2020, Vol. 68(2) 125–140
© The Author(s) 2020
Article reuse guidelines:
sagepub.com/journals-permissions
DOI: 10.1177/0038026120905489
journals.sagepub.com/home/sor

Annemarie Mol

Universiteit van Amsterdam [University of Amsterdam], The Netherlands

Abstract

When *words* are translated from one linguistic repertoire to another, their *resonances* stay behind. This is a challenge for those who write in academic English while working and living in another tongue. Here, I exemplify this with stories about the Dutch word *schoon*. The dictionary translates *schoon* into English as *clean*, but it is *not quite* clean. For a start, the songs, books and other cultural resources that resonate in *schoon* are distinctively local. Next, the particular sites (say, waste water treatment plants) where *schoon* is strived for differ from their (diverse) counterparts where English is spoken and the ambition is *clean*. And if *dirt* has notoriously been defined as 'matter out of place', this spatial thought would never have arisen in Dutch, because *vies*, the most prominent antonym of *schoon*, is invariably visceral. Finally, in urban settings in the Netherlands, *schoon* stands out as an aesthetic, a moral and a hygienic ideal; knowing whether this is also true for *clean* would require fieldwork in English (but where, in which English?). These examples suggests that hoping to purify one's theoretical notions of empirical filth is a monolingual delusion. For, however well-polished, English concepts will never have universal salience: they are just (a version of) English. Good academics therefore artfully, carefully, mind the gaps between different ways of knowing, acting and speaking.

Keywords

equivocation, material semiotics, multilingual, pollution

In academia, in my particular corner of the world as in many others, writing is first and foremost done in English. In the Netherlands, where I was born and raised and where I have been living for most of my 61 years, my colleagues and I are supposed to publish in so-called *international* journals – *international* being a euphemism for *English language*. But English is not our *first* language. We therefore live in translation, even those of us who never migrated.[1] Writing in English comes with rewards: it allows our texts to travel. In the 1980s, when I started out as an academic, I wrote texts in Dutch. It was frustrating that the authors on whose insights I gratefully built, or whose arguments I

Corresponding author:

Annemarie Mol, Department of Anthropology, Amsterdam Institute of Social Science Research, REC B5.10, Postbox 15509, Amsterdam, 1001 NA, The Netherlands.

Email: a.mol@uva.nl

proudly refuted, never took any notice.[2] And I couldn't blame them for it. I could read their English, French and German as Dutch schools insisted on the multilingual training of their students. But where and why should they have learned my Dutch? Once I started to go to international conferences, it became even more painful. I could tell people that I had written something that spoke to their concerns, but my texts remained opaque to them. So writing in English is wonderful in that it allows for intellectual exchanges beyond the relatively small circle of readers of Dutch. Exchanges, that is, with at least all academics who have had the chance and taken the trouble to acquire some proficiency in this particular imperialist tongue.[3] But this comes at a cost: within the Netherlands and Flanders what we write in English is, for all practical purposes, less accessible than what we write in Dutch.[4] And there are a few further complexities, too.

Of course it takes extra effort. A lot of it. With many years of training this improves a bit, but it doesn't go away. However, I am not out to seek your sympathy. Instead, I would like to take this occasion to address a matter of content. There are a lot of *resonances* to negotiate when one writes across different linguistic repertoires. For words do not just *refer* to entities that different languages cluster in different ways; with, say, the English word 'stone' representing a boulder, a pebble, a seed as well as a pit – entities not necessarily gathered together in other tongues. They do not just *do* things when used in practices; where, say, if one builder yells 'stone' to the other, this order, or request, may have the effect that a stone changes hands.[5] Words also *evoke*, there are absent/present realities that *resonate* within them; with the English word 'stone' calling up such things as stepping stones, including those that help people moving up socially, and rolling stones, including those that became legendary in the music scene. Such resonances are not simply characteristics of 'a language' – an allegedly well-rounded system of signs that may be caught within the confines of a dictionary. Instead, they have to do with all kinds of particularities of the practices in which words participate.[6] Some of these particularities I will touch upon in this text.

> *Touch upon*? That is English alright, but does it qualify as *academic* English? Maybe it sounds too light-hearted, superficial even, so that in one editorial round or another, someone with linguistic authority will change it into *present*. Should I maybe go for *exemplify* so as to underline that I am not after abstractions and generalities, but care about telling stories and specificities? *Analyse* is a possibility as well – that would also make things sound more serious, maybe, *analyse*, and stress that what I am up to is not just chatter but *theory*. Would it? And can I get away – in an academic text in English – with opening up questions and then never answering them?

The materials that I draw upon as I explore words-in-practices and their more or less elusive resonances all have to do with the positive qualification *clean*. But they are Dutch materials so what they turn around is *not quite* clean.

Cultural resonances

Anthropologists freely use the category of *Euro-American* when they make comparative contrasts with other large culture-clusters such as *Amerindian* or *Melanesian*. But as I move between different European languages I keep falling into gaps. These hinder smooth transitions from one tongue to another. They make life difficult for a Dutch scholar reading French and German and seeking to write in English. But they are also cracks through which the light gets in.

'There is a crack in everything; that's how the light gets in', Leonard Cohen sang. It is a beautiful line. And as it is widely known, in an English language text I might want to use it without even naming the source. That is what 'we' do. *We* use hidden references to constitute ourselves as a 'we', a collective in the know. The undertones resonating in such sentences pleasantly perform cultural connections between 'us'. But then again. Not every reader of the present text will *get* this reference. You may be too young to have absorbed Leonard Cohen songs; you may not like his music; or his lyrics; your head may be filled with Spanish, French or Bangla songs. Now that I have made my source explicit, though, you might want to look it up on *Spotify* or *YouTube*. The song where 'the light cracks in' is called *Anthem*.

Some resonances can be spelled out and explicated. With others this is far more difficult. Given that you are reading this text, it is likely that you have the technical facilities and the skills necessary to now trace Cohen's *Anthem* – even if you didn't know it before. But my guess is that (unless you happen to have been raised in Dutch) you will have more trouble with *Floddertje* and her dog, *Smeerkees*. While to me they loudly resonate in *schoon*, a Dutch word central to the research project that I just embarked upon.

The name Floddertje does not exist outside the stories about her written by Annie M. G. Schmidt in the early 1970s. It resonates with *sloddervos* – sloven – and *flodderig* – baggy – in a light, affectionate way, made manifest by the *tje*, a diminutive. Smeerkees is also a creative composition, this time of a *smeerpoets* – someone dirty, and *keeshond* – where *hond* is the Dutch word for what in English is called a dog and *kees*-hond a particular breed of dog. When I go online to find out if once again there are resources that I can point you to, I find a collection of Floddertje stories translated into English. But it is out of print. The blurb: '*Once there was a little girl called Scrumple who was always grimy and covered in dirt. Except when she'd just had a bath. But she could never stay clean for more than half an hour. Scrumple constantly needed another bath, together with her dog, Splotch, who was always filthy too . . .*' However hard the translator tried, these English names do not have as much splash as their Dutch not-quite-equivalents. They miss a particular poetry – rhythm, music – that enlivens the original.

'How do you know?' one of the readers of an earlier version asked. As if it were a scandal that I claim knowledge about how things sound in the English language even though it is not mine.

Annie M. G.'s humour does not easily transport either. She ingeniously plays with stereotypes to do with Dutch 'housewives' that stem from a historical moment when most women in the Netherlands were doomed to stay at home and overinvest in cleanliness. Annie M. G.'s way of surviving her sneakily sexist home country was to lighten it up with mockery.

An example. Floddertje's mother goes out to shop. Floddertje is eating but even so allows Smeerkees to climb onto her lap. He wags his tail which sends a slice of bread with jam into the air. As it falls, everything gets dirty – the tablecloth, Floddertje, her dress, Smeerkees. To solve this problem, Floddertje puts all these things in the bathtub along with the household's supplies of soaps and cleaning powders. Given that she is such a dirty child, supplies are ample. Floddertje opens the tap and as water pours into the bath, all too soon she cannot control the foam. To avoid drowning, she escapes into the street. The foam follows. People in the street get scared and call the fire brigade. The firemen disperse the foam with water. A lot of it. Until a brave fireman manages to enter the house, climb the stairs and close the tap. Now everyone is happy: the streets have never been this clean! Floddertje's mother comes back from the shop and reproves her for being naughty, but then again, look how clean you are! And so, too, are Smeerkees, the dress and the tablecloth.

I study the topic of *clean* with a heavy theoretical agenda and driven by serious societal and ecological concerns. At the same time, I cannot forget about Floddertje. I might, of course, use her as material; as an instance of a former *Dutchness* that by now has faded; a self-reflective figure lightly ironizing my field. But I wonder. That Floddertje resonates in the Dutch word *schoon* makes her absent/present when I study *clean*. But how exactly? Not just as a topic. I have been formed by Annie M. G. Schmidt's vicious humour and by the way she pointed out, time and again, the bizarre within the ordinary. This means that beyond being a part of my *field* Floddertje is a part of *me*. She has helped to shape my research abilities. She informs the *sensitivities* that inspire and direct my enquiries.

Floddertje is not the only Dutch figure to have shaped me. There are countless others. This being an academic text I might have foregrounded academic sources of inspiration. For instance, Lolle Nauta's argument that even theories that pretend to be abstract are best understood by foregrounding the 'exemplary situation' that, often by stealth, they reflect upon.[7] That is a relevant point of reference indeed. But when I study *clean* in everyday practices, my work is not just informed by theoretical repertoires, but also by the cultural resonances of the words relevant to those practices. *Schoon* resonates with *Floddertje*, not in 'the Dutch language', but in a gradually fading cultural repertoire articulated within that language.

Material resonances

In the Netherlands, waste water is pumped through the sewage system to what is called a *waterzuiveringsinstallatie*. *Water* = water; *zuivering* = purification; *installatie* = installation. When we were planning a field visit to one of these sites, I wrote to my colleagues, without having consulted a dictionary, that we were welcome at the Hilversum 'waste water cleaning plant'.[8] But in English, this plant doesn't *clean* waste water, it only *treats* it. Fair enough. Actually, in this instance, 'waste water treatment plant' is the better term, for while a lot of pollutants are retrieved in the plant, the effluent is far from *pure*. It has been purified only to the extent that it meets the legal standards of *clean* – which have to do with low enough nitrogen and phosphorus concentrations, on average, over the course of a year. But effluent still contains micropollutants – such as remnants of medicines and drugs and microplastics – and, added to that, it still contains microbes, too. You are not supposed to happily swim in water that a waste water treatment plant has just treated: it is not necessarily *swimmable*. And it is certainly not *drinkable*.

The plant in Hilversum that with six scholars based in Amsterdam we visit is remarkably clean. It is even its own kind of beautiful. The concrete of the buildings does not stand out as industrial white (like the waste water treatment plant two of us recently saw in Tilburg) and neither is it boringly grey (like the small one in De Meern where I went a few years ago on an open day). Different shades of warm red and light brown have been added irregularly, fluidly, to the sand-cement mixture and the result evokes *nature* rather than *technology*. The plant is adjacent to a small nature reserve and the hope was, we are told, that with its uneven, earthy colours it would blend in.

In the UK, Andrew Balmer and Susan Molyneux-Hodgson have explored the differences between waste water treatment plants and laboratories. 'Much like the laboratory, the sewage works is full of peculiar shapes, sounds and smells. But by contrast to our laboratory-experiences of bacteria as manipulable and yet vulnerable, and of the body as a danger to the bacteria, when one approaches the waste water sewage facility it is the body that is at risk in this immediately daunting and threatening landscape.'[9] Before reading the text from which I quote here, I didn't know the words 'sewage works' and 'sewage facility'. Apparently 'waste water treatment plant' is not the only name for this place in English. It is rather, or so I learn when asking someone in the know about it, a recent invention, crafted to avoid the harshness of 'sewage'. I am yet more surprised by the insistence on grime. In their field, or so Balmer and Molyneux-Hodgson tell, bacteria are lurking everywhere, not just in the sewage: 'in the water treatment facility . . . everything is a murky brown that has to be scrubbed and blasted off the body and other surfaces' (p. 68).

The library of the University of Amsterdam does not provide me with access to the journal *Engineering Studies*. Hence, I have only been able to read the article just quoted because Andrew Balmer was kind enough to send it to me after (even though we never met) I asked for it in an email. Grateful for his collegial kindness, I respond after reading. I quote from my email: 'what struck me, too, was that by contrast to the muddiness you describe, the waste water treatment plants in NL that we visited are meticulously kept clean – we didn't even have dirty shoes when we left. There are the tanks of course; and handling those, or otherwise doing maintenance work, will be messy and dirty (our field work did not yet include any of that, we just "visited") but my impression was that cleanliness was part of local pride.' Andrew, in an email back, presumed that we visited a place for purifying drinking water: 'we have a strict separation in the UK between the clean water facility and the waste water facility. This is reflected in the amount of time engineers put into maintaining the space surrounding the water. So it really is a muddy nightmare outside, and then very clean indoors.' But in our Dutch field, the separation between treating sewage and purifying drinking water goes a lot further. It is not an outdoors/indoors affair, drinking water is 'produced' in another site altogether. It is really the *waste water treatment plant* that is clean. When in a further email I underline this, Andrew jokes back: 'That is so impressive. Another reason to move to the Netherlands!'

Here is my puzzle. It is not that waste water treatment plants are different between the Netherlands and the UK. It is that getting to *know* about such differences seems to be necessary before I am able to write in English. And how do I get to know about the practices that English words incorporate, from the grime (mentioned in the original article) to the location of drinking water in relation to waste water cleaning (that I only learn about from Andrew's email)? There must be lots of further differences about which I have no inkling, even though they have serious consequences for what resonates in the English words that I may use when writing about this or that Dutch case. Learning that in English I should say 'waste water treatment' rather than 'waste water cleaning' is just the easy bit. The dictionary bit. It is a lot more difficult to find out about the realities that resonate within such words. The problems of writing in English stretch way beyond *English*.

The three waste water treatment plants that I so far visited in the Netherlands all have different colours: white washed; desolate grey; beautiful red-brownish. From that contrast I may conclude that the colour of the structures that make up waste water treatment facilities is not self-evident. But all three plants were clean. How, then, am I supposed to know that this is not the case elsewhere? And no, I do not insist on this cleanliness to suggest to my UK colleagues that the Netherlands is a better place to live. I say it to point at a particular difficulty of writing in a foreign tongue. Even if I use 'proper' English words, words that even a severe editor is unlikely to interfere with, they may not transport what I hope to say. For while for me they speak of my Dutch field, they may resonate with quite different realities for those who get to read my texts.

> If stories are about so-called 'far away' countries, we expect as much. *Of course* the treatment of sewage in Senegal or Bangladesh deserves to be explained to the readers of 'international' texts written in English. They – we? – are unlikely to have been there. But there also are differences between adjacent places in regions termed *Euro-American*. And how can I know what exactly these differences are without *doubling* my research and doing it in *English* as well as in *Dutch*? Added to that, in *which* English should I do added fieldwork – that of Durham UK, Durban SA, Dunedin NZ, or elsewhere yet again? And if I were to double, triple, quadruple my fieldwork, then what to attend to and what to leave be? Between different sites, there is no end to the specificities an author might try to explicate.

Words mean different things, not just between different languages, but also between different sites and situations. Different realities resonate within them.[10] In some cases and to some extent it is possible to spell this out. This is what fieldwork is about, after all. As a field worker you try to describe a site so that others, who haven't been there, get some sense of it. But here is my point. When it comes to it, ethnography is premised on the *exemplary situation* of the traveller who comes home to tell her tales. It presumes that someone who is one of *us* goes to a faraway place and then comes back to explain to *us* how *they* are different. *We* are the implied audience and since the author is a part of *us* she knows what about *them* to write down and make explicit. She knows what *we* take for granted and what *we* are bound to consider surprising.

But how can *I* know what *you* consider surprising? From language courses, novels and films I may learn *English*. But there is a lot that I do not know about 'readers of English' and their everyday realities. And if kind colleagues from the UK help me to attune my texts to the realities of 'sewage facilities' in that country, that still only goes so far. English is not euphemised as 'international' for nothing. *You* may be reading my words in Rio de Janeiro, Saint Petersburg, Osaka. How to guess what you hold to be self-evident, possible, or unimaginable? How to fine tune what needs to be said *in so many words* and what may be lightly skipped over? It is possible to tell fine stories, attentive to their details. But it is impossible to articulate all the resonances that echo in all their words. Hence, when texts travel, they are bound to transform along the way.

This is my point: Not only translations are betrayals. A lot also transforms between authors and readers of English who work in different sites and situations. Even a banal description of a waste water treatment plant cannot be properly tamed, but stubbornly defies transportation. So much, then, for the dream of stable analytic categories, firm concepts, universally salient theory.[11]

Semantic resonances

The most likely antonym of *schoon* – a Dutch word translating the English *clean* – is *vies*. If Floddertje and Smeerkees are *not* 'schoon', they are 'vies'. But that does not turn *vies* into an equivalent of *dirty*. If only translation were that simple! It isn't. Even in cases where two words map on to one another relatively neatly, their antonyms may go off in different directions. And here is what makes *vies* so interesting: it is not just an antonym of *schoon*, but also of *lekker*.

Lekker translates into English as *tasty* or *delicious*. While it used to pertain only to food, more recently it has widened out to other sensuous pleasures.[12] Yes, sex may be *lekker*, even if 50 years ago, when sex was more seriously sanctified, that sounded vulgar. Agreeable weather is *lekker*; pleasantly fitting clothes are *lekker*; and even work may be *lekker*: it is on days when things flow. *Vies* is a relevant antonym in some of these cases. Food is *vies* when it is unpalatable. Sex used to be *vies*, before it was *lekker*, as unless it was holy, it was shameful – but now it no longer is. The weather is *vies* when it is too wet to cycle. Clothing is *lekker* when it fits nicely, but when it is *vies* it needs a wash. Some work is *vies*, as it involves handling dirt or excrement, but working when one has no flow, while unpleasant, is not *vies*.

I greatly enjoy all these details, but I fear that for you they might be too much. So instead of further expanding this complex, criss-crossing semiotic network, I will zoom in on a *point*. Which is that the gap between *vies* and *dirty* may well be one of these cracks through which the light gets in.

In the social sciences Mary Douglas's assertion that *dirt is matter out of place* is repeated again and again. In its original incarnation – presented in the book *Purity and Danger* – it was an original idea.[13] But it has become a mantra and I wonder if it deserves to be endlessly reiterated. Douglas's concern was with categories. As she wrote that *dirt is matter out of place*, she was at the same time talking about situations in which categories need to be kept apart; circumstances in which it is ill advised to mix them up. Her *clean*, then, beyond its material incarnations, is about symbolic distinctiveness.

In English, it is possible to distinguish between 'cleaning up' and 'clearing up'. But if Douglas defines uncleanliness as 'matter out of place', she blurs that distinction and makes *cleaning* and *clearing* flow over into each other. What is matter *in* place? When I try to imagine that, I dream up the higher middle class English households that figured in the children's books that I read – translated into Dutch – around the time Douglas presented *impurity* as a categorical danger. There, children were tasked to tidy the room where they had been playing. Puzzles, dolls and Dinky toys: they all had their own particular spot on a shelf in a designated cupboard. This seems to be the *exemplary situation* that best illuminates what it means to have a *proper place*. This situation may not be *English* so much as *Douglas*. But it is definitely *not* Dutch.

The English expression 'clean and tidy' suggests that these are different things, but it also makes it easy for *clean* and *tidy* to flow over into each other. This is far more difficult in Dutch. For when things have been put in their proper place, a Dutch playroom (living room, bedroom, office) is *opgeruimd*. *Opgeruimd* bespeaks a spatial concern – the noun *ruimte* translates into *space*; the verb *ruimen* evokes displacing, and *opruimen* (which has *opgeruimd* as it past perfect) is putting things in their designated place. But *schoon* has nothing to do with places. As *vies* is its most prominent antonym, *schoon* sides with *lekker* in that something that is <u>not</u> *schoon* is disgusting. *Schoon* and *vies* bespeak concerns that, rather than spatial, are <u>visceral</u>.

Schoon calls up a floor that is no longer sticky, a dress without stains, a body that smells of soap, not sweat. The *schoon/vies* pair could never have illuminated a theoretical argument about the need to separate out categories. Instead, it suggests the need to spare sensitivities.

Do I have the right to claim this? When two so-called *native speakers* of English commented on an earlier version of this text, the first insisted that I am mistaken about English. In daily life, he noted, *clean* and *tidy* are *actually* markedly different and *clean* is about sensitivities, too. After all, next to *dirty* its antonyms also include *filthy* and *disgusting*. That was disappointing. Maybe I had to bow to his authority – English, after all, is not *my* language – but what, then, about Douglas and her 'matter out of place'? As I was wondering, the comments of the second reader came in. He wrote in the margins of my text that *clean* and *tidy* are *actually* hardly distinct at all. Or maybe, he added, this is just me, as in my daily life they amount to the same thing: housework that calls out to be done. The disjunction between my friends made me laugh.

Here is what I dare to write, then. I do not claim that infringing on the good of *cleanliness* is never sensitive. Instead, I claim that *schoon* is never spatial.

Words are not just spoken in practices, they also bespeak practices. This means that specific *exemplary situations* may hide, absent/present, within those words.[14] If you listen out for them, it is possible to hear them resonating. This helps in getting a better grasp on the strength and limits of the theories articulated in those words. The particular *pollution* that Douglas was concerned with in *Purity and Danger* could be remedied with *tidying*. It was dirt that, by putting it to one side, on a shelf, or in a bin, could be cleaned away. But the dangers that follow on from things being *vies* cannot be remedied in the same way. Cleaning something that is *vies* involves gut feelings. It is not a matter of transport but of transformation. Hence, theories articulated with the help of the *schoon/vies* pair are bound to go in different directions than theories informed by Douglas's *dirt is matter out of place*.

Mind you, I am not out to advocate 'Dutch theory'. I rather suggest that taking a detour through any language that is *not* English may help to shake up theoretical short-cuts that are *not just* specific to this or that theorist, but *also* depend on (a particular version of) English.

Douglas could never have written *Purity and Danger* in Dutch, for it would not have made sense to define *vies* in a spatial way. But what about English: do, after all these years, the dangers of uncleanliness still deserve to be theorised in a spatial way? Maybe that epoch is over. Who still dreams up nurseries to be tidied? And who, for that matter, still equates *pollution* with *dirt*? These days, the more striking *exemplar* of dangerous uncleanliness is rather the emptied plastic bottle.[15] Where is this *not* out of place?

Multilingual resonances

The dictionary suggests that the English word *clean* happily translates into the Dutch word *schoon*. But *schoon* is not quite *clean*. It has a more pronounced visceral twist. In addition, *schoon* also suggests an aesthetic pleasure that differs from the modernist ideals that have come to infuse *clean*. Clean calls up well-ordered categorisations, signals without noise, and buildings without frills – in a way that *schoon* does not.[16]

In Limburg, the southern region of the Netherlands where I grew up, *schoon* is pronounced as *sjoûn* and translates into English as *beautiful*. Despite almost two centuries of trying, language boundaries in this corner of the world do not coincide with those of nation states. The *sjoûn* of Limburg is quite like the *schön* of the German spoken only a few kilometres away, across the border. A dress that is *sjoûn* has not just been washed and ironed, but its colours are pleasant and its fit is flattering. A *sjoûn* house has fine windows and rooms of an appealing size, not too small, not too big. And then it is possible to compliment someone by saying that they have accomplished a task in a *sjoûn* way. In this usage, the word widens out from 'beautiful' to express a more general positive apprehension.

In the northwest of the Netherlands *schoon* no longer translates as *beautiful*. But *schoonheid* – the noun made out of the adjective – still translates as *beauty*. Small wonder, then, that for those who listen out for historical traces, dialects and adjacent languages, the aesthetic resonance of *schoon* is acute. When English words have such half-hidden resonances, I risk missing them. Hence, I make mistakes. I write sentences which, by stealth, say things that I do not particularly want to say. If I am lucky, an avid English colleague or editor remarks on this and – caringly, brutally – corrects me. I am truly grateful for this; even if sometimes I struggle to defend my points. However, while those of us who cannot claim authority over English are bound to err, we also have something to offer. We may *add in* a few resonances that echo within *our own words* and think with them. In the case in point: as I do fieldwork into *clean* – or rather *schoon* – I wonder about the aesthetics relevant to local practices.

For an evening, I trail a group of men and their machines as they energetically clean streets and squares after one of Amsterdam's day markets. Every morning the market stalls are laid out, every evening they are packed up again. Stall holders are supposed to put their debris in the large yellow plastic bags that they receive for this purpose from the organization that runs the market. But not all of them do. Customers, in their turn, are supposed to throw their waste in one of the bins that adorn the sides of the road. But not all of them do. Hence, by five in the afternoon, when the cleaners arrive, everything is messy and smelly. By nine, when they leave again, they have made an impressive, positive difference. That is part of what turns cleaning up after the market into a gratifying job. 'You arrive and the entire stretch is messy and *smerig* [filthy, like Smeerkees]. And then, when you leave, well – things look *mooi schoon* again.'

Here, the *mooi* is added to *schoon*. *Mooi* is a modest kind of beauty; or it may, as it does here, strengthen a word that already has a positive ring to it. In this little sentence fragment, the *mooi* stresses the *schoon*'s aesthetic undertones. When the street and squares are *mooi schoon* as all the debris has been trucked out (off to the incinerator), they are not simply well-ordered, but, more positive than that, look *nice*. All the cleaning efforts lead to them being *pretty*.

Harry, the foreman of the group, takes me on a walk through the neighbourhood in which the market is situated. In this part of Amsterdam, inhabitants are supposed to put their garbage in underground containers. If they have stuff that is too large, they are supposed to call a special phone number and set an appointment for the truck for *grof vuil* – large, bulky, heavy waste – to come and fetch it. But this isn't always done. People often put their bulky stuff out on the street, preferably near the underground containers. While this location shows their good will, it is counterproductive. For if there is stuff on the platforms attached to the underground containers, the designated machines are unable to lift up the containers and cannot empty their contents into the truck meant to carry it away. First, the garbage men have to get out and shift the stuff away. This is unpractical and when a single man is alone on his truck, it is often difficult, it takes time, it may be heavy. Pointing to a set of cardboard boxes, just next to a container, one that isn't full at all, Harry turns to me and asks: 'Do you understand that? Why do people *do* that?'

When Harry asks me why people 'do that', improperly putting boxes next to a container, he does not expect me to give an answer. I might have invented one. I could have replied that some people don't understand this business with the phone number; that the cardboard boxes are not easy to fold, especially for people who are not as strong as he is; or that it is interesting that people at least take the trouble to carry their boxes from their house to the container. But all of this would have been beside the point. Then and there, Harry is not inquisitive but exasperated. He himself is fully committed to making this neighbourhood *mooi schoon*. Then why are the locals so negligent, so insensitive, so painfully *improper*?

Schoon is not the only Dutch word that translates into English as *clean*. Another one is *proper*. Yes, this is a Dutch word. It is written in the same way as the English *proper*, but it is pronounced with a long o – proo-per. This term has moral undertones. This might come as no surprise for speakers of English, as the English *proper* is all about morality – the cleanliness having seeped out of it – despite its prominence in the French word *propre*.

When we walk back to the truck that brought us to the market, I come across a single spot where beneath my boots the stones feel slippery and sticky. The lingering smell is disagreeable as well. Carefully, I suggest this, but Harry immediately, defensively, replies that if only I had been here earlier, I wouldn't say this. The difference is truly impressive. This spot was very oily and very smelly only two hours ago. Here, the fishmonger has been selling fish, both fresh and deep fried. Fat leaks from his car. Added to that, people have discarded remnants of their fried fish on the pavement. So, too, have the herons, that also freely spread their excrement. 'A few years ago, there was a strike', Harry says, 'all cleaners were on strike. But I would still come here and work this part. For things need to be clean here. Hygienic. People come and eat here.'

If streets and squares are *aesthetically schoon* such prettiness is pleasing: it adds to Harry's job satisfaction. His dissatisfaction takes a *moral* turn: why do people *do* this? And then there appears to be yet another way of valuing that is highly relevant to cleaning up after the market, one in which the good to be served is that of *hygiene*. People who eat food from market stalls should not catch infectious diseases. Bugs are to be scrubbed away. They are to be killed with strong cleaning fluids. By men who are truly dedicated and who, beyond disputes about their salary, want eaters to be safe.

> *Schoon* is a composite value, it calls up different kinds of good. In trailing Harry and his men, I come across aesthetic, moral and hygienic repertoires of valuing.[17] I wonder if all three goods at stake – beautiful, proper, safe – resonate as loudly in *clean*. But how might I find out? I can ask my helpful English friends, but they have not done fieldwork with cleaners of a day market. They may know a lot about the word *clean* in other sites and situations, but not about the way it figures in my (or an equivalent, but what would be an equivalent?) field.

In the Dutch semantic network that includes *schoon* and *proper* and *puur* there are yet more related terms, notably *zuiver* and *rein*. If you speak German, you might recognise *sauber* and *rein*. A clean conscience is *zuiver*; and waste water, as we saw above, is submitted to *zuivering*. *Rein* is somewhat old fashioned, but the verb *reinigen* is still in use for particular kinds of cleaning, such as dry-cleaning, carpet cleaning and skin cleaning. What is more, these words are pertinent in practices beyond households, sewage systems, markets, hospitals and the beauty industry. In practices, that is, to do with theory.

> As I assemble resonances and slippages between the few closely related European languages that I have access to, I cannot help thinking of the different translations of the *clean reasoning* that stood out as an icon of the Enlightenment. In German, Kant wrote a *Kritik der **reinen** Vernuft*; in French this became the *Critique de la raison **pure***; in English it was translated into the *Critique of **pure** reason*; and while both *rein* and *puur* would have made sense in Dutch, the Dutch version contains a third term, it is called *Kritiek van de **zuivere** rede*. Should we indeed wash our words until they are clean and shining? I wonder whether calling for theory that is *schoon* might be an improvement here. My hope is not particularly with its hygienic or its moral overtones, but rather with its third layer, its promising aesthetics.

To conclude

Academic authors tend to put a lot of effort into closing down the gaps between the different variants of the terms they use. Hoping to build transportable theories, they celebrate 'the concept' – an honourable title given to a word defined in such a solid way that it is able to travel throughout a research project, between research fields, or even across disciplines, without transforming. However, if words are entangled with their semiotic as well as their practical contexts, it is impossible to make them immutable while they move between settings.[18] The dream of 'the concept' is faltering.

That words adapt is true *within* any so-called 'language', but the impossibility of semantic stability is all the more striking once you move *between* 'languages'. Elsewhere, this has been laid out and exemplified in work on the limits of translation.[19] In the present article, building on those insights, I have discussed it in the slightly different circumstances of the author who cannot claim full authority over English, but still knows enough English – but what is enough? – to write in it.[20]

But if words cannot be fully stabilised, the idea that this might be possible is consequential. It means that some words gain prominence while others are sidelined; and that dominant meanings are strengthened while lesser ones are marginalised or lost. In as far as academic work is done in English, this affects not just English, but also academic work.[21] It leads to an undue linguistic impoverishment of English language linguistic repertoires and, added to that, foregoes the enrichment on offer in other tongues. In the present text, I have attended to a particular kind of richness, that of the *resonances* that echo within words. I have provided examples of cultural, material, semantic and multilingual resonances by visiting a few situations where the words *schoon* or *clean* are *spoken* and to situations that these words *bespeak*.

> Can I use the word *bespeak*, is that okay? My first English reader edited it away. The second wrote in the margin that he liked the fact that I revitalised this *old fashioned* term. I had no idea it was old fashioned. Can I use it?

Recognising the fluidity, adaptability, multiplicity, relationality – the context dependency – of words has consequences for theory. For, as it is, the social sciences harbour *theories* about such phenomena as taste, values, morality, materiality, inequality, work – what have you. These *theories* are made to travel: from the UK to the Netherlands; from France to Brazil; from Chicago to South Africa and back again.[22] The suggestion is that 'taste', 'values', 'morality' and so on are the same *thing* from one site to the next. But they are not.[23] That even between English and Dutch, closely related languages, there are impressive gaps, might serve to underscore this.

> While the word *schoon* may resonate with Floddertje, the word *clean* does not. While in the Netherlands a 'waste water treatment plant' is a clean place, in the UK it is not. While Douglas used a spatial version of 'clean' to argue for washed out, distinct categories, in terms of 'schoon' this would never have made any sense. The word *schoon* moves between aesthetic, moral and hygienic repertoires of valuing – and to know whether the word *clean* does as well, I would have to do added fieldwork (but where?). In the semantic networks that afford words with their meaning, *schoon* is related to the Dutch *proper, rein, puur* and *zuiver* – but also to the German *schön, rein* and *sauber* and the French *propre* – in ways that *clean* is not. Such a small linguistic distance; so many gaps!

What to conclude? One possibility is to acknowledge slippages but still aim for a theory that is 'as coherent as possible'. The other is to attend upfront to *things that do not fit*. To control, or, better still, to care for equivocations.[24] To juxtapose stories without seeking to fuse them. To craft patchworks in which the threads that connect the pieces together are clearly visible. Or, to shift back from visuals to sounds again: to sing tunes that are polyphonous; or to keep diverse resonances audible, even if they are dissonant.

The format of this text resonates with this way of understanding *theory*. I have not presented you with a firm, overall proposition supported by subservient facts that are staged as if I am out to win an argument. Instead, I have assembled examples of what *resonance* may be and what, in these cases, its implications are. And no, this is not a *Dutch* format. Instead, it is informed by the pains and pleasures of moving and moving again between different linguistic repertoires.

Acknowledgements

Thanks for their support with the writing of, and their comments on, this particular text to a few so called 'native speakers' of English, notably John Law, Nick Bingham and Andrew Balmer; of Dutch, Mieke Aerts, Ignace Schoot, Thomas Franssen, Mandy de Wilde and Jeroen Boomgaard; of German, Anja Novak; and of French, Justine Laurent. Thanks as well to 'the informants', anonymised here as per my ethnographer's duty, who taught me/us a lot about *schoon* and other variants of clean. I also would like to thank the Netherlands Organization for Scientific Research for the Spinoza Prize that pays for half of my research time and for the salaries of shifting, spirited junior colleagues.

Funding

The author received financial support for the research and authorship of this article from the Netherlands Organization for Scientific Research.

Notes

1. That migration may come with bewildering effects of getting lost between languages is forcefully brought across in the remembrance, and analysis, of migrating from Polish in Poland to English in Canada in the book *Lost in Translation* (Hoffman, 1989). This title is used elsewhere, too, but this book stands out.
2. To remedy such lack of travel in at least a few cases, the journal *MAT* (*Medical Anthropology Theory*) started a series called *Found in Translation*. Here, in 2015, I was allowed to publish a belated translation of my 1985 article *Wie weet wat een vrouw is* – Who knows what a woman is. See for this, with a retrospective introduction, Mol (2015).
3. About how English got there, see De Swaan (2013). There are competing imperialist tongues around, like Spanish, but while they are imposed on in-country minorities, they have less traction across the borders of the nations where they are dominant.
4. This is not necessarily a matter of competence; the potential readership tends to understand English quite well. Other practicalities come into play. For example, Dutch language academic journals that used to cater to an interdisciplinary readership no longer exist because 'we' publish in specialist journals in English. There is of course discussion about this – in Dutch. Should I quote that? What does a reference to a Dutch book affect in a text in English (Boomkens, 2008)?
5. This stone-story forms the opening vignette of Wittgenstein's fabulous *Philosophical Investigations* that also leaves further traces in the present text (Wittgenstein, 1953/2009).
6. The shift from language-as-a-system to language-in-practice is clearly presented in Pennycook (2010).
7. For example, when Sartre theorised 'the stranger' in general terms he talked by stealth about the people one sees passing by when hanging out in a Parisian side walk cafe (Nauta, 1990). In a festschrift for Nauta, I first cast this idea in an auditory metaphor and wrote about *undertones* and *overtones* (Mol, 1994).

8. Thanks for a fun joint field visit and interesting discussions about it to Justine Laurent, Carolina Dominguez, Rebeca Ibañez Martín, Tait Mandler, Fenna Smits and Jeffrey Christensen.
9. Balmer and Molyneux-Hodgson (2013). I thank both authors for their work; and Andrew Balmer for his permission to quote from our email correspondence.
10. This is also why 'translation' has been mobilised as a metaphor for how realities (things, techniques) may relate from one setting to the next and why what later came to be known as 'actor network theory' was, early on, termed 'a sociology of translation' (Callon, 1984).
11. See also Strathern's to-and-fro between the categories of 'the field' and those used for 'analysis' (e.g. Strathern, 2004). Building on that, Law and Lin use Chinese terms to analyse fieldwork done in England (Law & Lin, 2018). What I am adding here is a further instability: that of ignorance about the empirical realities, not of 'the other', but of 'the reader'.
12. The term 'lekker' forms the focal point of a more extensive trailing (Mol, 2014).
13. The source text is more directly discussing categorisation and religion than dirty nurseries, water or streets (Douglas, 1966).
14. The notion absent/present is more extensively explored in Law (2002).
15. For how we got in this dire situation, see e.g. Hawkins (2011); and the contributions to Gabrys et al. (2013).
16. For a critique of the modernist dream of cleanliness and purity and a defence of the 'excluded third', the mess, the noise allowing for the signal, see Serres (2013).
17. Or, one might say in French, *économies de la grandeur* – translated into English as *economies of worth*. See Boltanski and Thévenot (2006).
18. The argument that here I make about *words* resembles – resonates with – earlier arguments made in *material semiotics* about the fluidity of techniques and technologies. See among others: Mol and Law (1994) and De Laet and Mol (2000).
19. For the case of philosophy, see the contributions to the fabulous Cassin et al. (2014).
20. Commenting on a previous version, Jeroen Boomgaard pointed out that in my analysis I follow the *author* and skip the work that *readers* do to remedy poor transportability. As readers, he insisted, we learn to adapt our understanding of what we read to what we know about the sources of a text. An intriguing further complexity, indeed.
21. For the argument that current academic repertoires are stuck in what can be said in English, argued through extensively analysed examples, see Wierzbicka (2013). Wierzbicka, however, believes that it is possible to use a simplified neutral language that travels across linguistic boundaries – thus disentangling 'language' from 'practices' in a way that goes in the opposite direction from what I am arguing here.
22. For more on the issue of *other kinds of English*, see Pennycook and Makoni (2019).
23. For the case of taste and tasting, see Mann and Mol (2019).
24. See for the notion of controlled equivocation, Viveiros de Castro (2004). And for the argument that equivocations may deserve care even as they defy control Yates-Doerr (2019).

References

Balmer, A. S., & Molyneux-Hodgson, S. (2013). Bacterial cultures: Ontologies of bacteria and engineering expertise at the nexus of synthetic biology and water services, *Engineering Studies*, 5, 59–73.

Boltanski, L., & Thévenot, L. (2006). *On justification: Economies of worth*. Princeton University Press.

Boomkens, R. W. (2008). *Topkitsch en slow science: kritiek van de academische rede*. [Superkitsch and slow science: critique of academic reason]. Van Gennep.

Callon, M. (1984). Some elements of a sociology of translation: Domestication of the scallops and the fishermen of St Brieuc Bay. *The Sociological Review*, 32, 196–233.

Cassin, B., Apter, E., Lezra, J., & Wood, M. (Eds.). (2014). *Dictionary of untranslatables: A philosophical lexicon* (Vol. 35). Princeton University Press.

De Laet, M., & Mol, A. (2000). The Zimbabwe bush pump: Mechanics of a fluid technology. *Social Studies of Science, 30*, 225–263.

De Swaan, A. (2013). *Words of the world: The global language system*. Polity Press.

Douglas, M. (1966). *Purity and danger: An analysis of the concepts of pollution and taboo.* Routledge.

Gabrys, J., Hawkins, G., & Michael, M. (Eds.). (2013). *Accumulation: The material politics of plastic*. Routledge.

Hawkins, G. (2011). Packaging water: Plastic bottles as market and public devices. *Economy and Society, 40*, 534–552.

Hoffman, E. (1989). *Lost in translation: A life in a new language*. Vintage Publishing.

Law, J. (2002). *Aircraft stories: Decentering the object in technoscience*. Duke University Press.

Law, J., & Lin, W. Y. (2018). Tidescapes: Notes on a shi (勢)-inflected social science. *Journal of World Philosophies, 3*, 1–16.

Mann, A., & Mol, A. (2019). Talking pleasures, writing dialects: Outlining research on schmecka. *Ethnos, 84*, 772–788.

Mol, A. (1994). Ondertonen en boventonen. Over empirische filosofie [Undertones and overtones. About empirical philosophy]. In D. Pels & G. de Vries (Eds.), *Burgers en Vreemdelingen* [Citizens and strangers] (pp. 77–84). Van Gennep.

Mol, A. (2014). Language trails: 'Lekker' and its pleasures. *Theory, Culture & Society, 31*, 93–119.

Mol, A. (2015). Who knows what a woman is . . . On the differences and the relations between the sciences, *Medical Anthropology Theory, 2*, 57–75.

Mol, A., & Law, J. (1994). Regions, networks and fluids: Anaemia and social topology. *Social Studies of Science, 24*, 641–671.

Nauta, L. W. (1990). De subcultuur van de wijsbegeerte: een privé geschiedenis van de filosofie [The subculture of philosophy: a private history of the discipline]. *Krisis, 38*, 5–19.

Pennycook, A. (2010). *Language as a local practice*. Routledge.

Pennycook, A., & Makoni, S. (2019). *Invitations and challenges in applied linguistics from the global South*. Routledge.

Serres, M. (2013). *The parasite*. University of Minnesota Press.

Strathern, M. (2004). *Partial connections: Updated edition*. Rowman & Littlefield.

Viveiros de Castro, E. (2004). Perspectival anthropology and the method of controlled equivocation. *Tipití: Journal of the Society for the Anthropology of Lowland South America, 2*, 3–22.

Wierzbicka, A. (2013). *Imprisoned in English: The hazards of English as a default language*. Oxford University Press.

Wittgenstein, L. (2009). *Philosophical investigations*. John Wiley and Sons. (Original work published 1953).

Yates-Doerr, E. (2019). Whose global, which health? Unsettling collaboration with careful equivocation. *American Anthropologist, 121*, 297–310.

Author biography

Annemarie Mol is a Professor of Anthropology of the Body at the University of Amsterdam. She has written about the coordination of different enactments of an allegedly single disease in hospital practice; theorised *care* as intertwined with, rather than opposed to, technology; explored how our theoretical tropes change if, instead of continuing to celebrate human thinking, we foreground human eating; and is currently embarking on an enquiry into *clean* as a *good*. All the while she reflectively attends to words and styles of writing.

Article

The Sociological Review Monographs
2020, Vol. 68(2) 141–157
© The Author(s) 2020
Article reuse guidelines:
sagepub.com/journals-permissions
DOI: 10.1177/0038026120905490
journals.sagepub.com/home/sor

Toward knowing: Engaging Chinese medical worlds

Lili Lai
北京大学, Beijing Daxue [Peking University], China

Judith Farquhar
Department of Anthropology, University of Chicago, USA

Abstract

This discussion opens with a puzzling statement from the analects of Confucius: *When you know it you know it, when you don't know, you don't know. This is knowledge.* Reflecting on various Chinese approaches to *zhi* (知), knowing/knowledge, in this article we re-explore the terrain we two authors covered together in recent research on minority nationality medical systems of southwestern China. Our itineraries drew us near to 'folk' approaches to knowing, evident both in practical medical work and in classic written sources. We found ourselves in that frictional field of medicine where expertise is not just possession of knowledge, it is also skills, politics, ethics, manipulations, ideologies, and more than one set of ontological assumptions. Reminded of some ancient Chinese metaphysical philosophy, we were led by healers to conclude that knowing and good action cannot be separated. The article reports visits to three mountain herbalists, describing the particular ways they practice knowing and use their expertise to treat difficult disorders. On the road through a mostly unknowable world, such Chinese healers expect transformations in both those who know and in what can be known and enacted. These lives teach us how to know not through concepts but through the irreducible patterning of life.

Keywords

Confucian epistemology, folk medicine, knowledge, southwest China

知之为知之，不知为不知，是知也。
Zhizhi wei zhi zhi, buzhi wei buzhi. Shi zhi ye.
Knowing it is knowing it, not knowing is not knowing. This is the way to know.

(*Analects* of Confucius, Ch. 2:17, 4th–3rd century BCE)

Corresponding author:
Lili Lai, School of Health Humanities, Peking University, No. 38 Xueyuan Lu, Beijing, 100191, China.
Email: lai_lili@pku.edu.cn

These lines come from the *Analects* of Confucius, which makes this proverbial statement very old indeed. The sentiment is ancient but far from forgotten. We doubt whether it has ever gone out of use in everyday speech since a disciple of the 'First Teacher' wrote it down and added it to a lot of other jottings from conversations with the Master.[1] As teachers, for example, we find '*zhizhi wei zhizhi*' a useful piece of advice for college thesis writers, who need to make the authorities for their arguments clear (show me how you know it) and state explicitly the questions that remain unanswered (which is to say, not knowing, *buzhi*, is not simple ignorance, or error, it has a structural job to do). More casual and proverbial usages abound.

There are many ways *zhizhi wei zhizhi* could be translated, and translations that make the statement more logical and didactic in English would, perhaps, render the thought of Confucius more globally respectable as epistemology and ethics, not just as homely 'Confucius says' advice.[2] But with our cryptic and very literal rendering above we are giving up at once, refusing to make non-circular commonsense out of it. Even so, *zhi* (知 knowing, usually translated as knowledge) is precisely the 'other term' we want to re-translate and problematize in this chapter. In place of definitions and commonsense distinctions (e.g., between knowledge and belief, between knowledge and ignorance, or even between knowing the truth and being in error), we propose in what follows to trace some paths trodden by people who take both *zhi* and *buzhi* quite seriously, even as their knowing practice evades all simple characterization. Their understanding slips through gaps in what is known, their itineraries find a way between *zhi* and *buzhi*.[3]

Our research over the last 10 years has focused on minority nationality medical systems as they are emerging among seven registered ethnic groups in China's south. Much to our surprise, writing about this experience has returned us to classical Chinese philosophy. What follows here, then, is both philosophical and ethnographic, but we mostly eschew anthropology and philosophy of science approaches to problems of knowledge in Chinese medical worlds. This discussion is not intended to be a critique of modern Anglophone epistemology, nor does it propose radical cultural difference as a challenge to commonsense. Instead we introduce a few terms of art from the Confucian tradition, and certain knowing practices found 'on the ground' in China, striving to connect something *other* with the way 'we' (we two authors and the diverse readers of this monograph) already know in practice. In other words, philosophical writing in Chinese has helped us, as anthropologists, better appreciate the knowing practices of the herbalists we have encountered in China's southern mountains.[4] Whatever was meant by that quasi-historical figure Confucius when he spoke of knowing and not knowing, his words can be used to open up unexpected new worlds.

Goldstamp Huang: Do you believe in fate?

In the course of anthropological field research in southern China, we met Dr Goldstamp Huang,[5] a senior practitioner in a Yao nationality medicine hospital. Having been introduced by Yang Jian, our research associate, who was interning with Dr Huang, we followed him one morning as he began his rounds in the inpatient ward of this 40-bed hospital. He went first to see a 50-year-old patient diagnosed with lymphoma. He told us she had been through six rounds of chemotherapy over the past six years. Her current main complaint was a terrible ulcer near her left popliteal lymph node. Dr Huang examined the open sore closely, then he left. Yang Jian told us that he was going downstairs to prepare a very special herbal plaster. She had already said that Dr Huang had been trying to find a certain special herb for this patient for a long time. He had asked almost every herb collector in town, even eventually riding on a motorcycle with one of them so they could go together deep into the mountains, where he himself dug up the precious root.

Very curious, Lili went with Dr Huang to see this special drug. He went into his clinic and took out a large tuber that looked rather like a bamboo shoot. Yang Jian told us later it is the tuber of *qiye yizhihua* 七叶一枝花, 'seven leaves per flowering stem.' We were impressed – this is a famously rare herbal drug. After peeling the tuber, Dr Huang told Lili that no metal should be in contact with the tuber as it was prepared, so he put down the knife and picked up a big rock. 'Step back a bit further,' he warned her, 'the herb is poisonous.' Then he put on gloves and safety glasses, and started to carefully smash and grind the tuber with the big rock. He was trying to make the paste as fine as he could, so it took quite a while.

'Will this freshly-made paste, put into a plaster, work for the patient?' Lili asked him. He first explained that the ulcer looked like what is called in Yao medicine a 'grievous toxic sore' (*da du chuang* 大毒疮), and the 'seven leaf stem' paste was known to be a specific treatment for this kind of ulcer. He also noted that he had already tried many different therapies on the patient, to see which might work better. Then he smiled, and asked Lili: 'Do you believe in fate (*ni xiangxin mingyun ma* 你相信命运吗)?' Sometimes the method that works on one patient will not work on other patients. You have to believe in fate, ride the waves of personal destiny (*mingyun* 命运).

Local knowledges

Dr Huang, it would seem, knew what he did not know. Yet he was not surprised that a couple of metropolitan anthropologists sought him out, trying to discern just what he did know. In what follows we want to re-explore some of the complex and uncertain terrain we two authors have covered, usually together, in our recent research on minority nationality medical knowledge and practice. New systems of traditional medicine are now emerging, with varying amounts of official support, in south and southwestern China. As we have worked, we have increasingly thought of these emergent medicines not as ethnic, or nationality, or folk, or vernacular, or indigenous, but as *local* knowledges.[6] There are readily understandable ways to speak of local knowledge in Chinese; no one was surprised, for example, to hear us announce that we had come to Dr Huang's Great Yao Mountains in search of *bendi zhishi* (本地知识), or local knowledge. They might have presumed that we had come from a world of knowing that was translocal or universal (e.g., the natural sciences), or that we were seeking to translate local knowledge into nationally-recognized information, and add it in purified form to the databases of the Chinese medicine pharmacopeia. At times we had occasion to explain to our interlocutors in the rural south that we tended to think of all knowledge as constrained by its knowers' local perspectives, practices, and aims.[7] Speakers of Chinese seem to have an intuitive understanding that all knowing is partial and informed by a point of view. (Are they keeping *zhizhi wei zhizhi* in mind?) Science and Technology Studies, moreover, showed us long ago that scientific facts depend on rigorous constraints and controls of variables locally put in place in particular laboratories. As China anthropologists of medical knowledge, moreover, and as speakers of a non-totalizing Chinese vernacular, we had long done research that relativized truth and refused most universalizing styles of thought.

So let's think again about Dr Huang and his several ways of knowing. He is a widely respected expert in the herbal medicine practiced by Yao nationality doctors in the Great Yao Mountains of northern Guangxi. He is one of the founders of a modern hospital of Yao medicine, he supervises junior residents and interns, and sufferers come from far and wide to receive his treatments. As is evident in the episode described here, he knew the natural medical resources of his home region better than almost any of his colleagues, and he was known for the many years of clinical experience that informed his therapeutic strategies.[8] He knew the unnamed and trackless places in the great forests near the hospital where 'seven leaf stem' might be found growing. He knew his lymphoma patient's sad history. He knew what the visible characteristics of her skin ulcer could tell him about the state of a disease process. He knew how this kind of 'grievous toxic sore' had been understood and managed by Yao practitioners in the past. He knew how to protect himself, his patient, and bystanders from the toxic fumes of the pounded root. And he worked hard to put his skills and understanding into service as good medicine, or healing.[9]

But he did not know what would happen in the future. Lili's question, 'Will this plaster help?', asked for a prognosis or a prediction and implied that there might be a knowable cause and effect chain linking natural drug, bodily lesion, and the progress of the lymphoma. But to answer such a question Dr Huang had to turn interrogative himself, and invoke not knowledge but belief: 'Do you believe in fate?' Even if for him and Lili (and Judith too, and possibly you, dear reader) 'fate' is a perfectly real force in our lives, we know that we cannot know our fate. There is nothing definitive or reliable or unalterable about personal fate or destiny, which is why it should not be thought of as knowledge *about* the future.[10]

The word he used for fate or destiny was *mingyun*, which literally means the (particular) flow of a (particular) life and death.[11] Though it is usually humans who have a *ming*, in this instance in which Dr Huang was putting several agents into close relationship with each other – the forest plant, the mashed root fibers, the gauze-wrapped plaster, and his own hard labor and devoted time – the fated particularity seems to be the relationship among these players, and their convergence upon a clinical problem. A therapeutic grouping has been conscientiously gathered. Perhaps as it nears the patient's body it will join with her particular destiny and help to redirect the flow of her life so far.

But *mingyun* cannot be known definitively even by skilled diviners (and it's possible that Dr Huang was such a diviner in his spare time). If anything, the practical divide between what can and cannot be known reminds us how many mundane practices of knowing are referred to in the paragraphs above. Dr Huang's knowledge of what has worked medically in the past is here found alongside his craft knowledge of how to control toxins. His experienced diagnostic and therapeutic judgment is noted along with his authoritative reputation: he is 'known for' his expertise. Expertise like Dr Huang's, relating to the forest and its natural agents (both toxic and healing), is far from universal among the residents of villages and towns near his Yao medicine hospital, so locally he is a rather unique expert knower. And even health policy-makers in Beijing hesitate to dismiss his medical expertise as mere belief, superstition, or folklore. Committed as the modern world may be to knowing translocal information, when faced with a knowing practice that heals in place, both its particular *zhizhi* (知之) and *buzhi* (不知) must be respected.

Knowledge: Is that a thing?

Treating these words for knowing and not-knowing as redolent terms, both ancient and modern, we hope in the remainder of this discussion to *other* knowledge as a problem. This effort to alienate a commonsense epistemology hardly makes us original among scholars who have studied Asian medical systems.[12] Various writers, faced with what seemed to be very different worlds and embodiments in Chinese medicine, yoga, Qigong, Ayurveda and so forth, found themselves speaking of 'styles of knowing,' emphasizing tacit, embodied, and 'ecological' assumptions (see, e.g., Hsu, 1999). Some found refuge in a concept of 'theory' that allowed non-structural entities to have a functional life (Porkert, 1974), and others translated Chinese medical realities into a materialist commonsense that was nevertheless full of surprises (Sivin, 1987). Judith Farquhar's (1994) ethnographic study of 'knowing practice' aimed to demonstrate the unity of knowledge and action in Chinese medicine. But the study included few descriptions that could clarify the 'action' side of this dynamic unity.

The relativism achieved by comparative research tended to multiply bodies of knowledge, but anthropology persisted in treating non-Western knowing practices as opinions, beliefs, or world-views, things that mostly take the form of cognition and systems of representation. We did not escape a certain idealism in the term knowledge itself. More recently, however, anthropology has recuperated a pointedly materialist or ontological way of thinking about our pluralistic universe (Blaser, 2010; de la Cadena, 2015; Kohn, 2013; Pedersen, 2011; Stevenson, 2014; Viveiros de Castro, 2004). As we began our fieldwork on nationality medicines in 2010, we found much inspiration in all manner of newly plural and concrete 'worldings' (Zhan, 2009). But as we worked, and stimulated by questions like those posed by the present volume, we came to ask – eventually, after some more engagement with healers in China's southern mountains – why we still care to investigate the genesis and practice of 'knowledge' at all? As a thing, knowledge became permanently elusive.

Doing ethnographic fieldwork, we found ourselves in that frictional field of medicine where expertise is not just (or even centrally) derived from a body of knowledge. Rather, it is a politics, an ethics, practices (lots of manipulations), ideologies, and (more than one) ontology (Law & Lin, 2017; Mol, 2002). Expertise also, as Confucius said, and as Dr Huang showed us, includes knowing how to cope with not knowing. We do not follow the (arguably half-ironic) example of the *Analects* and attempt to definitively state 'the way to know,' or *zhizhi* (etc.). But we still want to more sympathetically and better grasp how people go about knowing and acting in actual worlds. We hope the Chinese material, both pre-modern and recent, that we briefly introduce in the remainder of this chapter will help to address this desire, even if it just leaves us riding the waves of fate with Dr Goldstamp Huang.

So, before we seek in the Confucian tradition a terminology more suitable to the herb-alist expertise we have been exploring, let's consider the puzzles presented by a Lisu nationality healer working from his farmhouse above the eastern shore of Yunnan Province's Erhai Lake.

Lasting Loyalty Su: Thinking it up

Lasting Loyalty Su was 40 when we met him in his comfortable but isolated farmhouse. Both his father and grandfather had practiced in the same widely dispersed village as herbalists, but he himself took up medicine and herbal treatments only after his father died at the age of 67, six or seven years before we met him. His father didn't really teach him, though it was he, the ninth of 11 siblings, who had stayed in the house to care for his parents. As his father was dying, the old man expressed a wish for Su to practice heal-ing. To mark this agreement, Su said, he constructed a wall-hanging storage system for herbal drugs. It was sewn of pink silk, and had two long rows of pockets, each pocket labeled.

We asked Dr Su how he had learned his techniques and formulas. He said that he 'thought up' (*xiangchulai* 想出来) all his methods and medicines. Sometimes the solu-tions to stubborn therapeutic puzzles would come to him through dreams – his deceased grandfather or father would visit in a dream and tell him what drugs were good for what complaints. We felt he was speaking not only as a person who was able to 'learn from the yin side' (*yinchuan* 阴传, his term) through encounters with seniors who had passed away, but as a canny observer of his social and natural environment, over the years his father had been practicing and since.

Dr Su was reluctant to share with us many details of his clinical practice. It was important to him that only he, among all his siblings, had been designated as a kind of disciple after death by his father. He had a fated ability (*yuanfen* 缘分) that his siblings did not. (Recall Goldstamp Huang's turn to fate, mentioned above.) Asked to explain what he meant by *yuanfen*, he argued that healing skills cannot be passed on and taken up by just anybody. He really began to 'think up' medicine when the first patients came to him after his father died. His father had asked him to do something for them, so he began re-gathering his father's abilities,[13] going out into the forest and up into the moun-tains to find herbs. Sometimes he observed what sorts of plants were eaten by wild ani-mals to improve their health, and sometimes he gathered plants to use experimentally in addressing symptoms for which there was no usual cure.

Lasting Loyalty Su showed us his pharmacy. Our research team companions from the Academy of Chinese Medicine in Kunming were quite fascinated by this system of pink silk pockets. They took a lot of pictures, opened pouches to inspect the dried herbal con-tents, and noted the puzzling labels on the pockets. These labels at first seemed extremely simple: 'women's formula one' (and two, and three, up to seven), 'cooling drugs,' or 'summer wildflowers.' These medicines were a challenge to the scientific team partly because they were not identified by their proper names (i.e., those acknowledged by a universal botany) – Dr Su said he doesn't know the names of most of the things he col-lects, dries, makes into powders, and uses with patients; and there was not even one plant drug in each pocket but more often carefully crafted mixtures. Only someone who had a personal relationship with these particular plants could even read the labels, much less know how to use them safely and responsibly.

We suspect that our friends from a provincial research agency concluded that they had encountered here a particularly devious way for a mountain healer to maintain 'secret knowledge' away from the scientific eyes of the state.[14] But his labels were hiding in the full light of our camera lenses and notebooks. Our colleagues expressed a kind of grudging respect for Dr Su's complex expertise, and they probably began to think about how they could later collect and study his mixtures in the interest of developing and testing new drug compounds.

Dr Su told us he has an average of seven to eight patients a week. Every summer he hosts a three-day fête for the Medicine King: a small shrine to medical sage Sun Simiao sits above the family stove, near a more central shrine to the God of Heaven and Earth and set well above a much smaller family shrine with a few jars for burning incense to female ancestors. Many current and former patients bring offerings of food and a little money to the Medicine King fête to support their devotions. These satisfied patients treat the whole network of agents centering on Dr Su's own person as a source of healing efficacy. Do they think of him as a repository of knowledge? Perhaps, but we think they are more likely to see him as a conduit of healing powers over which he, as an individual expert, only has partial control.

For us this visit was an event that hit a cultural wall. How could we anthropologists comprehend the ghostly interlocutors, the mysteriously named herbal drugs, the stubborn chronic disorders brought by sufferers, the animals in the high forests, the devoted network of patients and supporters who visit Dr Su and the Medicine King Sun Simiao? We are tempted to see the medical work of grandfather and father Su, Lasting Loyalty Su, and the Medicine King as working on a continuum of forms of agency and service to the local people, bringing a healing tradition into the present, renewed. We know that nonhuman actors like Sun Simiao are built up in social practice over many years of the exchange of favors and gifts. So are actors like Lasting Loyalty Su, the herbalist, constructed as healers, with (at least) the continuing help of his forebears, the creatures of the forest, grateful patients, and the efficacious presence of the gods. But it is precisely because of this laborious process that we anthropologists – caught up in other networks, participating in other constructions – cannot know how in the world he knows what he puts into play as a healer.

Philosophy, cited

We have noted that medical anthropology, along with studies of Chinese medicine, has a rather long history of relativizing and localizing knowledge. But we anthropologists have not clearly delineated the place that knowing practices – sometimes known as expertise – occupy in the various social worlds that engage us. But the constant re-citation in contemporary Chinese medical practice of classical Chinese philosophy has impressed on us the importance of attending to something like knowledge.[15] (After all, even Confucius in his teaching constantly returned to whatever it was he meant by *zhi* 知.) In other words, if knowledge is what knowers do (just as 'science' is what scientists do, calling it science), then the living significations of this term 'knowledge' (but really *zhi*, of course) become an ethical, political, ecological, and very practical problem. Perhaps it bears repeating: In this reconsideration of a Confucian terminology, we are performing neither a philology nor an epistemology. We cite 'Confucius' not because we are in search of either origins or foundations of shared truths, but because many practitioners of Chinese medicine also find themselves citing Confucius and other early Chinese philosophers, as they try to explain what they are up to. We are trying to listen to those explanations.

The centrality of some process of knowing to the successful institution of an ethical sociality has long been asserted in Chinese philosophy. The 'Great Learning' (*c.* 3rd century BCE) is one of the Confucian Four Books to which scholars and thinkers in China have returned many times, generating tons of commentary and influencing debates far beyond intellectual and ruling circles. The short original text is, in part, a beautifully structured string of dominoes, first set up and then knocked over in reverse order: 'Of old, those who sought to emanate bright virtue in the world, first brought order to their kingdoms. Wishing to order their kingdom, they first regulated their families. Wishing to regulate their family, they first cultivated their persons . . .' and so forth. Positioned squarely between this sort of advice (to accomplish A, do B) and a parallel series of predictions (if B is done, A will follow, *if* the family is regulated, *then* the kingdom will be ordered . . .), are two sentences that work as the crucial pivot of the text: *Knowing* (*zhizhi* 致知) *comes from drawing near to things/As things are thus approached, knowledge is attained* (*zhizhi* 知至).[16] (For readers who are not comparing the Chinese characters, we should point out that these two phrases pronounced 'zhizhi' are not the same as the *zhizhi* [knowing it] in our epigraph on the first page.)

This is the key U-turn in the Great Learning's core text: once knowledge has been attained through a practice of drawing near to things, then the dominoes can fall in the proper order: 'Their hearts being rectified, their persons were cultivated; their persons being cultivated, their families were regulated . . ., ' right down to the achievement of 'world peace' (*tianxia ping* 天下平), which results from well-governed kingdoms, well-regulated families, and several more intimate self-cultivations. All of these great good things can be achieved, step by step, because a knowing comprehension can be reached through the action of drawing near to things.[17]

The Great Learning thus positions a practice of knowing at the turning point between aspirations to the good and successful achievement of the good; but this is not really a surprise in our scientific age, is it? It is almost taken for granted in modern popular epistemology, if we accept the commonsense meanings of these English terms, that good action, progressive social construction, wise governance, integral selfhood, and maybe even world peace, require the true facts that a scientific practice of knowing can provide. Read in a certain way, then, ancient philosophy in a foreign language once again confirms what we modernists already know about how the (one) world naturally works.

But some commentators on the Great Learning have rendered this commonsense more problematic with their genealogical work on 'the investigation of things' in the history of Chinese philosophy and scholarship.[18] We have noted above that the term usually translated as 'investigate' (*ge* 格) is literally and contextually better rendered as 'drawing near' to things. And the 'things' in question in the original text, our sources point out, are not external objects *dongxi* (东西) perceived by subjects and referred to with words, or other mental tools. They are more like the constructed entities we associate with STS epistemology or the gathered things present-at-hand, posited by Heidegger (1971). Knowing (*zhizhi* 致知) slippery social things is thus perceived in the text as being more difficult, more of a process of self-cultivation and world-building, than empiricist versions of investigation and cognition would admit: one doesn't come to terms with one's own family, heart-mind, intentions, sincerity, and personhood (all matters of concern in the Great Learning) through 'investigations' that measure, dissect, sample, represent, depict, conceptualize, or materially test a solid material thing. The Great Learning proposes instead that we need to cross a few distances, draw near to changing and unreliable things, catching them in the act of becoming manifest.

The implications of this critical translation of 'nearing' and 'things' are, in our view, massive. For one thing, the action of drawing near to gathering things is not served by a remote observer stance. The nearing to things that we read of in the original Great Learning is a turn both toward the widest world and toward the deepest self, extending its attention across both inner and outer spaces. To adopt a Latourian language, the 'things' in question are both quasi-subjects and quasi-objects, so the knower ideally would not be even a step away from the things known.

Our herbalist friends are experts at drawing near to things. They make their way up into the mountain forests seeking medicines conceived not as inert objects but as living and changing partners in healing. Dr Huang invoked a fated relationship between the seven leaf stem and a patient's illness; Dr Su insisted that only he among his many siblings had the fated ability to 'think up' herbal formulas by drawing near to things in the forest. Their knowing, then, is a rather strenuous practice.

Knowing the pattern, through-ing the way

This is not to say that some Chinese thinkers did not ask questions that were properly epistemological.[19] The very centrality of *zhi* knowing and *wu* things in the Great Learning seems to have demanded that later philosophers fill in a few (onto)logical blanks. Neo-Confucian thinkers Zhu Xi and the Cheng Brothers apparently asked themselves how, exactly, one gets from nearing things to fully attaining knowing.[20] The answer had to be more cosmological than psychological or cognitive: these philosophers turned to the patterns of things, *li* 理.

Before we try to approach their argument, however, we must confess that it is with this *li* that our own way of tracing an itinerary for knowing practice is interrupted: How should we translate or rigorously use this term? The Anglophone experts in classical, neo-Confucian, and evidential scholarship in China pretty uniformly translate *li* as 'principle.' But we cannot get over the fact that a more literal gloss of the word (per many dictionaries) is texture or grain (as in wood, the sources always point out): that is to say, *pattern*, a configuration that is inseparable from the materiality of the stuff in which it appears. *Li*-pattern, moreover, unfolds in time, as a kind of variable continuity, like the currents of a stream. If *li* is the pattern displayed in natural processes like the growth and branching of trees, or like the regularly repeating eddies in flowing water, then it is something – a very real and material process – that can be known.[21]

So, returning to Zhu Xi and his interlocutors, how did they fill in that troublesome gap between drawing near to things and actually comprehending them? Fan Hongye (1988) says that they interposed *li*. 'Thoroughly [engage] the patterns' (*qiongli* 穷理), they advised.[22] And following upon this intervention there were thinkers who clarified: *We can only know anything because pattern is shared by knowing heart-minds and known things.*[23] As a corollary of this position, 'things' cannot really be thought of – in objectivist, modernist fashion – as objects that a subject knows about. *Li* is that form of natural reason that brings pattern to all processes of generation, not just human creativity. Only by coming to terms with *li* can the knowing that concerned Confucius be successful, or attained (Fan, 1988).[24] In the phrase *qiongli*, *li*-pattern is the object of the verb 'thoroughly [engage]'; but *li* can be a verb itself: *li* is a patterning of processes of generation. (And when we get our hair cut, the barber *li*'s the hair. In Chinese medicine, the acupuncture needle might *li*, or nudge into motion, blobs of stagnant qi, blood, and fluids.)

We love this idea of a patterned flow that incorporates and unifies knower and known in an active field of structured practice (even if it might not be what most of the neo-Confucians really meant). The term *li*-pattern proposes a world of becoming that can underpin the social, moral, and political concerns of the Great Learning. Thoroughly engaging *li* becomes the only way to imagine the efficacy of 'drawing near to [social but not only] things' as this nearing achieves something that could be called – what? – an attainment of knowingness? (Thanks to Marisol de la Cadena, in this volume, for her awkward-felicitous usage of 'but not only.')

This is not just a technical point that only Song and Ming dynasty historians of ideas need to grapple with. Wang Hui (1995) argues that *lixue* (理学) (might we translate this as patterning thought, following Foucault [1970] and Timothy Reiss [1982]?) was the chief rubric under which much ethical-metaphysical thought, covering about six centuries, should be considered.[25] Partly due to the vast shadow cast over Chinese modernity by Ming period philosopher Wang Yangming (1472–1529) – who is sometimes presented as an East Asian rationalist who insisted on cognitive forms inherent to Mind – premodern *lixue* lent itself to a somewhat paradoxical translation into modern empiricism and science (*kexue* 科学). As anthropologists of medicine, we note that terms like physiology (*shenglixue* 生理学) and pathology (*binglixue* 病理学), pharmacology (*yaolixue* 药理学) and physics (*wulixue* 物理学) still incorporate that resonant old *li*-pattern that is so very non-empiricist (and not even rationalist). Is this patterning resonance heard among Chinese speakers? We have lots of casual evidence that it is.

We cannot move along the Confucian itineraries of knowing practice and matters of concern that fall under the rubric of *zhi* (知) without saying a bit more about Wang Yangming. This 16th century commentator on the Great Learning is famous among philosophers for his emphasis on the personal heart-mind, but he is more famous among the rest of us for his insistence on 'the unity of knowing and acting' (*zhi xing he yi* 知行合一).[26] Perhaps this is because Mao Zedong in his still-influential philosophical essays of the 1930s rather eerily channeled the epistemological pragmatics of Wang Yangming into the 20th century (Mao, 1971). Looking back over the translations of knowing practice that have occurred over the centuries in China, Wang Yangming helps us see the activity of knowing (*zhi* 知 and *xing* 行 together) as both taken for granted in the authoritative texts and as ever historically situated. Under his influence, for example, we notice that the terms 'nearing,' 'comprehending,' and 'attaining' in the pivotal sentences of the Great Learning are all verbs.

The word that Wang Yangming used for 'acting,' moreover, which is echoed in so much modern Chinese writing including Mao, was *xing* (行), which means first of all to walk along, to travel. Wang insistently reminded his 15th and 16th century readers that a unified understanding of knowledge and action presented not just conceptual but ethical challenges. Recalling again the matters of (social) concern evoked in the Great Learning, he insisted that a humane way of going along together required not a disembodied representation of objects, but a personal and exemplary practice of knowing the good (*zhi liangzhi* 致良知). And on that road through a vastly extended and mostly unknowable world, it is presumed that transformations in the itinerant knower take place even as more and more that can be known unfolds before us and within us.

Anthropology and philosophy have, we feel, returned us to the empirical. Looking back on our many encounters with working herbalists, we now see that the two doctors we have introduced thus far are actually representative of a certain situation of knowing. They were not the only southern mountain healers who tried to tell us something important about 'knowing it' and 'not knowing.' Indeed, our interviewees were much more interested in pointing to areas of not knowing than they were in claiming any special access to true knowledge. We had trouble hearing them at times, we now think. How in the world, we kept asking, do active knowers know? And how can our recent interlocutors, experienced healers in China's southern mountains, teach us about translating *zhizhi* (知之 or, for that matter, *buzhi* 不知) into an Anglophone and cosmopolitan term? We will address these questions with one more story. We hope that, through the ethnographic material we introduce in this article, readers can appreciate how some knowers we have known go about knowing, and how, like Goldstamp Huang and Lasting Loyalty Su, they live with also not-knowing, even as they are widely known for their efforts to know well how to ride the waves of an incalculable fate.

Virtuefont Li: All doing our best together

When we met him Virtuefont Li was a locally renowned doctor of Qiang medicine practicing in a new hospital built after the 2008 earthquake that had devastated Mao County. In our visit to his clinic, which he established to help a traumatized people, we encountered an anteroom full of patients who had come from all over the region to consult him. Local people in Mao County refer to Dr Li as a 'divine healer' (*shenyi* 神医), an appellation that refers mostly to the unusual effectiveness of his therapy.

Residents of a village near the county town all know, for example, how he brought a pancreatitis patient back from the brink of death with his effective treatments. We got the story of this dramatic cure from the patient herself, and she brought out all manner of documents and proofs to show us. She had been hospitalized in Chengdu for 70 days, some of that time in the ICU. This intensive and unsuccessful treatment completely depleted the family's savings and had them borrowing from all their relatives and neighbors. When doctors in the big city admitted there was nothing more they could do to save this patient's life, she was returned to the county hospital where hematemesis and hemorrhagic shock immediately developed. Everyone thought she was soon going to die. Her son showed us the firecrackers they had bought for the funeral, they had all been so despairing. But that evening a member of the patient's family had run into Dr Li on the street and asked him to try. Dr Li's son recalled that the patient's grown children had said, 'We won't blame you if you can't save her. We have nothing more to lose now by trying Qiang medicine.'

Later, recalling this case, Dr Li said: 'When I saw the patient, I could see her strong will to live. This is very important to me; also her family did not want to give up on her, her whole family was very close. Seeing all this, I gained confidence that we could all do our best together to take her life back.' Dr Li and his disciple-son went to see the patient that night, and then instead of going home they went back to the clinic – where they were surrounded by the herbal medicines they gather and process themselves – to discuss how to compose the first formula. According to Li Junior, the first eight sets of a drug formula are the most crucial. After eight sets of drugs, this patient was indeed able to get out of bed and walk a bit. Usually one set of drugs lasts for a week, but for this special patient, they compounded only three to five days' worth in each set, so they could adjust the prescription as the symptoms changed. When she was taking the third set, the symptoms worsened. Dr Li asked about her diet, and, discovering that she had eaten four fermented soybeans, 'for the flavor,' he changed the formula right away.

Throughout this patient's illness, Dr Li and his son paid close attention to her condition, especially how her bodily state changed as the drugs did their work. This was a 'dance of agency' unfolding in time (Pickering, 1993), one in which the skilled, experienced, and ethical doctor intervenes alongside the powers of drugs, symptoms, food, and diverse human affections. Dr Li's understanding of how to handle advanced pancreatitis (a term that meant almost nothing to him) was not something stored in his mind, ready to 'apply' in an outside world. Rather it was a constant coordination of powers and impulses in social time, working toward good ends with salient powers, only some of them 'known.'

On knowing and not knowing

The three healers we have briefly introduced, Yao Dr Huang, Lisu Dr Su, and Qiang Dr Li, show us different but similar situations of knowing. Dr Huang knows how to safely and therapeutically mobilize some rare powers from the forests of the Great Yao Mountains, but he can only do it by putting his own time, effort, experience, and hopes for success into the plaster applied to the wound. Dr Su gathers a network of powers that pre-existed his own medical practice, bringing nonhuman agents near and cultivating a relationship with the yin side, which is to say, the invisible, the un-nameable. And Dr Li works along the flow of pathological and therapeutic time, discerning and responding to the currents of change in a pancreas, a patient, a family and a supportive village. These embodied and emergent ways of knowing toward the good, rather than dominating illness with drugs, navigate between knowing and not-knowing, and in so doing participate in the currents or the grain of the world.

Our anthropological work of drawing near to nationality medicines in China's southern mountains has challenged us to look for patterns in particular unities of knowing and acting rather than facts, information, concepts, representations – the standard stuff of knowledge. We have been helped to understand a Chinese philosophy of knowing practice by witnessing the workmanlike ways in which three healers (Goldstamp Huang, Lasting Loyalty Su, and Virtuefont Li) draw near to things and attain both understanding and efficacy, seeking to build an ethical world of reliable interlocutors (intentions, heart-minds, families, even nations) while riding the waves of what can be known. The 3rd century BCE Great Learning still seems to describe a 'thorough engagement with *li*-pattern' as exemplified by these contemporary local medical men who, so passionately engaged, draw near to the myriad things that are local to them. If we were to circle back to reflect on and generalize their work, seeking deep insights about knowledge itself, this would be a betrayal, proof that we have not been paying attention. These lives teach us about knowing practice in their woody grain, in the changes of their flowing currents. To abstract from these stories would only foreclose what we can learn and delude us into forgetting how much we don't know.

This is the way to know

As anthropologists, we are in the knowledge game, as are you, dear readers. In this article, however, and in our other writings on these subjects, we make no pretense of thoroughly comprehending either the medical expertise of the herbalists Yao, Lisu, or Qiang,[27] or the consensus insights and translations gathered in the Confucian and neo-Confucian tradition of writing. The extreme partiality of our knowledge has been pointed out to us (usually irritably) both by disciplined China philologists and devoted ethnographers of rural places in China. But we take comfort in returning often to the program of research and self-cultivation, ethical social construction and peace in the world that we find condensed in the Great Learning. How do we read this program, *knowing comes from drawing near to things, as things are thus approached, knowledge is attained*? Now that we have rendered knowledge as a verb, insisting on the unity of knowing and acting; now that we have seen how experimental and interrogatory is the practice of some skilled healers; now that we have acknowledged how truly myriad are the things to be known; now, perhaps we can join mountain herbalists in efforts to more humbly draw nearer to more of the myriad things. Other worlds await us, asking us to attend to the powers and dilemmas in play in particular networks, the particular things that can be known under local conditions, and the stubborn areas of unknowability with which actors always must cope.

Funding

The authors received no financial support for the research, authorship, and/or publication of this article.

Notes

1. https://ctext.org/analects/wei-zheng. The Chinese Text Project provides a translation from James Legge, 'The Master said, "You, shall I teach you what knowledge is? When you know a thing, to hold that you know it; and when you do not know a thing, to allow that you do not know it – this is knowledge."' This translation is consistent with the context in Chapter 2 of the standard compilation of the *Analects*, in that this whole group of fragmentary sayings

tends to emphasize firmness of conviction about the truth, and humility in claiming expertise.

2. Here's a modern comic book version, which is widely popular: 知道的就说知道,不知道的就说不知道,要老实地说,这才是真知啊! This translates as 'If you know it, say you know it, if it is not known, say you don't know. One ought to speak honestly, this is the only true knowledge' (Cai, 2015, pp. 23–24). This version keeps Confucian ethics at the center, but drastically restricts the possible meanings.

3. The most important words in this sentence are the prepositions. Volker Scheid (2017) has shown the importance of 'through' (*tong* 通) in some currents of traditional Chinese physiology. François Jullien (2019) has argued in a recent conference paper that 'Between is not Being.' And Carla Nappi in personal communications has been urging historians to read for the prepositions.

4. Farquhar (1994) studies the logic of clinical encounters in modern traditional Chinese medicine under the title *Knowing Practice*. This book-length study of clinical reasoning emphasizes the many and various activities that concatenate to make knowledge authoritative and effective.

5. Goldstamp Huang's colorful first name is an example of how we protect the identity of people we interview.

6. But we must add a de la Cadena-style caveat: local knowledges, but *not only* 'knowledge.' See the argument below about the unity of knowing and doing in Wang Yangming. In our forthcoming book, *Gathering Medicines*, we define localness and local place-making at length and in detail through description of minority medicine activity.

7. Chinese has a proverb making fun of perspectives that are too constrained by local conditions: *jingdi zhi wa* 井底之蛙 [what can be seen by] a frog at the bottom of a well.

8. Dr Huang had embarked on his career as a herbalist after only a middle school education, many years before. But his family was known for its several generations of local healers, and as a young man he was selected also to receive about three years of medical training in Guangxi's capital Nanning. He had been grandfathered into his white-coated, certified, hospital practice as part of the minority medicine movement that began in the early 1980s.

9. In other cases we observed in Goldstamp Huang's practice, it was clear that he also knew how to use Daoist ritual to therapeutically manage bodily space and bodily disposition.

10. Putting this point in a Chinese way, '相信命运'不等于'知之'('Believing in fate' is not the same as 'knowing it').

11. See the discussion of words for life, including *shengming* (生命),in Farquhar and Zhang (2012). Fate is a topic for a different discussion, but here it can be seen that in China fate is closely allied to ways of knowing anything.

12. See the eponymous book edited by Charles Leslie (1976) for an early example. A later collection inspired by the Leslie volume (Bates, 1995) highlighted the place of 'scholarly knowledge' in Asian and early European medical traditions, in a project that stimulated considerable interest among those of us who had worked as historians or ethnographers in non-biomedical fields. The editor and contributors pluralized scholarly ways of knowing in this volume, directing attention to fascinating empirical presentations of diverse medical discourses and practices, all of which could be thought of as forms of expert knowing.

13. But really, what word should we use here? Was he re-gathering his father's 'knowledge' or 'expertise'? Was his effort more about true facts and reliable observations or about building his own relationships with the powers of the forest that could effectively address the suffering of his neighbors and clients?

14. Our project in China's southern mountains was usually assisted by research teams from county or province health departments. Quite often these researchers thought of their primary task as discovering specialist local knowledge about drugs and formulas for publication and

possible market exploitation. Because some healers resisted this kind of state project, many we worked with worried about healers 'keeping secrets.'

15. We often asked, in the households of rural healers, what textual resources they found useful. Quite a few would answer by pulling out a battered copy of the *Yi Jing* or *Book of Changes*, the most canonical Confucian writing of all.

16. The famous sentences are: *zhi zhi zai ge wu, wu ge erhou zhi zhi* 致知在格物,物格而后知至. Here's a more or less standard translation, from the Chinese Text Project: 'Such extension of knowledge lay in the investigation of things. Things being investigated, knowledge became complete.' Our different translation is influenced by famous points made by Zhu Xi, to wit: 格, 至也, 物, 犹事也. 穷推至事物之理，欲其极处无不到也. ('Ge'-investigate, this is to arrive; 'wu'-things are like matters of concern. Exhaustively reach toward the patterns of things, and you can go anywhere you want.) (Zhu Xi, 《大学章句》). Zhu Xi also has a briefer and equally salient formula about 'nearing' as the condition for thoroughly engaging *li*: 即物穷理, 'draw near to things in order to exhaustively grasp pattern.'

17. We cannot develop this very Confucian idea here, but a careful reading of the Great Learning should persuade you that the good that is imagined to arise from proper knowing practices, through a series of self-cultivations, is something like an achieved consonance with the flow of the great Way. This relation to knowing the good is not easy to achieve, however.

18. In this part of the discussion we are greatly indebted to Fan Hongye and Wang Hui, who cover the vast philological territory of Great Learning Confucianism, albeit with different critical purposes, to explore how 'the investigation of things and the attainment of knowledge' turned into a modern scientific, even a positivist and objectivist, epistemology. See Fan Hongye (1988); Wang Hui (1995).

19. This is a huge issue in philosophically inclined China studies. See Lloyd and Sivin (2002), Blum (2007), and Jullien (2004).

20. For an extensive introduction to neo-Confucianism via the original philosophical writings in translation, see deBary and Bloom (1999–2000).

21. Eduardo Kohn's *How Forests Think* (2013) verges on this depiction with his exploration of the natural-cultural semiosis discernable in his Amazonian field site. Perhaps we should be borrowing his metaphysical ambition by talking about 'how bodies know.'

22. Wang Hui's (1995) translator uses the phrase 'probe thoroughly the principle' for *qiongli*.

23. 心 (*xin*) is often translated as heart-mind for pre-modern Chinese. One of the stages in the attainment of knowing in the Great Learning is the rectification of the heart-mind.

24. The complexity of the debates and arguments that placed *li* at the heart of knowing, where, arguably, it still remains in a very scientific age even for writing in Chinese, is beautifully handled in Fan's paper, and carefully noted also in Wang Hui (1995). Our brief mention of this issue is only here to help us work our way back to the folk metaphysics of our knowing and doing herbalist friends in the mountains.

25. A very recent modern example of *lixue* in Chinese is Zhang (2016).

26. In other writing we have translated this very important phrase as 'knowing and going gather as one,' but here we wanted to resonate with the usual rendering 'the unity of knowledge and action.'

27. See our forthcoming book, *Gathering Medicines: Nation and Knowledge in China's Mountain South*. In that study we engaged with seven 'minority nationality' groups: the Achang, Li, Lisu, Qiang, Tujia, Yao, and Zhuang.

References

Bates, D. (Ed.). (1995). *Knowledge and the scholarly medical traditions.* Cambridge University Press.

Blaser, M. (2010). *Storytelling globalization from the Chaco and beyond.* Duke University Press.

Blum, S. (2007). *Lies that bind: Chinese truth, other truths*, Rowman and Littlefield.

Cai, Z. (2015). *Lunyu: Ruzhede zhengyan* 论语: 儒者的诤言 [Analects: The Confucian's admonition]. Shandong Renmin Chubanshe.

deBary, W. T., & Bloom, I. (Eds.). (1999–2000). *Sources of Chinese tradition (2 vols*, 2nd ed.). Columbia University Press.

de la Cadena, M. (2015). *Earth beings: Ecologies of practice across Andean worlds.* Duke University Press.

Fan, H. (1988). 从'格致'到'科学 *Cong 'Gezhi' dao 'Kexue'* [From 'the investigation of things' to 'science']. *Journal of the Dialectics of Nature, 10*(3), 39–50.

Farquhar, J. (1994). *Knowing practice: The clinical encounter of Chinese medicine.* Westview Press.

Farquhar, J., & Zhang, Q (2012). *Ten thousand things: Nurturing life in contemporary Beijing.* Zone Books.

Foucault, M. (1970) *The order of things: An archaeology of the human sciences.* Pantheon.

Heidegger, M. (1971). *Poetry, language, thought.* Harper and Row.

Hsu, E. (1999). *The transmission of Chinese medicine.* Cambridge University Press.

Jullien, F. (2004). *A treatise on efficacy: Between Western and Chinese thinking.* University of Hawai'i Press.

Jullien, F. (2019, May 22). *Between is not being.* Paper presented at the Seoul Symposium on East Asian Medicine as Alternative Potential.

Kohn, E. (2013). *How forests think: Toward an anthropology beyond the human.* University of California Press.

Law, J., & Lin, W. Y. (2017). Provincializing STS: Postcoloniality, symmetry, and method. *EASTS, 11*(2), 211–227.

Leslie, C. (Ed.). (1976). *Asian medical systems: A comparative study.* University of California Press.

Lloyd, G., & Sivin, N. (2002). *The way and the word: Science and medicine in early China and Greece.* Yale University Press.

Mao, Z. (1971). On practice. In *Selected readings from the works of Mao Tsetung* (pp. 65–84). Foreign Languages Press.

Mol, A. (2002). *The body multiple: Ontology in medical practice.* Duke University Press.

Pedersen, M. A. (2011). *Not quite shamans: Spirit worlds and political lives in northern Mongolia*, Cornell University Press.

Pickering, A. (1993). The mangle of practice: Agency and emergence in the sociology of science. *American Journal of Sociology, 99*(3), 559–589.

Porkert, M. (1974). *The theoretical foundations of Chinese medicine: Systems of correspondence.* MIT Press.

Reiss, T. J. (1982). *The discourse of modernism.* Cornell University Press.

Scheid, V. (2017). Promoting free flow in the networks: Reimagining the body in early modern Suzhou. *History of Science, 56*(2), 123–130.

Sivin, N. (1987). *Traditional medicine in contemporary China: A partial translation of revised outline of Chinese Medicine (1972).* Center for Chinese Studies, University of Michigan.

Stevenson, L. (2014). *Life beside itself: Imagining care in the Canadian Arctic.* University of California Press.

Viveiros de Castro, E. (2004). Perspectival anthropology and the method of controlled equivocation. *Tipiti*, *2*(1), 3–22.

Wang, H. (1995). The fate of 'Mr. Science' in China: The concept of science and its application in modern Chinese thought. *Positions*, *3*(1), 1–68.

Zhan, M. (2009). *Other-worldly: Making Chinese medicine through transnational frames*. Duke University Press.

Zhang, D. (2016). *Yuanqi, Shenji: Xianqin zhongyi zhi dao* 元气。神机：先秦中医之道 [Origin qi, divine machine: The way of pre-Qin Chinese medicine]. World Library Publishers.

Author biographies

Lili Lai earned her PhD in Anthropology at the University of North Carolina-Chapel Hill in 2009, after college training in Chinese medicine and public health in Beijing. Since then she has been teaching at Peking University and pursuing medical anthropology research in China. Her first book is *Hygiene, Sociality, and Culture in Contemporary Rural China: The Uncanny New Village* (2016). A second major research project, on the development of minority nationality medical systems in China, has produced a forthcoming book and numerous articles and chapters. Lai has also published STS research on the practice of biomedicine in Beijing.

Judith Farquhar has been studying traditional Chinese medicine in an anthropological and philosophical vein since the early 1980s. The present article extends some concerns that animated her first book, *Knowing Practice: The Clinical Encounter of Chinese Medicine* (1994). And it demonstrates the value of a commitment to collaboration that has been at the root of her research since 1999. The most recent ethnographic monograph to result from a lengthy collaboration is *Ten Thousand Things: Nurturing Life in Contemporary Beijing* (2012), co-authored with Professor Qicheng Zhang of the Beijing University of Chinese Medicine. Farquhar is Max Palevsky Professor Emerita in the Department of Anthropology at the University of Chicago.

Harraga: **Burning borders, navigating colonialism**

The Sociological Review Monographs
2020, Vol. 68(2) 158–174
© The Author(s) 2020

Article reuse guidelines:
sagepub.com/journals-permissions
DOI: 10.1177/0038026120905491
journals.sagepub.com/home/sor

Amade M'charek
Universiteit van Amsterdam [University of Amsterdam], The Netherlands

Abstract
In this article I introduce the non-English word, *harraga*, to address the convoluted nature of migration, death, borders and colonial legacies. My empirical material comes from the south of Tunisia. I draw on practices of migration from Tunisia, the extraction of resources and its effect on the economy of the country, and the washing ashore of bodies on the southern Tunisian coast. I also reflect on the recent European border management in this area that is intended to stop migration from both Tunisia and Libya. *Harraga* (الحراقة) is an Arabic word used in Tunisia, Algeria and Morocco. It could be translated as *those who burn*. A pragmatic or accommodating translation would be 'sans papiers', or 'undocumented migrants'. However, *harraga* is not a word for a group of people, but for an activity. The activity of *moving out of the Magreb*. Those who engage in *harga*, 'burn' borders in order to enter European territories, or overstay their visa. Yet enfolded in the word *harraga* is much more than the activity of leaving for Europe. I will slowly unpack this word and show that (1) *harraga* is not about identity (the migrant/the refugee), but an activity, the activity of burning borders and of expanding living space; (2) *harraga* is not about burning bridges or leaving histories behind, but about crafting *connections* as well as colonial *extractions*; (3) *harraga* problematizes Europe's borders by siding with those who burn them, human beings.

Keywords
colonial extractions, colonial flows, European borders, migration, Zarzis

By way of introduction

Harraga (الحراقة) is an Arabic word used in Tunisia, Algeria and Morocco. It could be translated as *those who burn*, with the Arab word for 'to burn' being *ahrag* (أحرق). This, however, is too literal a translation to make sense. More meaningful, already, is 'sans papiers', or 'undocumented migrants'. However, also this misses the point, as *harraga* is not a word for a group of people ('illegal migrants') and neither does it apply to those who, after their travels, find themselves *in Europe* ('we live here, too'). It is rather a word

Corresponding author:
Amade M'charek, Department of Anthropology, University of Amsterdam, PO Box 15509, Amsterdam, 1001 NA, The Netherlands.
Email: a.a.mcharek@uva.nl

for an activity, that of *moving out of the Magreb*. Crucially this moving out is in defiance of the bureaucratic rules and their elaborate visa systems. Those who engage in *harga*, 'burn' borders to enter European territories. They do not, however, burn the bridges to the people and places they depart from. To these they keep all kinds of links. For, as they burn borders, they don't move away from their place of origin. *Harraga* is about expanding living space.

Initially the word *harraga* was not so much related to Europe. It started to be used in the 1970s in Tunisia for the illegal crossings of the border between Tunisia and Libya. Southern Tunisian men burned the Tunisian–Libyan border in the hope of finding jobs in prosperous Libya.[1] More recently, in the early 1990s and related to the introduction of a visa system in France, *harraga* started to be used for 'burning' *visas*. This doesn't mean that papers were set aflame, but rather that people disregarded their papers and stayed in France or another European country for longer than they were officially allowed. Gradually, also in Europe, *harraga* changed from the burning of papers (visas) to the burning of borders. The borders of Europe. Those who engage in *harraga* brave boundaries that are meant to stop them in their tracks.

In addition the word *harraga* mobilizes history. Folded into *harraga* is a story of colonial and postcolonial relations. For a long time after official independence it was easy to travel from the Maghreb countries to the former colonizer, France.[2] Many would travel back and forth between France and Tunisia, and many would in the end prefer to settle down in Tunisia (Natter, 2014, 2015). France would occasionally introduce a visa system and then lift it. But since March 1995, a more rigid visa system has been in place, as part of the Schengen Convention. While this Convention was aimed at the free movement of people and goods *within* the borders of Europe, it made it more difficult for those *outside* Europe to access this area. The Convention led to a common visa-system, also called the Schengen Visa, and as a result of this the borders of Europe became ever more severely controlled.[3] That doesn't mean that nothing and nobody is allowed to pass them. Tunisian salt is eagerly shipped across to the EU, and so are phosphorus, olive oil, fish and other profitable resources. Also, while the so-called tourist visa is highly restricted, some people are invited into Europe. Recruitment bureaus in the capital Tunis draw highly educated young people in. Those who are trained as medical doctors, ICT specialists or engineers are especially likely to be offered a job in European countries (see Lakhal, 2019; Musette, 2016).[4] But not so the people who have nothing going on for them in the villages and small towns where they were born. Not the people who find themselves in a dead end; who feel immobilized by the standstill left after salt and brains have been mined and shipped out. These people, cornered, seek to break out. They are the ones who consider *harraga*.

In what follows, I will unfold *harraga* in three steps. The first is condensed in something we might think of as a road sign; the second starts out from the carriage of a truck; and the third speaks from a work of art made out of rubbish found on the Mediterranean shore.

A 'road sign' pointing at the sea

A rock among other rocks, some tilted, others straight. Behind them a wide-open sea. This is the Mediterranean. Next to an arrow on the rock, a text in Arabic reads:

Figure 1. 'Europe this way'.

أوروبا من هنا. Translated into English this means: 'Europe this way'. A crown on the word *Europe* (أوروبا) is suggestive of a top destination, a royal one (Figure 1).

These rocks are to be found on the coast near the southern Tunisian town of Zarzis. They carry a message and index a route. If you want to go to Europe, you do not necessarily have to drive to Djerba, a nearby island connected to the mainland by a bridge and the location of an international airport. Neither is it necessary to first visit Tunis, the capital 600 kilometres to the north, to file for a visa from one of the European embassies. You simply cross the Med. Right here. All you need to do is get yourself a *flouka*, a small wooden fishing boat, and sail away. Preferably with the help of an engine.

With this image full of irony, as with the term *harraga*, this text deliberately starts out from the perspective of the potential traveller: the person in Zarzis who might want to burn borders. Not that this person would need a sign: everybody in Zarzis knows where to find Europe. The problem is not which direction to take. There are plenty of other problems.

Within Europe, in what has been called 'the refugee crisis', the focus of attention has been on classifying who each and every migrant is, e.g. a genuine refugee, an economic migrant, a trafficker, or a latent terrorist (Magalhães, 2015; and this volume). Migrants may be called *irresponsible* because they take so many risks in travelling; or they may be called *victims* who need to be helped, or they might be labelled *thugs* involved in the trafficking of people. But one way or another, there is a constant need for identifying and ordering. The key question is by which label to classify *these people* in order to act. However, from the perspective of those facing the rock, who are thinking about whether or not to cross the sea, *harraga* is not an identity, but an activity. It requires a lot of preparation, the kind of work that needs to be done to move, and to get yourself to moving. And it doesn't end when you are in Europe. You're still this *harraag*, this person doing *harraga*.

One of the documentaries recently made in Tunisia has a scene in which a number of young men are sitting in a rundown place.[5] It is late in the afternoon, getting dark, they share a stack of beer cans, Tunisian beer, they are drinking. When the journalist asks them a question about their situation, the first thing to come up is the issue of *harraga*. One of them says: 'Well you know, it is better to die than to be a living dead man.' The others confirm that, of course, they are waiting for their chance to go. They are all set, they have paid for the crossing and are waiting for better sea conditions. So it is there, constantly, the possibility of moving. This is a potentiality that might happen, is bound to happen. And if formerly *harraga* was something for adventurous young men who wanted to achieve something big, who hoped to come back with lots of valuables, it is nowadays also a matter of survival. You risk being accused of inertia if you are not prepared to go. So everybody is prepared to go. Because there is nothing to stay for.

As *harraga* requires you to do a lot, it depends on a lot. Here is the story of Majid, a 16-year-old boy.[6]

> Over the past years he has seen his group of peers diminish. All of them have taken the boats and arrived in Italy and France. For more than a year he has been constantly nagging his parents about *el harga*. His parents acknowledged that he has little to stay for. Young men tend to populate the terraces of the many Zarzis cafés; an indication that youth unemployment is sky-high. Knowing that the future of his son is not likely to be different from that of these young men, Majid's father has been stealthily saving from the little he earned, while his mother has borrowed additional money from her brother who lives in France. Majid's father has looked out for an experienced shipper. 'You know an older man, not these youngsters who do not know how to navigate a boat', his sister told me. They paid 3500 Tunisian Dinars (approximately 1000 euro) for the boat journey. The shipper had indicated that the sea is best in September and October. So they'd better be ready by then. Majid will need a mobile phone and some 300 euros cash, to purchase phone cards once on Lampedusa and to travel from Sicily to mainland Italy and then to the French border where he will be picked up by relatives. The first attempt was cancelled because of bad weather, but the second was already successful. No one around Majid knew about his plans to leave, except for his immediate family, in Zarzis and France. In particular one of his sisters in Zarzis was the key to navigating him through Italy: keeping contact with him and his relatives in France to coordinate their journeys, sending online bus tickets to her brother as it appears that long distance buses in certain parts of Italy do not sell tickets on board etc. After a journey of one long week, Majid arrived in France safely and was soon to be enrolled in a schooling scheme to continue his education, in France rather than Zarzis.[7]

So *harraga* is an activity. It requires preparation and a state of preparedness, to take the chance when it comes. You need to collect trustworthy information about shippers, about the journey, about the duration of the trip (when to start panicking in the absence of telephone contact with your loved one), and about the scenarios and sequences of events upon arrival, so that family members can help you navigate your route at a distance; scenarios such as: a medical check upon arrival in Lampedusa, followed by shipping over to mainland Italy, buying bus tickets online, walking 2 hours from the reception centre to take the bus to the Italian–French border. But you also need money, more or less money. You might need to sell your mother's gold, borrow from close relatives or take the savings that were meant for mending the roof of the house. If the family has some olive trees, well, you try to sell them, even if the family is dependent on them. You sell whatever valuables there are in order to be able to go, because you have to pay the price.[8] Because being a dead man alive, or a living dead man, is not a situation to stay in. So you try to get out of that situation. For whatever it is that you might want to achieve in your life, it cannot be done in where you are. Not in Zarzis.

In the north of Tunisia poverty can be worse. In the south it is more or less rural, so there are ways of getting food. People are not hungry. You may eat from the land, from your extended family. So if you seek to engage in *harraga* to survive, it is not hunger you are dying from, but boredom. There are no jobs, no prospects; only the fear of things getting worse.[9] Nowadays complete families leave. Not just young men, or girls by themselves, but families. Families including grandparents, families including babies, everybody goes. And takes the boat. Europe, that direction. Arrow.[10]

Writing about this in English and trying to translate the term *harraga*, in one way or another, its genealogy gets lost. For along with the word, the activity, too, has a history. As I said above, the word emerged in the south of Tunisia in the 1970s to be taken up later in Algeria, for people crossing borders illegally, without the proper papers. In some cases they did not have a passport, or they did not have the visa that was needed. In other cases they overstayed their visa. The English word *migration* includes all sorts of formal state-obeying, law-obeying, movements of people from one country to another. But *harraga* assumes a situation of challenging the boundaries of the state and of going on where states try to stop citizens from moving about. It assumes the activity, the impetus to cross borders, whatever the rules of the states involved. Or, stronger still, despite the rules of the states involved.

This makes *harraga* into an activity that interferes with the way states imagine the relations between states and individuals. It makes *harraga* into an activity that *burns* state-rules: rules that stipulate that *this* border can only be crossed in *this* way and not in another; or that papers are only legal in *this* way and not in another. And so *harraga* evokes an immediate relation between the person who does *el harga* and the state. Thus what people engaged in *harraga* do is mess up boundaries.

All this is implied in the sign on the rock, and in the crown making Europe into this royal something that everybody is aspiring to. If there had been only the words, then you might have been tricked into believing that somebody had written this sign trying to help others. *There* is Europe, arrow, in that direction. But there is irony in the crown.

There is also irony in the very fact of this sign on the rock being, as I call it, a road sign. For road signs, along with roads, are things that you find in modern places, like Europe. A road sign signals modernity. A colloquial joke, often heard in the south of Tunisia about someone who is not savvy or up to date with what is going on in the modern world, is: 'Ah, he lives behind the road signs (Men wra L'blayek, من وراء البلايك).[11] Living on the wrong side of the road signs then means that the person is from a place where modernity has not arrived. A rural place. Somewhere backward, where nothing happens. A dead end. A place that has not been *developed*, but may still be implicated in colonial relations. In quite different ways.

Figure 2. The salt truck.

Persisting colonial relations

Figure 2 shows a truck. Now a truck is not a remarkable thing – but this one deserves to be remarked upon. I was angry when I first saw it and cannot help being angry whenever I see it again. It carries salt from Zarzis to France for the company Cotusal. This extraction of salt from Zarzis has quite a history as it is entwined with Tunisia's colonial past, that stretched from 1881 to 1956. Salt has been shipped to France since 1903 by various French companies.[12] Cotusal, active in various Tunisian cities, has praised the Zarzis salt in particular for its high quality and rich minerals, making it suitable not only for bulk use, such as keeping European roads accessible in winter, but also for pharmaceutical purposes.[13] The price that Cotusal currently pays for the salt is still the same as under colonial rule: 5 Tunisian cents for a *tonne* of salt (1000 kilos). By contrast, local consumers will have to pay between 500 and 2500 cents for one *kilo*. In May 2014, after the Tunisian revolution, the concessions for Cotusal were ratified again, along with their old colonial conditions.

So the salt is shipped out of Zarzis. Before it is loaded onto the trucks, it has been 'harvested' in the basins of the *sabkha* (سبخة), a saline flat, a huge area surrounding Zarzis.[14] From there it is transported first to be purified and dried; and then deposited with the help of bulldozers in large heaps in the open air. This saline flat, usually featuring three large white 'mountains, is right next to a temporary cemetery for the dead migrants whose bodies have been washed ashore in considerable numbers since the late

1990s. While the salt ships easily to Europe, the people who are buried here, halted and immobilized *harraga*, had more difficulty crossing the Mediterranean. The currents in the sea somehow push back the bodies of those who tried to cross but drowned and wash them ashore in Zarzis. They died because of bad boats, bad traffickers, bad luck. Over the years volunteers from the town and the local police and coast guards, who take this as an obligation, have been burying them – but the land in which they are permitted to do so is a former landfill. It is unstable and shifts easily after periods of heavy rain. Litter and human remains get mixed together in deeply uncomfortable ways.

And if you climb the hill right next to this cemetery-cum-landfill, you see the white salt heaps shining brightly and towering in the flat landscape. The salt travels from here to France without too many obstacles. It does not need to go in a rickety boat. It is welcomed. Just like the well-educated who go to the migration desks of France and Germany in Tunis (others are following their lead). There, if you have the right papers, diplomas this time, you can cross European borders without problems (Lakhal, 2019; Mahroum, 2001; Musette, 2016).[15] At the same time, Tunis has become the NGO hub of Northern Africa. All the good intentions of the West seem to be gathered there. Many of the NGOs involved provide all sorts of economic programmes aimed at helping to build the country. Help the country: while depleting it of the people with the most promising education. Is that not an irony? The colonial legacy is therefore not just a legacy. It persists in the extraction of all sorts of goods and intellectual capital.

This persistent set of colonial relations is folded into *harraga*. For example, it is not an accident that people from Tunisia tend to go to France, and not to Italy. Thus, the bridges that are being built by *harraga* are not only built by the travellers, but by others as well. This is because, as I indicated above, *harraga* is not a matter of moving away from somewhere and of leaving everything behind. Even though it literally means *burning*, it is about *crafting connections*. It is about the possibility of doing something, both at the site from which you depart and in the site that you go to. *Harraga*, then, keeps connections going, just as they are kept going when salt and brains are exported. Connections that are too easily hidden in discussions on 'migration'.

These connections have to do with money – the money that you need to leave and the money that you send back to your family, or that you hope to send back to your family, once you are doing well at the other side. But connections also mean personal networks, links with the people who went earlier and with the people who are coming after you. Such networks make living in the margins of French society possible, they allow newcomers to arrive.[16] So that people from Tunisia go to France not just because of the colonial legacy between the states, and not just because of a shared language, French,[17] but also because in France they are likely to have an infrastructure: cousins of cousins, people who you can go to and who will help you to find a job, to find shelter, to get going.

There are, however, agreements between Europe and Tunisia that oblige Tunisia to keep its citizens within its territory, or at least to control their movement (e.g. Badalič, 2019). So Tunisia has been active in bringing people back and occasionally jailing them, or giving them a choice between paying a huge fine or going to jail. Everyone, including the airlines, has been enrolled in this process of stopping people from moving illegally. This, too, is a persistent colonial connection.

Except that in 2011 it was, for a while, interrupted. In December 2010 the Tunisian street vendor Mohamed Bouazizi set himself on fire as a response to the confiscation of his wares and the constant humiliation by police officers. This event set in motion a social movement against unemployment, corruption and lack of political freedom. It was the start of the Tunisian revolution, which led to the expulsion of President Ben Ali on 14 January 2011. In the aftermath the state became lenient, absent. The police would just be standing by and letting people go. It was all in the open. People were saying: are you sure, can we go? The police were not sure, but they stepped back and in this way, in February 2011 almost 4000 people, at that time still mostly young men became, did, *harraga*. They took the boat from Zarzis to Lampedusa.

With the president having fled the country and expelled from office, for a moment the military sided with the people. They decided not to shoot, but to say: there is a reason for people to hit the streets. At that same moment, the governors of jails opened their doors to political prisoners who were free to go. So while the state reconfigured itself, it became momentarily absent. The miserable economic situation, the unemployment, the lack of safety, the corruption: they were a shared concern. With poor wages and inflation that was skyrocketing due to neoliberal state politics, police officers were in the same boat as everyone else.

But that moment did not last. In came the IMF with its structural adjustment policy, and an even fiercer commitment to neoliberalism.[18] The call was to reduce bureaucracy, leave more and more to the market (as if the market was functioning), the typical focus of the IMF. Meanwhile, in the tumultuous year of 2013, two secular politicians were assassinated, which prompted the ruling Islamist party Ennahda to hand over power to an interim government. By that time regular citizens had also started to feel the unpredictability of the retreating state. And things became really scary in Tunisia. For the police would stand by, watch how conflicts escalated and do nothing. There would be a conflict on the street, among people demonstrating and blocking a road on the one hand, and passers-by on the other, and the police would not interfere. In the south and in rural areas, crime was rising to the point where people did not dare to go out at night anymore. The absence of the state became palpable. Which indicates that there are different versions of states doing nothing. One is out of solidarity, of understanding, we won't stop you, just go. The other is that of a retreating state that no longer heeds its responsibilities.

By now things have changed again. The coast guard has become more and more active. If you hope to do *harraga* they will stop you.[19] This has changed the way people move. Before they would leave in big boats, but nowadays people often leave in really small feluccas, fit for no more than six people. They used to ask a fisherman, but nowadays many buy their own feluccas and go. So a strong market for small boats and for motors that fit them has been developing in the past two years or so. And indeed, despite the heightened surveillance by the coast guard, the numbers of people that are managing to leave have been increasing throughout 2018 and 2019. And as those involved know about the weather and the sea, there are remarkably few casualties. Still hundreds, but not the thousands that we see for those who leave from Libya.

Figure 3. Mohsen's 'Basta harraga' artwork.

Basta harraga

The people who engage in *harraga* do not all stay in Europe, quite a few of them return. Europe is not all that kind to migrants. However promising the dreams, things can be sad in reality. Because of that and because *harraga* depletes the country, some, like Mohsen Lihidheb, turn against *harraga*. They think it has to be stopped. There has been enough, too much of it. *Basta*.

Figure 3 depicts one of Mohsen's artworks. The round object, with the bulb on top, that is Europe, shining in the distance. And in front of it you see the masses that are moving in its direction. The artwork puts us outside Europe looking at these objects that are organized around it.

The plastic ball that calls up Europe is actually the float of a fishing-net. For his art, Mohsen uses objects that he finds on the beaches of Zarzis. So that is one of them and on top of it there is another find, a bulb. Maybe it stands for enlightenment or the lure of Europe: an illusionary shine on top of this Europe that is self-contained and has everything. Around it there is an empty-looking space, that may be water. And then there are lots of shoes and slippers. Mohsen finds shoes and slippers on the beach. For him, they indicate the human beings who have lost them while moving towards Europe. They may have just lost their footwear, but, tragically, of course, more likely they have lost their lives. And around those shoes there are lifejackets that should have been lifesaving. Maybe they stand for human beings. I think they do because of the black balls that resemble heads. But they are also indicative of safety and danger. Of the risks that people take when they try to get to Europe.

But there are also words: *basta harraga*, they read. *Basta* from the Italian, stop. Stop *harraga*. Enough *harraga*. And this is not a moral but a political statement. It does not accuse those who leave of behaving improperly, of taking undue risks, of betraying their home country. None of that. This statement is sensitive to the fact that *harraga* is not about identity anyway. It is therefore *basta* to the system that causes people to leave. That causes them to view Europe as their only possibility for a good life. To survive. If they survive the crossing of the sea.

Harraga is thus about a politics of *life* and *death*. While it is an effect of a lack of possibilities in life, the risk of death, death at Europe's borders, is never far away.[20] A risk that many who are not welcomed are willing to take because they lack a diploma as engineer, ICT specialist or medical professional. But doing so they are confronted with an exceedingly securitized border. Ever since 2011 and the series of revolts in Arab countries, the southern border of Europe has been cast as vulnerable.[21] One that requires care and attention, in the form of huge investment and the use of state-of-the-art technologies. But since all this high-tech surveillance did not stop people from coming, Europe has been looking for ways of stopping them earlier on their journey, and has been trying to execute its border surveillance elsewhere. Such as in Turkey, after the Turkish deal of 2016 (e.g. M'charek, 2018; Rygiel et al., 2016).

Tunisia has been constantly on Europe's list for an equivalent to this deal with Turkey. Even though its new democracy is still fragile and its economy not moving forward, it has been pressured by various European countries to take the deal. Recently it has complied with a so-called 'Contingency Plan' for providing shelter to some 25,000 refugees that are expected to move out of Libya in the near future as a result of continuing and increasing violence.[22] Yet the number of refugees that leave Libya to come to Tunisia is decreasing, because people know that by being in Tunisia, a so-called safe country, they reduce their chances of ever entering Europe. In addition to actively stopping people moving in its direction, Europe has implemented a large programme called EU Emergency Trust Fund for Africa (EUTF), a 4.5 billion euro programme as a whole and with current funding for North Africa of 656 million euros. The management of 'vulnerable' borders is a key concern in this programme. Its website tells us:

> The BMP [Border Management Programme] Maghreb programme aims is [*sic*] to mitigate *vulnerabilities* arising from irregular migration and to combat irregular migration. The action aims to do so by enhancing the institutional framework of Morocco and Tunisia to protect, monitor and manage the borders, in line with internationals [*sic*] standards and human rights that identifies and mitigates risks to rights holders at borders, while ensuring the free movement of bona fide travellers and goods.[23]

A lot can be said about this programme and its goals, such as indeed 'an emergency for whom?' (Kervyn & Shilhav, 2017). Its focus on migration and borders seems to underline the constant panic about the integrity of Europe's borders. Now in Zarzis its effect has just started to take shape. As part of this EUTF, 20 million euros have been dedicated to innovations in the *Garde Nationale Maritime* of Tunisia, because they are often involved in what are called search and rescue operations. Many have said that these are illegitimate ways of stopping migration. The *Garde Nationale Maritime* will be equipped with new communication technologies and boats, and its staff will be trained accordingly. In addition, it is expected that EUTF money will be invested in innovations in the national police. Although the coast guard might stop people on boats, currently the police does not interfere with them getting on these boats in the first place.

As I said *harraga* is about a politics of life and death. And so is Europe's border management regime. Many have therefore argued that the thousands upon thousands of dead in the Med are co-produced by the way Europe seals its borders off (e.g. Cuttitta & Last, 2019). *Harraga* interrogates this focus on borders precisely by burning these, by pointing the arrow, right there. And it addresses the problem of borders by siding with those who cross them, human beings.

Now there is something tantalizing about the work of Mohsen, the artist. He uses waste to evoke humans. This work calls into question how humans, some humans, are treated as waste. At the same time it seeks to sensitize people to the ecological disasters that are ongoing. He collects waste and displays it. Look, what a lot of waste! But in the artwork pictured in Figure 3, it is important that this is not just any waste.[24] Mohsen has collected traces of movements, traces of *harraga*, to visualize the magnitude of *harraga*. To evoke what *harraga* is all about. If you go, you need decent shoes to walk away, you need bottles of water to take with you, a lifejacket, a boat.

And these are just a few of the objects on display in Mohsen's domain. When you enter his yard and see the heaps of shoes and slippers that he recently collected, of clothing and of other things not always easy to determine, it is shocking, shocking every time. There is so much. The multitude is overwhelming.

This puzzling work of art is laid out on the ground, next to where Mohsen lives at the edge of Zarzis. The setting is mundane: when the photo was taken, a chicken wandered about, seeking worms or something else to eat. But on a day like any other, Mohsen has made this photo to display it on his website. If you enter his museum, he takes you by the hand, there are conversations, he tells you about his work. But at the same time, he does not just address people nearby, people in the village, passers-by. He deliberately reaches out.[25]

To you as well. While the artwork puts its viewers outside Europe to look at it from a distance, the *basta harraga* that underlines the artwork is directed to people in Europe and beyond. It is, after all, not written in Arabic script like the text on the rock. The juxtaposition of the Italian and the Arabic words are in the Roman alphabet. This is a political call. That should not have to be translated into English to make its point.

Conclusion: Moving on

In this article I have used the word *harraga* to complicate what is often addressed as 'irregular migration'. I did not rush to translate this word, but explored it, chewed on it. This has allowed me to write about things that the term 'migration' risks hiding. Such as, for one, that 'migrating' is not necessarily about others, migrants, 'those people', however they may be identified, but that it is something a 'we' may be compelled to do if we find ourselves being buried alive, living in a dead end. Next, that colonial relations are not over or a history left behind but leave traces in the present, persist, take ever-new forms (e.g. Stoler, 2016). And then, crucially, that the separation between Europe here and the rest there, beyond its boundaries, does not hold in practice. For the borders of Europe are exported and protected in various locations in the world, by various actors (e.g. Afailal & Fernandez, 2017; Badalić, 2019).

Rather than presenting different views on irregular migration, here I have mobilized three material objects – rock, salt and rubbish – to unfold what *harraga* is. In the context of the present publication, I have done so with a particular question in mind, namely: how does *harraga* move social theory?

To address this question head-on, the rock provided a good starting point. The rock allowed me to put Europe out-of-focus, for a moment, and to start from a specific place outside Europe, Zarzis. From the salience that it has in this place, the word *harraga* allowed me make seven interventions in current ideas about migration.

First, *harraga* is quintessentially an activity that interferes with imagined relations between states and individuals. While the word *migration* is tightly related to formal state-obeying, law-obeying, movements of people, *harraga* is about burning borders. It assumes a situation where states try to stop citizens from moving about. *Harraga* is thus an activity that *burns* state-rules and messes up boundaries.

Second, *harraga* is an activity rather than an identity. This became clear as I explored *harraga* from the perspective of those facing the rock-cum-road sign, 'Europe this way'. I did not introduce this perspective by soliciting their views on migration, but by attending to where they are in the world and what they do when engaging in *harraga*. By attending to the preparation work, knowledge, networks and money that are required for the crossing, which tells that moving out of the Maghreb is not only a risky but also a demanding activity.

Third, *harraga* is about crafting connections and expanding living space. From the perspective of Zarzis it became visible that migration is not so much about leaving one place for another, but rather about expanding living space. It is about making movement possible rather than staying stuck, buried alive in a dead end. *Harraga* thus sensitizes us to connections made between there and here, but also to the ways in which movement both depends on already established connections and in its turn brings about links that are new.

Fourth, *harraga* is about colonial flows and extractions. Flows of people from Zarzis to France and back. Extractions from Zarzis to France only. For while people from Zarzis get on small boats in the hope of a better life in Europe, salt is being carried away on trucks and shipped to France with only very little return. Salt leaves Zarzis for France at prices set under colonial rule.[26] While in current debate on migration the movement of people is cast as a problem, the circulation of goods such as salt is part of formal, free economic trade. *Harraga* brings this to light. It makes us attend to hidden but enduring colonial relations which mean that burning borders and the shipping of salt are part of the same socio-political reality.

Fifth, *harraga* intervenes with the politics of borders. For the currents of the sea bring the bodies of *people* who did not make it to Europe alive, and washes these ashore in Zarzis. This puts salt in a further and different relation to migration, as the *sabkha* from where salt is extracted is adjacent to a provisional cemetery for drowned migrants. *Harraga*, then, is not simply about migration and migrants knocking on Europe's door, but also about dead bodies at Europe's borders. Many have argued that heightened securitization of Europe's borders are contributing to increased numbers of dead in the Mediterranean (Cuttitta & Last, 2019; Spijkerboer, 2007). Yet Europe is investing even more in protecting its borders as well as exporting these to other parts of the world. Those who arrive alive in Europe are typically submitted to heightened surveillance. The dead, by contrast, have long been conveniently overlooked (Last & Spijkerboer, 2014) and still receive little political attention (Kovras & Robins, 2016). *Harraga* calls attention to dead-bodies-at-the-border (M'charek, 2018).

Sixth, *harraga* intervenes in the separation between the dead and the living. Death is folded into *harraga* for those facing the rock.[27] It is not something they shy away from, even if they may stumble over the bodies of those who did not make it to Europe alive as these are washed ashore on the very beaches that they will depart from.[28] *Harraga* thus brings the realities of the dead and the living together.

Seventh, *harraga* calls into question what is litter and who is disposable. Rubbish, configured in an extraordinary piece of art, evokes the lure of Europe and the risk of death for those trying to reach it. It is crafted with objects found at the shore, objects that belonged to those who tried to engage in *harraga* but died along the way. Litter of people treated as if they were disposable. At the same time, it also displays words: *Basta harraga*. This political statement questions the various issues that I addressed in this article. It addresses the problem of borders by siding with those who cross them, human beings. It decries problems of persisting colonial relations, lack of opportunities and unemployment, state surveillance and border management. It is to this spiral of disparities and death that *Basta harraga* is a call. *Basta*.

Acknowledgements

I am grateful to Mohsen Lihidheb for his friendship and for sharing his stories and wisdom whenever we have a chance to meet. I thank Annemarie Mol and John Law for encouraging me to write about *harraga* and for their patience during a slow process. Guiding and gently pushing me further, yet giving me the space to explore the unexpected narratives that emerged. Thank you! Fredy Mora-Gámez I thank for reviewing my article and for his generous feedback. I also thank the members of the TemaT team (Linköping) for their careful reading and discussion of the article, and the members of RaceFaceID team, especially Lisette Jong, Ildikó Plájás and Clément Dreano for feedback on an earlier daft.

Funding

I am grateful to the European Research Council for supporting my research through an ERC Consolidator Grant (FP7-617451-RaceFaceID-Race Matter: On the Absent Presence of Race in Forensic Identification).

Notes

1. In this way, Libya is part of the story. A few decades ago, half of the people in the south of Tunisia could be found in Libya. Not so now. There used to be jobs but there is nothing you might want to go to Libya for now. With the discovery of oil in 1957 Libya's economy started to boom and the demand for labour was steady until the fall of the Gaddafi regime in 2011. The political relations between Libya and Tunisia in the period 1973–1987 were whimsical, ranging from extreme tensions and military battles to dear friendship. This led to a highly

securitized border that was under the direct control of the army. Both this border politics and the fact that many (male) citizens were hesitant to acquire a passport (because of the risk of being called up for military service, or because it was too expensive) provoked *harraga* (Chandoul & Boubakri, 1991). Some would engage in the trafficking of Tunisian sugar and Libyan tea, others would go for seasonal labour (olive harvest), still others would find more permanent jobs in the Tripoli area. Since 1988, the Tunisia–Libya *harraga* became obsolete, as it became easy to legally cross the border with an ID card rather than a passport.

2. In 1956 both Tunisia and Morocco were *declared* independent by France; Algeria, however, had fought a bitter war between 1954 and 1962 to win its independence from France.

3. To be sure, as many border-studies scholars have argued, Europe's borders are not necessarily geographical borders. Given the severe surveillance of people who apply for a visa, especially if they are from so-called black-list countries, Europe's borders have extended way beyond its geographical location (M'charek et al., 2014; Van Houtum, 2010). This export of Europe's border controls has assumed great vigour with the so-called refugee crises (e.g. Zaiotti, 2016).

4. Or, see www.youtube.com/watch?v=DnZHM5glkxE (accessed 6 January 2020).

5. See www.youtube.com/watch?v=d6ggJ-u8j9s&t=1550s (accessed 6 January 2020). In the summer of 2018 I was contacted by the makers of the documentary because they were producing a series on migration and were wondering whether they could follow me and my research in Tunisia. This programme thus came to be centred on drowned migrants and the work of fishermen and volunteers to dignify the dead. See M'charek (2018) for an overall sketch of this research

6. Majid is a pseudonym.

7. These are the legal rules concerning so-called 'unaccompanied minors' in Europe. Even when you are not considered a refugee you have the right of residence in the country of destination and are entitled to education.

8. Economics is an important aspect of *harraga*. To be sure this does not only include the money made by traffickers. If one starts to think of the economics of the visa system, the securitization of movement and borders, the scale of the *harraga* market becomes tangible. This aspect of *harraga*, however important, goes beyond the scope of this article, but see e.g. Andersson (2014), Cranston et al. (2018), Gammeltoft-Hansen and Nyberg-Sorenson (2013) and Schapendonk (2018).

9. This fear is real, and many have grown disappointed that the recent political changes did not translate into social equity and economic development. Things have got worse in many ways, with increasing government debt, rising inflation and the dramatic devaluation of the Tunisian Dinar as economic facts on the ground.

10. See e.g. https://nawaat.org/portail/2019/05/07/tunisia-illegal-migration-and-brain-drain-two-sides-of-the-same-coin/ (accessed 6 January 2020).

11. Those who understand the Arabic will enjoy this rap, moving between France and Tunisia, in which the road sign figures as a motif. In the song the identity of 'living behind the traffic signs' is proudly claimed, in an angry response to a statement made by a well-known Tunisian TV presenter, Mariem Belkadhi, who said that she is not 'Men wra L'blayek' and thus knows what goes around in the world. The song addresses the extractions and exploitation of those considered 'Men wra L'blayek', the focus of (post)colonial policy on the metropolis and thus the discriminating separation between urban and rural Tunisia. Enjoy! www.facebook.com/truth.ha9i9a.news.2/videos/vb.277524315642123/2336267746587937/?type=2&theater

12. Cotusal has been active in Tunisia since 1949, but it is claimed that the company was involved much earlier than this date, see http://nawaat.org/portail/2018/03/16/cotusal-exploitation-francaise-de-lor-blanc-tunisien/

13. www.cotusal.tn/le-salin-de-zarzis/

14. Whereas Zarzis town covers 34 hectares, Cotusal is allowed to use 1774 hectares of the Zarzis area; see http://nawaat.org/portail/2018/03/16/cotusal-exploitation-francaise-de-lor-blanc-tunisien/ (accessed 6 January 2020).

15. The problems of brain drain in the Mediterranean region is now internationally recognized and (partly) addressed through various projects that are developed as part of the so-called Emergency Trust North Africa (EUTF) and its aim of governing migration: https://ec.europa.eu/trustfundforafrica/region/north-africa/tunisia (accessed 6 January 2020).

16. These days, such networks are also extending into other countries, especially to Germany (Musette, 2016).

17. French is the second language in Tunisia and is taught from primary school level onward. It is used actively in social traffic and in the media.

18. See e.g. http://nawaat.org/portail/2013/03/18/tunisia-and-the-imf-a-beggar-state-and-an-impoverished-people/ (accessed 6 January 2020). In the same vein, the EU and Tunisia are involved in negotiations about an international trade deal (ALECA) which forces Tunisia to liberalize its markets. This deal is met with harsh criticism by Tunisian experts: 'some have argued that the liberalization of agricultural markets would allow heavily subsidized European agricultural goods to be dumped onto the Tunisian market'. See http://mesh-kal.com/2019/05/20/calls-to-block-tunisia-eu-trade-deal-get-louder/ (accessed 6 January 2020).

19. This is also part of the so-called externalization of Europe's borders that we have encountered and which I further elaborate below. The coast guard are supported by the EU to help stop all irregular migrants, resulting e.g. in jeopardizing people's rights to seek refuge, see e.g. Badalič (2019).

20. Literature about these so-called border-deaths is accumulating. From work that tries to map the magnitude of death, its numbers (e.g. Last & Spijkerboer, 2014), to work that focuses on the process of identification (e.g. M'charek & Casartelli, 2019).

21. See, inter alia, Broeders and Hampshire, (2013), M'charek et al. (2014), Van Reekum and Schinkel (2017).

22. www.ansamed.info/ansamed/en/news/sections/generalnews/2019/05/28/libya-unhcr-plan-in-tunisia-ready-for-25000-refugees_0ac21198-03e6-4219-bd93-0ed07041dad2.html (accessed 6 January 2020).

23. https://ec.europa.eu/trustfundforafrica/region/north-africa/regional/border-management-pro-gramme-maghreb-region-bmp-maghreb_en (accessed 6 January 2020). My emphasis.

24. If you are interested in Mohsen's work you might want to watch a documentary dedicated to his work, broadcast by Aljazeera in November 2017: '*Garbage artist of Zarzis*, at: www.youtube.com/watch?v=rttsYj_aj7E (accessed 6 January 2020).

25. See e.g. the documentary *Garbage artist of Zarzis* or the various websites of Mohsen: http://art.artistes-sf.org/mohsen; http://zarziszitazarzis.blogspot.com (accessed 6 January 2020); http://zarzissea.skyblog.com (accessed 6 January 2020).

26. On the perfomativity of circulations, see M'charek (2016).

27. This observation is an obvious one for people who have lost their loved ones on their way to Europe. This makes the forensic identification of the dead, in various ways, about dead and living people (see M'charek & Black, 2019).

28. See for an impression, a newspaper article I published at: www.nrc.nl/nieuws/2019/07/17/de-lijken-blijven-op-de-kusten-aanspoelen-a3967427 (accessed 6 January 2020).

References

Afailal, H., & Fernandez, M. (2017). The externalization of European borders: The other face of coloniality Turkey as a case study. *Athens Journal of Mediterranean Studies*, 4(3), 215–224.

Andersson, R. (2014). *Illegality, Inc. Clandestine migration and the business of bordering Europe.* University of California Press.

Badalić, V. (2019). Tunisia's role in the EU external migration policy: Crimmigration law, illegal practices, and their impact on human rights. *Journal of International Migration and Integration, 20,* 85–100.

Broeders, D., & Hampshire, J. (2013). Dreaming of seamless borders: ICTs and the pre-emptive governance of mobility in Europe. *Journal of Ethnic and Migration Studies, 39*(8), 1201–1218.

Chandoul, M., & Boubakri, H. (1991). Migrations clandestines et contrebande à la frontière tuniso-libyenne [Undercover migration and smuggling at the Tunisia–Libya border]. *Revue Européenne des Migrations Internationales, 7*(2), 155–162.

Cranston, S., Schapendonk, J., & Spaan, E. (2018). New directions in exploring the migration industries: Introduction to special issue. *Journal of Ethnic and Migration Studies, 44*(4), 543–557.

Cuttitta, P., & Last, T. (Eds.). (2019). *Border deaths: Causes, dynamics and consequences of migration-related mortality.* Amsterdam University Press.

European Commission. (2017). *Securing Europe's external borders.* http://ec.europa.eu/dgs/home-affairs/what-we-do/policies/securing-eu-borders/fact-sheets/docs/systematic_checks_at_external_borders_en.pdf (accessed 15 November 2019).

Gammeltoft-Hansen, T., & Nyberg-Sørensen, N. (Eds.). (2013). *The migration industry and the commercialization of international migration.* Routledge.

Kervyn, E., & Shilhav, R. (2017). *An emergency for whom? The EU Emergency Trust Fund for Africa-migratory routes and development aid in Africa.* Oxfam Briefing Note.

Kovras, I., & Robins, S. (2016). Death as the border: Managing missing migrants and unidentified bodies at the EU's Mediterranean frontier. *Political Geography, 55,* 40–49.

Lakhal, M. (2019). Tunisia: Illegal migration and brain-drain, two sides of the same coin. *Nawaat.* https://nawaat.org/portail/2019/05/07/tunisia-illegal-migration-and-brain-drain-two-sides-of-the-same-coin/ (accessed 6 January 2020).

Last, T., & Spijkerboer, T. (2014). Tracking deaths in the Mediterranean. In T. Brian & F. Laczko (Eds.), *Fatal journeys tracking lives lost during migration* (pp. 85–108). International Organization for Migration (IOM).

Magalhães, B. (2015). *Enacting refugees: An ethnography of asylum decisions* (Doctoral dissertation). The Open University.

Mahroum, S. (2001). Europe and the immigration of highly skilled labour. *International Migration, 39*(5), 27–43.

M'charek, A. (2016). Performative circulations: On flows and stops in forensic DNA practices. *Tecnoscienza, 7*(2), 9–34.

M'charek, A. (2018). Dead-bodies-at-the-border: Distributed evidence and emerging forensic infrastructure for identification. In M. Maguire, U. Rao, & N. Zurawski (Eds.), *Bodies of evidence: Security, knowledge, and power* (pp. 89–110). Duke University Press.

M'charek, A., & Black, J. (2019). Engaging bodies as matter of care: Counting and accounting for death during migration. In P. Cuttitta & T. Last (Eds.), *Border deaths: Causes, dynamics and consequences of migration-related mortality* (pp. 85–103). Amsterdam University Press.

M'charek, A., & Casartelli, S. (2019). Identifying dead migrants: Forensic care work and relational citizenship. *Citizenship Studies, 23*(7), 738–757.

M'charek, A., Schramm, K., & Skinner, D. (2014). Topologies of race: Doing territory, population and identity in Europe. *Science, Technology, & Human Values, 39*(4), 468–487.

Musette, M. S. (2016). Brain drain from the Southern Mediterranean. *IEMed Mediterranean Yearbook.* European Institute of the Mediterranean.

Natter, K. (2014). *Fifty years of Maghreb emigration: How states shaped Algerian, Moroccan and Tunisian emigration* (Working Paper 95). International Migration Institute, University of Oxford.

Natter, K. (2015). Revolution and political transition in Tunisia: A migration game changer? *Migration Information Source: The Online Journal of the Migration Policy Institute*. www. migrationpolicy.org/article/revolution-and-political-transition-tunisia-migration-game-changer (accessed 6 January 2020).

Rygiel, K., Baban, F., & Ilcan, S. (2016). The Syrian refugee crisis: The EU–Turkey 'deal' and temporary protection. *Global Social Policy, 16*(3), 315–320.

Schapendonk, J. (2018). Navigating the migration industry: Migrants moving through an African-European web of facilitation/control. *Journal of Ethnic and Migration Studies, 44*(4), 663–679.

Spijkerboer, T. (2007). The human costs of border control. *European Journal of Migration and Law, 9*, 127–139.

Stoler, A. L. (2016). *Duress: Imperial durabilities for our times*. Duke University Press.

Van Houtum, H. (2010). Human blacklisting: The global apartheid of the EU's external border regime. *Environment and Planning D: Society and Space, 28*(6), 957–976.

Van Reekum, R., & Schinkel, W. (2017). Drawing lines, enacting migration: Visual prostheses of bordering Europe. *Public Culture, 29*(1), 27–51.

Zaiotti, R. (2016). *Externalizing migration management: Europe, North America and the spread of 'remote control' practices*. Routledge.

Author biography

Amade M'charek is Professor of Anthropology of Science at the Department of Anthropology of the University of Amsterdam. Her research interests are in forensics, forensic anthropology and race in the criminal justice system as well as humanitarian settings. M'charek is the Principal Investigator of the ERC-Consolidator Project RaceFaceID (http://race-face-id.eu), a project on forensic identification, face and race.

Article

The Sociological Review Monographs

The Sociological Review Monographs
2020, Vol. 68(2) 175–191
© The Author(s) 2020
Article reuse guidelines:
sagepub.com/journals-permissions
DOI: 10.1177/0038026120905492
journals.sagepub.com/home/sor

鮭鱒論 (salmon trout theory) and the politics of non-Western academic terms

Shiaki Kondo
北海道大学 Hokkaido Daigaku [Hokkaido University], Japan

Heather Anne Swanson
Aarhus Universitet [Aarhus University], Denmark

Abstract
This article probes how scholars might give nuanced attention to the power-laden dynamics of knowledge practices within non-Western settings at the same time that they seek to become more alert to the challenges of Anglophone academic domination. This inquiry arises from our focus on 鮭鱒論 (*sake masu ron*), a Japanese term that can be translated as *salmon trout theory*. While 鮭鱒論 holds unique insights for the growing fields of the environmental humanities, multispecies anthropology, and other forms of more-than-human scholarship, it is fundamentally tied to Japanese colonial projects and the marginalization of Ainu knowledges. By tracing the development of 鮭鱒論, we demonstrate that while non-English-language academic terms can open up new analytical possibilities, they can also carry their own imperial histories and politics of knowledge. At the same time that we explore how careful attention to 鮭鱒論 might be a useful scholarly move, we also show why it is important to robustly understand the term's Japanese context as we consider its wider scholarly possibilities. How, we ask, might the term be productively remade in dialogue with Ainu activisms, indigenous studies, and postcolonial theory? Through this case, we offer some preliminary insights about how to simultaneously respond to the marginalization of non-Anglophone academic traditions and to the violences of non-Western imperialisms.

Keywords
Ainu studies, archeology, Japan, North Pacific, salmon

Corresponding author:
Shiaki Kondo, Center for Ainu and Indigenous Studies, Hokkaido University, Kita 8, Nishi 6, Kita-ku, Sapporo, Hokkaido, 060-0808, Japan.
Email: shiaki.kondo@let.hokudai.ac.jp

This monograph asks how English, an academically dominant language, can be enriched through more careful attention to other words and their conceptual worlds. In this final article, we seek to build on this suggestion by exploring how the need to question absences, silences, and exclusions is not limited to standardized social science English, but is also relevant across a range of academic languages that have developed together with imperialist, nationalist, and/or colonialist projects. While we fully share this monograph's move to create more space for non-English concepts to expand and disrupt existing English social theory, we also seek to show how it is essential to simultaneously remain alert to the often complicated politics of other language concepts themselves.

Our concerns emerge from our focus on 鮭鱒論 (*sake masu ron*), a Japanese term that can be translated as *salmon trout theory*. While 鮭鱒論 holds unique insights for the growing fields of the environmental humanities, multispecies anthropology, and other forms of more-than-human scholarship, it is also tied to Japanese colonial projects and the marginalization of Ainu knowledges. This term pulls us into this article's core concerns: despite their ability to productively enrich English-language scholarship across multiple disciplines, Japanese language concepts have often been marginalized within English-dominant academic spaces (Asquith, 1996; Kuwayama, 2004). Yet, at the same time that English-language scholarship needs to consider what it might be losing in its mono-lingual form, Japanese-language scholarship calls out for an analogous inquiry. Like European and American social science conversations (in many languages), the historical development of Japanese social science was profoundly entangled with imperial and nation-building initiatives, and many 20th-century Japanese concepts – both academic and popular – themselves emerge from complicated and problematic practices of colonial knowledge-making and dubious racial ideologies.

As scholars who work within (Kondo) or alongside (Swanson) Japanese-language social science institutions and conversations, we approach this monograph issue's concerns about English-dominance, conceptual difference, and questions of translation through a particular regional lens. In contrast to the Netherlands and Scandinavian countries, where non-English academic publishing has already been substantially marginalized, Japanese language publication remains robust. While Japanese scholars in some fields prioritize English publications, others feel greater pressure to publish in Japanese than English, especially in their early career phases. In short, scholars' relations to English-dominant academic debates take many forms.

Broadly speaking, Japanese scholars have long been alert to the challenges of what Mol and Law, in the introduction to this volume, call 'academic submission': the process of being judged through academic practices that often dismiss research conducted on other terms. However, in Japanese contexts, the problem has been framed less as one of language-based Anglophone dominance and more as a general issue of 'Western' intellectual hegemony (Kuwayama, 2008), which some Japanese scholarship, including ethnology and folkloristics, has actively sought to resist (Hudson, 2006, pp. 413–414). Because 20th-century Japanese academics often read German-language scholarship alongside English texts, they frequently considered them together as 'Western' modes of thought, and in this context, Roman-character/Chinese-character distinctions have often been the more important categorical distinction.

In this article, we move rapidly among words such as Anglophone, Western, and European in ways that may seem awkward to some readers. The challenges in using these terms are part of the very questions of translation and untranslatability that are so central to this monograph. Common terms for expressing difference – such as 欧米 (*oobei*, roughly Euro-American), 洋風 (*youfuu*, roughly Western style), ローマ字 (*romaji*, roman letters), 外来語 (*gairaigo*, words from non-Japanese languages other than Chinese), and 白人 (*hakujin*, white people) – embody a logic of civilizational thinking that is not quite identical to that expressed by the English-language terms. As we explore in more depth within the context of 鮭鱒論, Japanese-language imaginaries often divide the cultures of the world into bread people (Europeans and Americans) and rice people (Asians), while giving little attention to the world-making force of other peoples and lifeways.

Overall, we see Japanese social science as a productive site from which to further contemplate this monograph's core themes, as its scholarship has emerged jointly out of concerns about subordination within European and American imperial projects and its own imperial conquests. Within this fray, both academic and popular notions of 'Japanese-ness' have typically come to be defined in ways that variously subsume, erase, or render other identities, modes of practice, and knowledge traditions as constitutive outsides. As we describe below, 鮭鱒論 allows us to probe such dynamics through attention to Japanese social science theory about Ainu and other indigenous peoples.

We take up these issues as cultural anthropologists – i.e., as members of a discipline that continues to grapple with its own colonial roots. Anthropology, as a field, developed within practices of colonial governance, and today, the field continues to grapple with the ways this history shapes ongoing practices. In one sense, anthropology is a field that seeks to take non-Western concepts seriously as analytics, and 'emic' concepts often structure anthropological inquiries. Non-English terms set off by italic font are a common feature of ethnographic description and analysis, marking their untranslatability and otherness in relation to the surrounding sea of English prose. Such use has been the subject of much debate and critique: Does anthropology inappropriately domesticate non-English and non-Western concepts in its efforts to make them legible and assimilateable to the Euro-American academe? Or does it allow them to disrupt dominant discourses? Is the very distinction between emic and etic inherently colonialist as the etic is merely the unmarked emic of European thought? And overall, who gets to make translations, and whose terms are used to 'write culture' (Clifford & Marcus, 1986)?

What is 鮭鱒論?

Such questions inform our approach to 鮭鱒論, an important concept in Japanese anthropology and archeology. In contrast to many of the concepts presented in this monograph, 鮭鱒論 is a term that emerged within practices of academic analysis, specifically those of Japanese scholars to interpret and narrate the pre-history of Japanese and Ainu people, in part through comparisons with the West Coast of North America. In one sense, 鮭鱒論 is not especially difficult to translate or explain in English. It names the scholarly claim that there is a region in which salmon are important not only materially, in the form of nutrients, but also spiritually, i.e., in the nearly ubiquitous presence of First Salmon ceremonies. The area is nearly co-extant with the home range of Pacific salmon, stretching from northern Japan, the Kurils, and Kamchatka to Alaska, Western Canada, and south to northern California. The primary argument of 鮭鱒論 is that salmon and sea-run trout facilitated the development of rich, complex indigenous cultures with relatively high population densities around the North Pacific Rim, i.e., that particular worlds emerged through the interactions of people and salmon. By drawing attention to these relations, the term offers significant resources for multispecies scholarship, which we discuss in more depth below.

Yet the simplicity and utility of the concept obscures the stakes and questions with which it is entangled. 鮭鱒論 has a deeply problematic history in relation to the Japanese islands of Honshu and Hokkaido, where it was used to explain why some areas (those without salmon) developed agriculture, while others (those with abundant salmon) did not. This split became essential to narratives about the emergence of 'Japanese culture' through rice cultivation that frame both the culture and mode of cultivation as products of creative invention and ingenuity borne of relative resource scarcity. While Japanese anthropologists and archeologists were captivated by salmon as such, some scholars typically framed the abundance of these fish as an impediment to cultural development. In elaborations of 鮭鱒論, salmon allegedly provided so much natural wealth that the people who depended on them remained 'backward' because they did not need to develop civilization, industriousness, or complex social institutions to survive. In this way, the concept developed within conversations that depicted North Pacific indigenous groups, including Ainu people, as 'primitive.'

Throughout the late 19th and 20th centuries, Japanese academic debates have been central to projects of national identity-making, as Japanese intellectuals and elites have struggled to define what it means to be at once 'modern,' 'non-Western,' and 'Japanese.' As in Europe and the US, anthropology and ethnology in Japan developed in large part as projects of colonial administration and national identity-building, respectively. 鮭鱒論 gained prominence in post-World War II Japan, during the period of intense reflection about Japanese identity that followed the war and American Occupation. At the same time, it also evokes multilayered histories of imperial identity projects that stretch back to the Meiji (1868–1912) and Tokugawa (1603–1868) periods. For centuries, ethnic Japanese elites sought to distinguish themselves from Ainu people, whom they termed 土人 (*dojin*, or barbarians), while allowing the Matsumae Han (an ethnic Japanese trading institution) to exploit Ainu labor and salmon runs as they profited from the export of fish and other northern products to mainland Japan. Beginning in 1869, the Japanese state (formed in 1868) began to officially claim, settle, and colonize *yaunmosir*, an island the new government renamed Hokkaido. In the following decades, Japanese colonial officials sought to forcibly assimilate Ainu people, drawing inspiration from American Indian policies (Medak-Saltzman, 2015, 2018). Recognizing the centrality of salmon for Ainu lifeways, the government-run Hokkaido Colonization Commission banned Ainu salmon fishing and forced Ainu people into farming (Yamada, 2011). For more than a century, the Japanese state refused to acknowledge Ainu as native people, referring to them as *kyuudojin*, or 'former barbarians.' Such projects of dispossession, discrimination, and dismissal of Ainu lifeways and knowledges were part and parcel of efforts to define and constitute a celebrated Japanese-ness by invoking Ainu people as lesser 'others' (Morris-Suzuki, 1994).

鮭鱒論 sits within these histories as it is bound up with efforts to probe what it means to be Japanese by explaining the origins of Japanese culture – and by doing so vis-a-vis Ainu people who were deemed to be the remnants of those who did not develop proper civilization. It is far from the only Japanese social science concept to embody such a logic: it was part of widespread academic and popular efforts to develop new and ostensibly better modes of 民族主義 (*minzokushugi*, or ethnic nationalism) in the wake of WWII. Although many aspects of this school of thought – often referred to as 日本人論 (*nihonjinron*, or theories about the Japanese/Japanese-ness) – remain embedded in academic and public discourse, younger generations of Japanese anthropologists typically consider it to be a reformulation of wartime nationalism and explicitly distance themselves from what many consider to be its racist and imperialist underpinnings.

As we will explore in more depth in the following sections, 鮭鱒論 is a thoroughly 'Japanese' concept in that it developed within the conversations of Japanese academics and in dialogue with projects of Japanese nation-making. Yet we want to stress that the concept came into being within Japanese academic traditions that are at once highly international, specifically positioned, and cross-disciplinary. 鮭鱒論 emerged at the intersections of anthropology and archeology, as well as in the encounters between Japanese scholars and German/Austrian theories of cultural diffusion. We first trace the intellectual history of 鮭鱒論 in greater depth to show how this concept formed within a complicated mix of transnational academic conversations, nationalist desires, and colonial relations. We then probe why the term has not gained much traction in English-language debates, as well as why it has fallen out of favor within contemporary Japanese anthropology. Lastly, we explore why, despite the histories we outline here, we want to attempt to engage with the concept and what we see as its latent possibilities. In doing so, we probe why social scientists might want to re-engage this concept, and how they might carefully and productively remake it in dialogue with Ainu activisms, indigenous studies, and postcolonial theory.

While there are many analytical reasons to consider 鮭鱒論 within the context of this monograph issue, we have also chosen the term because it is intertwined with our own research. We are two anthropologists who research the relations among people and salmon – one of us is Japanese, studied in the US, and now works at an indigenous research center in Hokkaido, while the other is American and conducted research on fisheries in Hokkaido. For both of us, 鮭鱒論 has shaped our work in significant, albeit different ways.[1]

鮭鱒論 and Marxist history

鮭鱒論 played a central role in post-World War II Japanese archeology, a discipline that, in turn, became core to widespread debates about national and ethnic identity in the second half of the 20th century. 鮭鱒論 was originally proposed by Sugao Yamanouchi, a prominent Japanese archeologist known for his pioneering work on Jomon (archaeological) culture. In the late 1940s, Yamanouchi began to talk about salmon and trout as an important food source for Jomon people who lived in (what came to be) northeastern

Japan. For more than a decade, Yamanouchi orally presented this idea on various occasions, and it was even cited by his colleagues. However, it was only in 1964 that Yamanouchi first published an outline of his 鮭鱒論 idea.

Yamanouchi (1964/1996) characterized the Jomon as a neolithic-stage culture with pottery and polished stone tools, but lacking agriculture and non-canine animal husbandry. Based on the faunal remains in shell middens, he argued that Jomon people likely had an economy based on hunting, fishing, and gathering, and he drew on comparisons with ethnographic descriptions of contemporary indigenous groups in California to argue that Jomon people may have used acorns and salmon/trout as their principal food sources, in a way similar to peoples on the other side of the Pacific. According to Yamanouchi, while nuts and acorns were widely available in the Japanese archipelago, salmon and trout were available only in its northeastern parts. The distribution of fish could explain the seemingly uneven distribution of Jomon archeological remains, which are numerous in northeastern Japan and less so in southwestern areas. Overall, Yamanouchi depicted the Jomon people in ancient northeastern Japan as the southern limit of a salmon/trout area, stretching from California to Hokkaido and northeastern Honshu islands.

Some Japanese archeologists and historians enthusiastically accepted Yamanouchi's idea, while others remained skeptical (Watanabe, 1967/1996). Japanese Marxist historian Seita Toma was an early supporter of what quickly became known as 鮭鱒論. Toma (1951) theorized that Jomon culture split in its final developmental stage into an artistically-refined northeastern culture (ex. Kamegaoka) and a down-to-earth western culture. The difference between the two was explained by the presence/absence of salmon and trout, explicitly building on Yamanouchi's 鮭鱒論 idea. Toma (1951) speculated that the affluent northeastern culture was able to develop a magnificent artistic tradition, evidenced by the Kamegaoka-style potteries, due to its relatively well-off economic status. However, in Toma's analysis, the people who created this beautiful artistic tradition had 'already lost the internal power to develop in the future' due to their excessive salmon wealth (1951, p. 31). In contrast, Toma described western Jomon culture as plain yet more inventive, in that its people began to adopt 'primitive' agriculture. According to Toma, western Jomon people thus eagerly accepted rice cultivation when it was introduced from overseas because they had some previous experience in agriculture and were interested in exploring new ways of living. In essence, Toma's narrative is one of how a group of poor forager-horticulturalists 'developed' into rice cultivators, while their domestic neighbors to the northeast, the original affluent salmon people, remained undeveloped and slid behind.

The title of Toma's 1951 book, *Formation of the Japanese Race: In Terms of the Relations with East Asian Peoples*, reveals its aim to re-narrate Japanese-ness in the wake of Japan's defeat in World War II and the severe criticisms of its imperial ideologies. In the postwar period, Toma's argument was considered progressive in the sense that he was trying to break away from the mystified emperor-centered view of Japanese history. Toma was part of a cohort of Japanese social science and humanities scholars who were looking for a new theoretical framework through which to envision a new 'democratic' society. In contrast to Yamanouchi, Toma made 鮭鱒論 a more politically charged theory with a refined Marxist twist. For many Japanese archeologists and historians, Marxism, which was oppressed during the war period, assumed prominence as an influential paradigm.

It should not be assumed that because 鮭鱒論 emerges out of contact with Western scholars and Marxist theories that it is not also 'Japanese.' While the concept has resonances with the work of English-language Marxist anthropologists, such as Marvin Harris (1979), it is also 'other' to them, as 鮭鱒論 took on its unique conceptual form in deep dialogue with Japanese ethnographic traditions and situated political concerns that differed markedly from European and American contexts. 鮭鱒論 is not part of a universal Marxist materialist cannon, but a term that emerges out of encounters between Marxist theory and other lines of thought specific to Japan.

In the case of Japanese archaeology, Marxism allowed scholars to emphasize developmental trajectories over both divine and multi-ethnic origin stories. While the official narrative of wartime Japan continued the assertion that Japan was an emperor-centered monoethnic nation-state with divine origins, some Japanese scholars, including Shogoro Tsuboi, described the Japanese as fundamentally multi-ethnic in order to justify Japanese colonial expansion and its rule over other Asian people (Yamaji, 2011, pp. 11–12). In this context, discussions of ethnic hybridity were as politically problematic as those of racial purity. Within this academic atmosphere, 'any discussion of "indigenous people" or "ethnic origins" in ancient Japan . . . seemed to provide support for that [colonial] expansion' (Hudson, 2006, p. 414). Thus, as early as the 1930s, Japanese archeologists began to stay away from any discussion of ethnicity as a resistance against these types of imperial narratives.

As an historian who received much inspiration from archeological discoveries at that time, Toma inherited this caution around ethnicity, indigenous peoples (e.g., Ainu and Okinawan), and colonial justification. Yet he also tried to re-establish the concept of ethnicity in a Marxist framework (Toma, 1951, p. 11, note 18). Throughout his 1951 book, Toma discusses the historical development of three regions in 'Japan,' namely Tohoku/Kanto (northeast), Kinai (contemporary Kansai area), and northern Kyushu in relation to the Chinese continental dynasties and nations in the Korean peninsula.

However, by today's standards, his arguments are also highly problematic. As previously mentioned, Toma (1951, p. 199) characterizes Tohoku as an originally affluent salmon region which was left behind in later development.[2] This is reminiscent of mono-linear evolutionary theories in which farming societies were assumed to be superior to foraging societies. While Toma celebrated the resilience of relatively minor nations (e.g., Japan) amid political turmoil in ancient times, as we have seen, he does so in a way that characterizes its northeastern peoples as caught in a nonadaptive society that failed to develop beyond the original abundance provided by salmon. In addition, by defining the Japanese archipelago (Ryukyu to Hokkaido, Sakhalin and Kuril Islands) as the (only) homeland for ancestral Japanese, Toma conveniently erased the continuing indigenous voices of resistance after 1868 to the Japanese colonization of Hokkaido and other northern islands.

Debates in anthropology and folkloristics

The same search for origins that underlies 鮭鱒論 also drove debates in other fields, even when 鮭鱒論 was not itself present. Kunio Yanagita, the founder of Japanese folkloristics, argued in his final book that rice cultivation, the foundation of Japanese culture, was introduced from the Eurasian continent to Honshu from the south, through the Ryukyu Islands, taking salmon and northeastern Japan out of the story altogether[3] (Yanagita, 1961).

This was in contrast to interpretations by Masao Oka, Eiichiro Ishida and their colleagues, who insisted on the northern origins of the Japanese (cf. Ishida et al., 1958). The two ethnologists led the 'General Ethnological Research on the Ainu アイヌ民族総合調査' (1950–1954) sponsored by the Japanese Ethnological Society (Ishida, 1952). As part of this expedition, a young human ecologist named Hitoshi Watanabe (not to be mistaken with Makoto Watanabe, a critic of 鮭鱒論) conducted ethnographic fieldwork on the Ainu people's traditional patterns of natural resource utilization, including that of chum salmon, and later became the author of the well-known *Ainu Ecosystem: Environment and Group Structure*. These works of H. Watanabe (1964, 1972) soon came to play a significant role in 鮭鱒論 debates as an ethno-archeological baseline.

While Oka and Yanagita had different ideas about the origin of the Japanese and were influential in different disciplines (ethnology and folkloristics, respectively), it is important to note that both were outspoken against conceptual colonialism from the West and were strong advocates of what cultural anthropologist Takami Kuwayama calls 'native anthropology.' It is well known among Japanese folklorists that Yanagita did not like to see his followers use 'Western' anthropological concepts, even though he himself read works of Western scholars (Kuwayama, 2008, p. 138). Oka was similarly committed to developing Japanese scholarship. In a paper published in 1944, Oka advocated East Asian ethnology 東亜民族学 conducted not by Euro-American scholars but by East Asian researchers – at the same time that the militaristic Japanese government was using the rhetoric of the Greater East Asia Co-Prosperity Sphere to justify imperial expansion. During the war, he was also actively involved in the National Institute of Ethnology, which disseminated ethnological information for colonial governance (Yamaji, 2011).

As Kuwayama (2008) points out, Japanese scholars have long been alert to the academic structures and practices that marginalize them. However, as we mentioned in the introduction, in Japanese contexts, the problem has been framed less as one of language-based Anglophone dominance and more as a general issue of 'Western' intellectual hegemony. Japanese traditions of ethnology and folkloristics can be seen as forms of resistance against such academic dominance, and this sensibility continues within contemporary Japanese anthropology (Hudson, 2006, pp. 413–414).

Yet, as the case of 鮭鱒論 makes clear, this opposition to Western-colonialism within Japanese ethnology and folkloristics is also deeply entangled with problematic projects of national identity-making. As Emiko Ohnuki-Tierney (1993) points out, rice – a key part of 鮭鱒論 narratives – has emerged as a potent tangible symbol of Japanese national identity. Ohnuki-Tierney (1993, pp. 117–118) discusses the importance of the staple food as a metaphor of the self: Japanese people are discerning about the differences in Japanese rice, while Western Europeans carefully distinguish among French, German, and Italian breads. Inspired by Ohnuki-Tierney's argument, we argue that Japanese academic identity-making projects of 鮭鱒論 represent a process of making 'Rice People' (Japanese) in opposition to 'Bread People' (Westerners) within social science research.

Yanagita and Toma have been powerful in this focus on rice as the central food of Japanese-ness. Toma's argument, under the influence of Yamanouchi's 鮭鱒論, shares with Yanagita a commitment to praising rice cultivation as a technology that is central to Japan's state formation, while relegating salmon fishing to a marginal position. This identity-building project has been remarkably durable, spanning the period from the colonial expansion of the Meiji Restoration to World War II to the long postwar period. Throughout this time, Japanese ethnologists and anthropologists have remained concerned about Japanese uniqueness and the threats of Western academic hegemony, but have given little thought to how they might be entangled in the material and conceptual colonialisms of Ainu people in the rice/salmon people distinction.

Today, 鮭鱒論 is considered a classic debate in Japanese archeology, ethnology, and folkloristics (cf. Obayashi, 1971/1996; M. Watanabe, 1974/1996). Yet, while the topic still fascinates many Japanese biological anthropologists and archeologists, younger generations of cultural anthropologists are relatively indifferent to questions about the origin of the Japanese (Sasaki, 2009, pp. 225–226). Thus, while the use of salmon in Ainu and Japanese societies continues to be discussed by culturally-focused scholars (Segawa, 2005; Suga, 2005), 鮭鱒論 is viewed primarily as an historical, rather than as a contemporary term.

The potential of 鮭鱒論

Within English language scholarship, 鮭鱒論 has been generally ignored, with the exception of coastal archeology, where the term has received some limited attention. Through their English language texts, Akira Matsui (2013) and Junko Habu (2004, p. 60) have introduced 鮭鱒論 as a theory of Jomon subsistence, and a handful of others have used it to explore the significance of salmon around the North Pacific Rim (e.g., Tushingham & Bettinger, 2013). Yet overall, the concept has had a relatively limited life beyond the borders of Japan. We want, however, to propose that despite its troubling pasts, English-language scholarship might benefit from closer attention to 鮭鱒論 as the concept holds salient insights for the growing bodies of scholarship in the environmental humanities and multispecies anthropology, as well as building forms of scholarship more alert to colonialisms and their ongoing effects. In particular, we see 鮭鱒論 as a term that can encourage further reflection about the ways more-than-human, multispecies, and environmentally-focused scholars engage East Asia. By fostering extended discussion about the non-universality of nature/culture binaries, scholars working within the so-called 'ontological turn' have generated substantial attention to the ways that non-Western peoples – including in East Asia – often enact ways of being and thinking in which the categories of nature and culture play little role (Descola, 2013; Strathern, 1980). Yet overall, English-language social science scholarship has given far more attention to generalized East Asian nature/culture principles than to specific East Asian concepts that have emerged within particular analytical, theoretical, and political debates (e.g., Asquith & Kalland, 1997). In contrast, 鮭鱒論 insists on attention to specific more-than-human relations, while also foregrounding East Asian theorizations of nature.

Our contemplation of the analytical possibilities within 鮭鱒論 emerges in large part from our own research on salmon–human relations: in the North Pacific, in Alaska, and Japan for Kondo and Japan and the Columbia River region for Swanson. As anthropologists committed to more-than-human scholarship (cf. de la Cadena & Medina, this volume), we see 鮭鱒論 as a term that offers conceptual resources for developing multispecies-based forms of 'area studies' scholarship. While many regions in academia are partially defined via climate and biological parameters (i.e., the Arctic, Tropics, and Mediterranean), the notion of region-making itself as a multispecies process remains under-explored. 鮭鱒論 invites scholars to consider in depth how the North Pacific *becomes* a region not through the sheer presence or absence of salmon, but through the particular intimacies of people and fish; it pushes us toward scholarly imaginaries that take the constitutive relations between people, other beings, and landscapes more seriously in the ways in which we conceptualize the geographies and grounds of our analyses. 鮭鱒論 pushes us to more fully consider what a region is, and more precisely, how the multispecies relations that make the North Pacific or the salmon-trout culture area might lead us to narrate more-than-human histories at regional scales.

In this way, the concept also directly intervenes in North Pacific scholarship. For an area cross-cut by both World War II and Cold War divisions, 鮭鱒論 transgresses lingering (post)communist/capitalist, as well as Asian/European divides. Even today, many conversations about salmon – both academic and more popular – remain decidedly national or continental in their frame of reference. In contrast, 鮭鱒論 consistently insists that northern Japan, Kamchatka, Alaska, and the West Coast of North America belong in the same frame. This insight can be extended beyond its largely archeological concerns to explore how – contra the 20th-century focus on divisions – this region has a powerfully intertwined history of trade, sea mammal hunting, frontier colonialism, resource extraction, indigenous disenfranchisement, and fisheries industrialization (including canneries and fish hatcheries). Telling linked North Pacific histories – rather than only national narratives – is crucially important because doing so can activate possibilities for new kinds of transnational political initiatives.

Second, 鮭鱒論 indeed offers an interesting interdisciplinary method for developing robust materialist approaches to multispecies relations, one that illustrates how scholars can study empirical details of more-than-human relations across multiple temporal scales by integrating archeology and anthropology. By moving between these fields, 鮭鱒論 shows how ontologies – entire worlds – are brought into being through *longue durée* interactions of people and fish. While the crudest versions of the concept veer close to environmental determinism, the more subtle versions of 鮭鱒論 point to the ways that people and salmon 'become with' each other not only in direct interactions (as described in Haraway [2008] and Despret [2004]) but also over many human generations and on what are evolutionary timescales for salmon. They pull together research on numbers of salmon bones in middens with attention to salmon-related rituals, songs, and stories.

A recent English-language text that grapples with salmon–human relations in the North Pacific illustrates how further attention to 鮭鱒論 might matter. In *Keystone Nations* (2012), one of the most important edited volumes on salmon–human worlds, Colombi and Brooks describe salmon as 'cultural keystone species' in indigenous societies of the Northern Pacific region with case studies from Sakhalin, Kamchatka, Aleutians, mainland Alaska, and the Canadian/US Northwest Coast region. Yet while Colombi and Brooks (2012) offer a valuable framework to see the Northern Pacific region as assemblages of 'salmon nations,' they did not include a chapter devoted to Ainu relations with salmon, nor do they mention any of the accumulated works on 鮭鱒論. It is likely that the language barriers between Anglophone and Japanese-speaking academia made it difficult for them to engage with such work. But if they had, this might have changed their broader theorization of ethnicity, salmon, and history in North Pacific worlds. Today, Hokkaido salmon worlds look 'industrial,' as the majority of Japan's salmon are se04ranched, i.e., raised in hatcheries before they are released into rivers and the ocean. Yet this industrialization is not external to stories of Ainu–salmon relations. Rather it is a process fundamentally bound up with practices of Japanese nation-making and the marginalization of Ainu fishing rights. In addition, if they had thought with and against 鮭鱒論, it might have encouraged the contributors to give more attention to connectivity, i.e., to rich trans-Pacific indigenous connections and alliances in the past and present, a point to which we return below.

More generally, 鮭鱒論 highlights the simultaneous necessity and highly fraught politics of materialist identity-claims. While it productively focuses on how human ways of life are constituted together with those of other beings, many versions of 鮭鱒論 indeed rely on and promote problematic notions of bio-ethno-nationalism. As described in the previous sections, 鮭鱒論 often invokes racial logics that track through relations among plants/animals, eating, and human bodies. These lines of thought directly contribute to the exoticization and marginalization of those who are not ethnically Japanese. The recollections of renowned Ainu scholar Mashiho Chiri of his youth in Tokyo illustrates how stereotypical versions of this biocultural logic have shaped pervasive notions of identity and belonging:

> When I entered the First High School, I was just getting to know Tokyo and, even if it wasn't necessary, I was nervous all the time, due to a sort of sense of humility. The First High School students . . . encircled and showered me with kinds of questions that some would interpret as very stabbing. They asked something like 'You grew up with bear meat and salmon as staple food. Are you feeling alright here [in Tokyo], eating steamed rice all the time?'. . . which made my faint-hearted self cry in secret. (Chiri, 1935/1981, p. 165)

Yet, while they are often little more than simplistic racializations, assertions of biocultural identity cannot and should not be dismissed outright. North Pacific indigenous life worlds are indeed co-emergent with salmon: while indigenous peoples do not 'vanish' when their access to salmon is blocked, it is a serious form of cultural violence to impede indigenous fisheries because for many North Pacific indigenous communities *being* means being-with these fish.

During ethnographic fieldwork, one of us (Swanson) had a conversation with an Ainu man who actively took on the 鮭鱒論-linked notion of a world divided into rice people (Japanese/other Asians), bread people (Westerners), and salmon people (Northern indigenous people). For him, the designation of 'salmon people' was not limited to archeological conversations that positioned salmon cultures as 'backward' but was an idea that could be productive within his own identity-work, as well as within efforts to craft transnational North Pacific indigenous alliances. His comments illustrate how 鮭鱒論 may contain some powerful insights about the way that Ainu-ness is a biocultural assemblage in which salmon have a critical role. At the same time, the very history of 鮭鱒論 that he repurposes offers a cautionary reminder about the ever-present challenges of articulating material identities in non-essentialist ways.

While 鮭鱒論 has been entangled in the academic history of ethnic Japanese identity-making and Ainu marginalization, it also strongly resonates with projects of indigenous connection and revitalization. The geographical links and material connections emphasized in 鮭鱒論 are very similar to those that underpin North Pacific indigenous alliances. For example, in 1982, the Sapporo Ainu Culture Association publicly revived *asircepnomi*, the Ainu ritual to celebrate the arrival of the first salmon of the year, and in more recent years, the ritual has also included the harvest of salmon with a traditional fish spear called *marek*. The annual event has sometimes been attended by indigenous groups from outside of Japan, most significantly Northwest Coast indigenous groups in Canada and the US, where similar First Salmon Ceremonies are widely held (Sapporo Ainu Culture Association, 2013). In this way, salmon become a boundary object (Star and Griesemer, 1989) for indigenous collaborations in Northern Pacific region. Such Northern Pacific alliances appear to add strong support for ongoing Ainu activist efforts to regain food sovereignty, as indigenous rights to salmon have more legal recognition in Canada and the US.[4] By drawing on observations similar to those of 鮭鱒論 – namely, that entanglements with salmon are fundamental for indigenous communities around the North Pacific – indigenous peoples are cultivating their own transnational biocultural alliances.

Overall, 鮭鱒論 pushes us to more deeply consider the negotiations and tensions of biosocial politics in their specific contexts – an insight that resonates far beyond regional and thematic debates.

Conclusion

As this monograph asserts, Anglophone theory needs to be diversified and decolonized. But so do many parts of non-English-language scholarship. It is crucial to remember that while 鮭鱒論 is a 'Japanese' concept, it is also one built from Ainu knowledges and lifeways, yet one that is part of political structures that marginalize Ainu people and their voices.

The point of our article is not to foster a quixotic search for terms that are 'clean' or 'innocent.' Rather, it is to argue that it is important to know and engage the histories of the terms we use – Anglophone and otherwise – at the same time that we seek to re-shape and use them in new ways. We see this as a form of the practice that Donna Haraway (2008, pp. 97–98) has called 'inheriting histories' – in this case, in the material-semiotic liveliness of concepts and terms – in order to make worlds otherwise. While words are highly mutable, genealogies matter, and active engagement with terms' histories is a key part of transforming unequal knowledge practices into multiple ones.

One of our goals in this article, in line with this monograph edition, has been to present 鮭鱒論 as a non-English-language concept that could contribute to and intervene in Anglophone theory, especially within more-than-human, multispecies, and environmentally-focused scholarship. And we think the term does indeed have substantial utility in that regard. Yet we have also wanted to highlight the layered complexities of 鮭鱒論, because we think our concerns about the concept signal an issue that stretches beyond it. Thus, the second goal of this chapter is to encourage further reflection about how scholars working in Anglophone traditions might engage knowledge politics and conceptual plurality not through an Anglophone/rest binary, but through deep engagements with the histories of multilayered imperialisms, colonialisms, and otherings that are entangled with terms that originate in many different contexts.

鮭鱒論 has been entangled in a clearly problematic history, but the same goes for most Anglophone scholarly fields, which have long equated the 'human' of the humanities with Western people (cf. 'model-system' in Chernysheva & Sezneva, this volume). Our field of anthropology is no exception when it comes to dark histories and problematic politics of othering. Yet rather than dismiss such approaches entirely, a growing number of scholars seek ways to enact them otherwise, torquing them into alternative practices. The same approach, we suggest, should be taken with non-Western concepts. They should not be seen de facto as a savior or escape from colonialist knowledge-making simply because they do not further Western imperialisms. Rather, we must engage them carefully, with attention to their histories and resonances, asking how they might, indeed, be powerful in certain Anglophone contexts, while also noting that they may need to be decolonized in other ways, i.e., that they may need to be deliberately remade. Such work calls out for collaborative scholarship of the kind we try to enact in this article, where scholars alert to Ainu concerns, Japanese intellectual histories, and Anglophone concerns open up such issues together.

In this type of scholarship, attention to Ainu concepts, not just those that are Japanese and Anglophone, is the next step toward building academic theory that is more responsive to histories of colonial relations. The Ainu word *cep* can be translated as 'what we eat' and usually indexes chum salmon. It also refers to 'fish' in general when used in conjunction with other words. Likewise, *kamui cep* can be translated as 'god's fish' and typically refers to a species of salmon called *Oncorhynchus keta* by most biologists and 'chum salmon' in many, but not all, vernacular Englishes. In some cases, *kamui cep* is used to refer more specifically to particular chum salmon that have been offered to the gods. These expressions suggest that chum salmon is *the* food for the Ainu, who are entangled with the gods-in-the-environment through subsistence activities and fishing-related rituals. The contemporary Japanese word for salmon (*sake*) (the first character of 鮭鱒論) completely misses this human–salmon–god entanglement, even though there is a possibility that the Japanese word *sake* might be borrowed from the Ainu words. When we think about decolonizing Western concepts, what we need is a triangulation of concepts, one that engages *cep* together with 鮭鱒論, as we continue to confront the layered complexities of academic terms.

Taking Ainu concepts seriously can also mean stepping out of academia into the places where Ainu people actively engage in revitalization of their traditional culture. For example, one of the co-authors (Kondo) has participated in Ainu culture workshops, in which participants including Ainu youths and Japanese students learned to make a *mus*, a jelly made out of gelatin extracted from chum salmon skin, which is part of traditional cuisine of Sakhalin Ainu people. In other programs, the Ainu youths also learned how to use *marek* (described above) as well as *isapakikni*, a fish club which is necessary to kill salmon in a respectful manner. Nowadays, revitalization of salmon-related culture is considered by some Ainu people and their Japanese collaborators as an important arena in which to address the still ongoing marginalization and neglect of indigenous rights in Yaunmosir/Hokkaido as well as in trans-North Pacific contexts. It is also a site of conceptual creativity.

While we do not dismiss 鮭鱒論, neither do we argue that one *must* keep the term as a central analytical concept. That is not something we should decide. Rather, we have tried to illustrate how 鮭鱒論 points us toward a profound need – indeed, an obligation – to build conceptual language together with indigenous peoples. Perhaps, in such dialogues, 鮭鱒論 will be reclaimed. Or, alternatively, it may be set aside as new terms that actively couple analysis with revitalization emerge from collaborative engagements (see Joks, Østmo, & Law, this volume, on a call for conversation between Sámi herders and biologists). Regardless, attention to 鮭鱒論 matters here, as it points out the ways that multilayered histories of colonialism and marginalization continue to haunt theory and theory-making. It reminds us that scholars need to create languages that are at once analytical and world-making together with Ainu (and other indigenous) communities, and not just with national traditions of non-English scholarship.

In relation to other articles in this monograph edition, ours is different in that we have focused on a non-English academic term and its history rather than vernacular, folk or indigenous terms themselves. However, our points resonate with many of the others in this publication. First, concepts clearly reflect the socio-political history of the country where they are created. While Chernysheva and Sezneva (this volume) touch upon Russian *obshcheye* in relation to nostalgia for a Soviet past, our article describes Japanese academics' struggles in the postwar period to break away from an emperor-centered view of Japanese history via Marxism. Second, categorization of human groups, in some cases, are deeply entangled with those of non-humans or humans' relations with them (cf. de la Cadena & Medina, this volume). In this sense, it is interesting to note that many of the contributions, in one way or the other, grapple with the nature–culture divide, which is arguably a characteristic of the English language. Third, we also agree with Joks, Østmo, and Law (this volume), who explore the fundamentally relational character of the Sámi term *meahcci*, in that misunderstanding and marginalization of indigenous lifeways begin with and are continuously reinforced by what we can call 'conceptual colonialism.'

Acknowledgements

The authors would like to thank Mai Ishihara for her comments on an early draft, as well as John Law and Annemarie Mol for their feedback on multiple versions of the text.

Funding

The authors received no financial support for the research, authorship, and/or publication of this article.

Notes

1. We first met at an international conference in Osaka called 'World Multiple: Everyday Politics of Knowing and Generating Entangled World' in December 2016. Then, we met again in Tokyo at the workshop titled 'Fisheries Management and Multispecies Relations in the Anthropocene: Perspectives from Environmental Humanities' (December 2017). We subsequently met for a week in Aarhus, Denmark to develop the arguments and some of the initial text for this article. Lastly, we have continued to exchange ideas and drafts with each other and with other colleagues (see acknowledgments) via email and Skype.

2. Moreover, he does not really mention the Ainu, the indigenous group of the northern Japanese archipelago including northern Tohoku, Hokkaido, Sakhalin, and Kuril Islands. We do not know the exact reasons for this neglect of the Ainu. However, if we consider the academic contexts of the time, it is likely that Toma wanted to stay away from (misused) types of 'multiculturalism' such as Tsuboi's work, which stressed the racial and cultural hybridity of the Japanese as a proof of its superior resilience and adaptability (Yamaji, 2011, pp. 11–12). It is also possible that Toma might have avoided mentioning Hokkaido and ancestors of the Ainu in his theory of the formation of the Japanese because it would have drawn attention to an ongoing colonial situation in Japan.

3. Although Yanagita intentionally turned away from discussions about the Ainu later in his career (Yamada, 2017), he was initially quite interested in legends and folklore regarding salmon, as well as scholarship about them (Suga, 1998). After reading James G. Frazer's *Golden Bough*, Yanagita thought that some Native American folklore on salmon was structurally similar to what he had encountered in Japanese folk tales (e.g., the salmon's special relationship with twins). However, around the 1930s, Yanagita became critical of Frazer and Frazer's Japanese followers who used the term 'totemism,' as he sought to create a 'national' academic tradition distinct from those of Europe and the US. Because totemism and the salmon totem were originally proposed by a non-Japanese scholar and carried theoretical baggage from 'Western' academic traditions, he actively excised them from his work (Nakayama, 1924). Furthermore, because ethnic Japanese folklore on salmon forces researchers to pay attention to connections between northern peoples and the Japanese, it was at odds with the vision of an ancient rice-based Japanese culture that Yanagita promoted in his later work (Suga, 1998).

4. For example, 'Kotan-no-kai,' an activist group, and others held a workshop titled 'Ainu's Right to Harvest Salmon: Learning from Native America' in December 2017. Furthermore, some Ainu communities have sent delegates to North America to learn about indigenous salmon fisheries and fisheries rights there. In September 2019, Mr Hatakeyama, President of the Monbetsu Ainu Association, harvested chum salmon without applying for the Special Harvest Permission required by Hokkaido Prefecture. The prefectural government urged him to apply for this permission, while Mr Hatakeyama believes that he does not need to do so because Ainu people have indigenous rights to harvest salmon.

References

Asquith, P. J. (1996). Japanese science and western hegemonies: Primatology and the limits set to questions. In L. Nader (Ed.), *Naked science: Anthropological inquiry into boundaries, power, and knowledge* (pp. 239–258). Routledge.

Asquith, P., & Kalland, A. (1997). *Japanese images of nature: Cultural perspectives*. Curzon Press.

Chiri, M. (Ed. Trans.). (1981). *Collection of Ainu folk tales, with The Lives of Yezo Monsters*. Iwanami Shoten. [In Japanese] (=知里真志保『アイヌ民譚集 付，えぞおばけ列伝』岩波書店) (Original work published 1935).

Clifford, J., & Marcus, G. E. (Eds.). (1986). *Writing culture: The poetics and politics of ethnography*. University of California Press.

Colombi, B. J., & J. F. Brooks (2012). *Keystone nations: Indigenous peoples and salmon across the Northern Pacific*. School for Advanced Research Press.

Descola, P. (2013). *Beyond nature and culture*. University of Chicago Press.

Despret, V. (2004). The body we care for: Figures of anthropo-zoo-genesis. *Body & Society, 10*(2–3), 111–134.

Habu, J. (2004). *Ancient Jomon of Japan*. Cambridge University Press.

Haraway, D. (2008). *When species meet*. University of Minnesota Press.

Harris, M. (1979). *Cultural materialism: The struggle for a science of culture*. Random House.

Hudson, M. J. (2006). Pots not people: Ethnicity, culture and identity in postwar Japanese archaeology. *Critique of Anthropology, 26*(4), 411–434.

Ishida, E. (1952). About the joint research report on the Saru Ainu. *Japanese Journal of Ethnology, 16*(3–4), 186. [in Japanese] (=石田英一郎「沙流アイヌの共同調査報告について」『民族学研究』16巻3-4号)

Ishida, E., Egami, N., Oka, M., & Yawata, I. (1958). *The origin of the Japanese people*. Heibonsha. [In Japanese] (=石田英一郎・江上波夫・岡正雄・八幡一郎『日本民族の起源』平凡社)

Kuwayama, T. (2004). *Native anthropology: The Japanese challenge to western academic hegemony*. Trans Pacific Press.

Kuwayama, T. (2008). *Native anthropology and folklore: Japan and world system of knowledge*. Kobundo. [In Japanese] (=桑山敬己『ネイティヴの人類学と民俗学―知の世界システムと日本』弘文堂)

Matsui, A. (2013). Salmon exploitation in Jomon archaeology from a wetlands point of view. *Journal of Wetland Archaeology, 5*(1), 49–63.

Medak-Saltzman, D. (2008). *Staging empire: The display and erasure of indigenous peoples in Japanese and American nation building projects (1860–1904)* (Unpublished doctoral dissertation). University of California, Berkeley.

Medak-Saltzman, D. (2015). Empire's haunted logics: Comparative colonialisms and the challenges of incorporating indigeneity. *Journal of Critical Ethnic Studies, 1*(2), 11–32.

Morris-Suzuki, T. (1994). Creating the frontier: Border, identity and history in Japan's far north. *East Asian History, 7*, 1.

Nakayama, T. (1924). Essay on Keta god. *Journal of History in Hida, 8*(3) [In Japanese] (=中山太郎「気多神考」『飛騨史壇』8巻3号)

Obayashi, T. (1996). Social organization in Jomon period. In K. Tanigawa (Ed.), *Folklore of salmon and trout* (Collection of materials on Japanese folk culture, Vol. 19, pp. 398–409). San-ichi Publishing. [In Japanese] (=大林太良「縄文時代の社会組織（抄）」谷川健一編『鮭と鱒の民俗』日本民俗文化資料集成　第19巻) (Original work published 1971).

Ohnuki-Tierney, E. (1993). *Rice as self: Japanese identities through time*. Princeton University Press.

Sapporo Ainu Culture Association. (2013). *Asircepnomi: Thirty years' progress of the ritual to welcome new salmon*. [In Japanese] (=札幌アイヌ文化協会編『アシリチェプノミ：30年の歩み：新しい鮭を迎える儀式』札幌アイヌ文化協会)

Sasaki, K. (2009). Research on the ethnogenesis of the Japanese people: Review and outlook. *Bulletin of the National Museum of Ethnology, 34*(2), 211–228. [In Japanese] (＝佐々木高明「戦後の日本民族文化起源論」『国立民族学博物館研究報告』34巻2号)

Segawa, T. (2005). *The Formative History of Ainu Ecosystem*. Hokkaido Center for Publishing Projects. [In Japanese] (=瀬川拓郎『アイヌ・エコシステムの考古学』北海道出版企画センター)

Star, S. L., & Griesemer, J. R. (1989). Institutional ecology, "translations" and boundary objects: Amateurs and professionals in Berkeley's Museum of Vertebrate Zoology, 1907–39. *Social Studies of Science, 19*(3), 387–420.

Strathern, M. (1980). No nature, no culture: The Hagen case. In C. MacCormack & M. Strathern (Eds.), *Nature, culture and gender* (pp. 174–222). Cambridge University Press.

Suga, Y. (1998). Northern cultures for Kunio Yanagita: On the problem of neglecting the folklore regarding salmon. *Folk Material Culture Monthly, 31*(4), 1–5. [In Japanese] (=菅豊「柳田国男にとっての北方文化―サケをめぐる民俗の看過の問題から―」『民具マンスリー』31巻4号)

Suga, Y. (2005). *To whom does the river belong? Folklore of people and environment.* Yoshikawa Kobunkan. [In Japanese] (=菅豊『川は誰のものか―人と環境の民俗学』吉川弘文館)

Toma, S. (1951). *Formation of the Japanese race: In terms of the relations with East Asian peoples.* Iwanami Shoten. [In Japanese] (=藤間生大『日本民族の形成―東亜諸民族との連関において―』岩波書店)

Tushingham, S., & Bettinger, R. L. (2013). Why foragers choose acorns before salmon: Storage, mobility, and risk in aboriginal California. *Journal of Anthropological Archaeology, 32*(4), 527–537.

Watanabe, H. (1964). Ecology of the Ainu and problems in prehistory in Japan. *Anthropology Journal, 72*(1), 9–23. [In Japanese] (=渡辺仁「アイヌの生態と本邦先史学の問題」『人類學雜誌』72巻1号)

Watanabe, H. (1972). *The Ainu ecosystem: Environment and group structure.* University of Tokyo Press.

Watanabe, M. (1996). Problems of 'salmon-trout theory' in studies of Lithic period culture in Japan. In K. Tanigawa (Ed.), *Folklore of salmon and trout* (Collection of materials on Japanese folk culture, Vol. 19, pp. 393–397). San-ichi Publishing. (=渡辺誠「日本石器時代文化研究における『サケ・マス論』の問題点」谷川健一編『鮭と鱒の民俗』日本民俗文化資料集成 第19巻) (Original work published 1967).

Yamada, S. (2011). *Modern Hokkaido and the Ainu people: Hunting restriction and land issues.* Hokkaido University Press. [In Japanese] (=山田伸一『近代北海道とアイヌ民族―狩猟規制と土地問題』北海道大学出版会)

Yamada, Y. (2017). Ryuzo Torii and Kunio Yanagita: Two discourses on the theory of the Ainu being an indigenous people of Japan. *Bulletin of the National Museum of Japanese History, 202*, 181–212. [In Japanese] (=山田康弘「鳥居龍蔵と柳田國男：『先住民＝アイヌ』説をめぐる二つの対応」『国立歴史民俗博物館研究報告』第202集)

Yamaji, K. (Ed.). (2011). *Japanese anthropology: Colonialism, studies of foreign cultures, and history of academic research.* Kansei Gakuin University Press. [In Japanese] (=山路勝彦編『日本の人類学―植民地主義、異文化研究、学術研究の歴史』関西学院大学出版会)

Yamanouchi, S. (1996). Jomon culture. In K. Tanigawa (Ed.), *Folklore of salmon and trout* (Collection of materials on Japanese folk culture, Vol. 19, pp. 371–379). San-ichi Publishing. (=山内清男「縄文式文化」谷川健一編『鮭と鱒の民俗』日本民俗文化資料集成 第19巻) (Original work published 1964).

Yanagita, K. (1961). *Road of the ocean. Chikuma shobo.* [In Japanese] (＝柳田国男『海上の道』筑摩書房)

Author biographies

Shiaki Kondo is Assistant Professor at the Center for Ainu and Indigenous Studies, Hokkaido University. Kondo has conducted intensive ethnographic research among Athabascan-speaking groups in Interior Alaska, US, since 2012. He co-edited *Anthropology of Human and Animal* [in Japanese] (Shumpusha) and *A Human History from Canine Perspective* [in Japanese] (Bensei Publishing). He is on the editorial board of *Tagui*, a new Japanese-language journal on multispecies ethnography and environmental humanities.

Heather Anne Swanson is Associate Professor of Anthropology at Aarhus University, where she also co-directs the university's Center for Environmental Humanities. Swanson has conducted long-term research at the intersection of salmon and human worlds in Japan and the US. She is a co-editor of *Domestication Gone Wild* (Duke University Press) and *Arts of Living on a Damaged Planet* (University of Minnesota Press), as well the author of numerous chapters and articles on fisheries, watersheds, and social science approaches to studying more-than-human landscapes.